The Legal System

CORE TEXT SERIES

The Legal System

Fourth Edition

KATE MALLESON
Professor of Law, Queen Mary, University of London

RICHARD MOULES
Lecturer, Fitzwilliam College, University of Cambridge

Series Editor
NICOLA PADFIELD
Fitzwilliam College, Cambridge

OXFORD
UNIVERSITY PRESS

OXFORD
UNIVERSITY PRESS

Great Clarendon Street, Oxford OX2 6DP

Oxford University Press is a department of the University of Oxford.
It furthers the University's objective of excellence in research, scholarship,
and education by publishing worldwide in

Oxford New York

Auckland Cape Town Dar es Salaam Hong Kong Karachi
Kuala Lumpur Madrid Melbourne Mexico City Nairobi
New Delhi Shanghai Taipei Toronto

With offices in

Argentina Austria Brazil Chile Czech Republic France Greece
Guatemala Hungary Italy Japan Poland Portugal Singapore
South Korea Switzerland Thailand Turkey Ukraine Vietnam

Oxford is a registered trade mark of Oxford University Press
in the UK and in certain other countries

Published in the United States
by Oxford University Press Inc., New York

© Oxford University Press 2010

The moral rights of the authors have been asserted

Crown copyright material is reproduced under Class Licence
Number C01P0000148 with the permission of OPSI
and the Queen's Printer for Scotland

Database right Oxford University Press (maker)

First published 2003

This edition 2010

British Library Cataloguing-in-Publication Data
Data available

Library of Congress Cataloging-in-Publication Data
Malleson, Kate.
   The legal system / Kate Malleson, Richard Moules. — 4th ed.
     p. cm. — (Core text series)
   ISBN 978-0-19-956018-9 (pbk.)
   1. Justice, Administration of—England. 2. Law—England. 3. Justice,
Administration of—Wales. 4. Law—Wales. I. Moules, Richard, lecturer.
II. Title.
   KD7100.M35 2010
   349.42–dc22
                                          2010001523

Typeset by MPS Limited, A Macmillan Company
Printed in Great Britain
on acid-free paper by
Clays Ltd, St Ives plc

ISBN 978-0-19-956018-9

2

Preface to the fourth edition

Previous editions of this book have highlighted the pace and scale of change to the legal system. The last three years have been no exception. October 2009 was a landmark in legal history as the Judicial Committee of the House of Lords ceased to exist and the new UK Supreme Court opened for business. But change is seldom uncontroversial and rarely does it come free of charge. As this book shows the legal system has many competing aims and functions and it is intimately connected to the economic and political priorities of society. It is unclear which, if any, of the many recent reforms will prove to be successful and long lasting. Nevertheless, in an era of change one thing is certain: the legal system will remain a dynamic, contentious, and intellectually stimulating subject to study.

Preface to the first edition

Most people know something about the legal system without ever having opened a textbook. The police, judges, juries, lawyers, courts, and Parliament are subjects which fall within almost everyone's field of general knowledge. The advantage of such familiarity is that the legal system is one of the least intimidating areas of the law to study. The disadvantage is that the preconceptions which people bring to the subject often make it difficult to approach its study with an open mind. Much of our common knowledge of the legal system comes via the news and fictional accounts on television and film. The preoccupations and content of this material is often skewed and sometimes inaccurate. It also gives rise to a range of common myths; for example, that most criminal trials are heard by a jury, that contested trials of any kind are the norm, that most convicted offenders are sent to jail, that barristers spend all their time in court and solicitors in offices (and that judges in England and Wales have gavels!).

The job of disentangling fact from fiction and redirecting attention to neglected but important aspects of the process requires detailed attention to empirical data. Some of this is available but passed over because it is not considered newsworthy, such as statistics on the functioning of the magistrates' courts or the detailed workings of police powers. Other data are simply not collected. We only have a very partial picture, for example, of how the civil justice system works which has hampered the assessment of the impact of recent reforms in that area.

In addition to the empirical difficulties faced by a student of the legal system, the familiarity of the subject matter can obscure the fact that many aspects of it are complex and require considerable analytical rigour to make sense of them. For example, it is difficult enough to grasp the various arrangements by which legal services are funded; the task of determining which of these works well or badly and assessing the effect of various changes to the funding system requires the combined skills of a lawyer, an economist, and a political scientist. The result is that it is relatively easy to say *something* about the legal system, but much more difficult to make an empirically informed and intellectually rigorous contribution to the subject.

The task of building up an accurate and comprehensive analysis of the legal system is not made any easier by the fact that the legal system is a moving target. Barely a week goes by when some aspect of the system is not subject to review. The Human

Rights Act 1998, the restructuring of Legal Aid, the introduction of Conditional Fees Agreements, and the Woolf reforms to civil justice have all had a profound impact on the legal system in recent years. As I write, the Criminal Justice Bill is going through Parliament, bringing significant changes to the criminal justice system. On the horizon is a full review by the Government of the way legal services are regulated, while looking further ahead the role of the Lord Chancellor, the judicial appointments process, and the organization of the highest courts are all areas in which criticism is building up and change looks increasingly likely.

One effect of this stream of reform is that it is inevitable that by the time this book is being read it will be out of date in some important respects. To deal with this problem it is necessary for students of the legal system to be equipped with a variety of sources with which to supplement and update their knowledge. For this reason, the text has pointed to a range of additional sources of information such as websites and journals which are a vital addition to any textbook, however recent.

Although the speed of changes to the processes and institutions which make up the legal system poses challenges for the student and author alike, the good news is that many of the issues which inform our understanding of it remain relatively constant. One of the main aims of this book is to identify and analyse these underlying themes and trends. The general editor of this series, Nicola Padfield, has described its aim as being to write at several levels simultaneously; to strip the subject to its core while continuing to point out the intellectual challenges and difficulties within it. This book is structured with this aim in mind. In the first chapter I identify a series of themes, trends, and tensions which run through the system and which provide a framework for analysing the subject. These are then picked up and expanded in the following chapters as they relate to individual topics.

The book seeks to show that the system is run through with different and inevitably competing aims and functions. Which of these takes precedence at any one time will affect the detailed arrangements of the system. It is essential that anyone wanting to understand the legal system in England and Wales is aware that the policies which shape it are ultimately decided not merely, or even very greatly, with reference to its own internal logic or needs, but on the basis of the political and economic priorities of society more generally. There is no such thing as a strictly legal reading of the legal system. Law is not politics by a different name, but the legal system is intimately connected with the political system. What follows should always be read with that in mind.

Dr Kate Malleson
April 2003

Contents

Detailed contents

Online Resource Centre

www.oxfordtextbooks.co.uk/orc/malleson4e/

This edition is accompanied by an **Online Resource Centre**, an open-access website designed to support the book. The English legal system is a constantly moving area and by keeping up to date with the latest developments, you can use current examples and cases in your coursework and exams to display your knowledge and understanding in the most effective ways.

Updates to the law will be added to the website twice per year, providing an easy source of reference to the current law. There is also a list of live web links to supplement those websites recommended in each chapter, so you have handy sources of information for more in-depth study.

Guide to using the book

FEATURES

There are a number of features throughout the textbook designed to help you in your studies.

SUMMARY

This chapter outlines a number of trends and themes which link the topics covered in the book. It highlights the increase in size and the economic and political importance of the legal system. It argues that th of this expansion includes an acceleration of the pace and amount of the legal system and an intensification of the debate about its role and This debate raises questions which go to the heart of the legal syste

---

Chapter summaries highlight what will be addressed in each chapter, so you are aware of the key learning outcomes for each topic.

FURTHER READING

Judicial Statistics 2005 (http://www.official-documents.co.uk/docu 6799.asp).

Information on the Criminal Justice System in England and Wales (1 publication) (http://www.homeoffice.gov.uk/rds/digest41.html).

The Runciman Royal Commission on Criminal Justice (Cmnd 2263 1993), ch 1, paras 11–16.

Jacqueline Hodgson 'Reforming French Criminal Justice' (Noverr Action 6.

At the end of each chapter is a list of recommended **further reading**.

These suggestions include books and recent journal articles, and will help to supplement your knowledge and understanding of key topics.

USEFUL WEBSITES

Expenditure and costs of the Criminal Justice System
http://www.homeoffice.gov.uk/rds/digest4/chapter9.pdf
Department for Constitutional Affairs home page
http://www.dca.gov.uk/
Ministry of Justice
http://www.justice.gov.uk/

Most chapters also include a selection of **recommended websites** that you will find useful. In a fast-moving subject such as this, it is important to keep up to date with the latest developments, and these web links provide a platform for accurate and reliable online research.

SELF-TEST QUESTIONS

1 List three definitions of the common law.

2 What is the difference between primary and secondary legislation?

3 What changes were brought about to the legal system in England European Communities Act 1972?

4 What role is played by the European Convention on Human Right as a result of the Human Rights Act 1998?

5 In the light of the growing importance of statutory provisions, is it a ful to describe England and Wales as a common law legal system

---

Each chapter concludes with a short selection of **self-test questions**. These allow you to check your understanding of the topics covered, and to engage fully with the material in preparation for further study, writing essays, and answering exam questions.

GENERAL APPROACH

The aim of books in the Core Text Series is to strip the subject to its core while also pointing out the intellectual challenges and difficulties within the law. The early chapters identify a series of themes, trends, and tensions which run throughout the legal system. These issues are then picked up and expanded in the following chapters as they relate to the individual topics. This approach offers clarity as you progress through your studies, as the authors introduce the issue in its wider context, before describing its practical application in detail, to give you a fully rounded picture. One example of this approach is the treatment of the Human Rights Act 1998.

> 3.17 The UK was one of the states which played a leading role in dr
> was also one of the first countries to ratify it. However, until t
> 1998 was passed, the provisions of the Convention were not
> courts and citizens who wanted to claim that their rights had
> go to Strasbourg to the ECtHR to do so. The provisions of the
> more detail in chapter 4 below.
>
> 3.18 The decisions of the ECtHR, in contrast to the European C
> binding in the UK so that victory in Strasbourg does not gua
> will be put right in the UK. In practice, however, when ther
> finding in Strasbourg against the UK Government, it has bee

Chapter 3 addresses the 'Sources of law' and introduces briefly how the Human Rights Act 1998 came about, and introduces the concept of it impacting on the UK courts.

> **The Human Rights Act and the judiciar**
>
> 4.46 Even before the recent anti-terrorism and asylum cases descri
> that the new role which the Human Rights Act 1998 gives th
> legislation and official decision-making is having a significant
> tutional and institutional arrangements of the legal system.
>
> 4.47 One consequence of the greater power which the HRA 199
> branch of government has been to focus attention on the com

Chapter 4 is dedicated solely to the Human Rights Act 1998, and takes a more detailed look at the effects it has on the domestic legal system, the process which led to its enactment, and its ongoing role and effect on UK law. Specific case examples are provided so you can see the law in action.

Introduction

SUMMARY

This chapter outlines a number of trends and themes which link the different topics covered in the book. It highlights the increase in size and the growth in economic and political importance of the legal system. It argues that the impact of this expansion includes an acceleration of the pace and amount of reform to the legal system and an intensification of the debate about its role and function. This debate raises questions which go to the heart of the legal system: Is the justice system private or public? How much do we want to spend on civil and criminal justice? Can an acceptable quality of justice be maintained if costs are cut? Do we want more civil litigation or less? Is there still a place for lay personnel? Are inquisitorial methods better than the traditional adversarial system? Should judges make political decisions? Does the executive have too much control over the law-making process? What are the implications for the legal system of the increasing importance of human rights? These questions help to frame our analysis of the legal system and recur in different contexts throughout the chapters which follow.

Trends and themes

1.1 The institutions, procedures and personnel which make up the legal system of England and Wales are at first sight only a very loosely connected set of subjects. It is not immediately obvious that there is much to link, say, the rights of suspects, the court structure and the judicial appointments process. Indeed, these and other topics which are commonly found in most legal system courses are often taught as distinct areas connected only by the overarching subject of the law. For this reason, many authors choose to describe the subject as a process rather than a system to emphasize

the fact that the different areas are not driven by a central goal or bound by a set of coherent underlying principles. While it is true to say that there is no unifying entity holding the legal system together, the various institutions, procedures and personnel are shaped by a number of common trends and themes. The aim of this book is to articulate these throughout the different substantive topics so as to provide a framework within which to make sense of the different parts of the system.

1.2 The most pervasive of these trends is the general expansion in the size of the system in recent decades. The numbers of cases processed and people employed by it (directly or indirectly) is greater than at any time in the past. As the legal system has become larger and more economically significant, affecting the lives of more and more people, it has inevitably moved up the political agenda, and public interest in its workings has intensified. Governments are now expected to introduce policy changes which affect the legal system on an ongoing basis. This has led in turn to an intensification of the scrutiny of the system beyond a narrow legal forum. How much public money should be spent on it, who should staff it and how it should function have become more frequently heard questions in general public debate.

1.3 The answers to these questions ultimately depend on underlying political values. Our views on such subjects as the use of no-win-no-fee funding arrangements for litigation, the attack on restrictive practices in the legal profession and the erosion of the role of the jury are all affected by whether the system is conceived of as essentially a private enterprise driven by and responsive to market forces or a public service requiring state subsidies and public participation. Likewise, attitudes to such changes as the reduction of access to the appeal system and the curbs on the rights of suspects and defendants are driven by different views on how the balance should be struck between the requirements of cost-saving, efficiency, crime control and the rights of individuals. These, and other, underlying questions of principle, are evident as unresolved tensions in every area of the legal system. Nor are they new. The debate about the purposes and goals of the legal system is as old as the system itself. What has changed is that the increasing size and significance of the legal system has given it new intensity.

The expansion of the legal system

1.4 All developed societies have complex legal systems, and England and Wales is no exception. But for most of its history the legal system has affected relatively few people since, until quite recently, the law in any formal sense did not generally impinge on the day-to-day lives of the majority of the population. Throughout the twentieth century as the volume and scope of law grew, so too did people's willingness, need and ability to use the legal system. Whole areas of life such as family breakdown or employment disputes, which would previously have been dealt with privately or by other institutions such as the church or the trade unions, have come to be handled by lawyers and courts. Thirty years ago relatively few people had any contact with the legal profession. Today, most people will use a lawyer at some stage in their life in order to purchase a house, obtain a divorce, make a will or seek advice about a claim arising from a traffic accident. As a result, the number of solicitors and barristers has expanded from fewer than 30,000 in 1970 to over 110,000 in 2009, while the judiciary has experienced a ten-fold increase in numbers over the same period – from under 300 judges to over 3,000. Though we may still have some way to go before we reach the dizzy heights of the litigation culture of the US, there is no evidence to suggest that this process is slowing down. As more and more areas of life are drawn into the jurisdiction of the courts and tribunals the trend would appear to be toward further expansion of the legal system in the years ahead.

Political and economic significance of the legal system

1.5 One inevitable consequence of this expansion of the role of law and the legal system has been a growth in its economic significance. The most costly part of the system – the criminal justice process – accounts for about £14bn per year of public spending. This figure is low compared with the bigger spending areas such as defence, social security, and health. Nevertheless, the total sums are now substantial. As a result, successive governments have looked for ways to reduce these costs. In common with almost all areas of public expenditure, the reforms of the last 20 years or so have primarily been designed to reduce the size of the budget or to ensure that it is spent more effectively.

1.6 These direct costs of the criminal justice system are matched by the indirect costs incurred in damages awarded in the civil courts. In recent years these costs have risen to the point where they have an impact on the budgets of some government departments, such as the Department of Health, where litigation costs have increased particularly sharply.

1.7 The direct and indirect cost of the system in terms of public spending does not, however, tell the whole story of the economics of the legal system since it is also an income generator. As the economies of England and Wales have become increasingly service-based, the provision of legal services has grown into a sizeable industry. In 2003, the turnover of the legal services market was a record £18bn. Large city firms, in particular, now each have turnovers worth hundreds of millions of pounds. In 2006–7 the turnover of the legal profession reached £23.3bn; a figure which doubled since 1997. Despite the short-term effects of the economic recession, this increasingly global market in legal services looks likely to grow substantially in coming years. One example of this is the fact that the High Court now generates significant revenue in court fees and legal costs by adjudicating overseas commercial disputes in which contracts have stipulated that disputes be settled in the UK courts as a result of the British judges' general reputation for incorruptibility and high intellectual standards. As the political and economic importance of the legal system has grown, the Ministry of Justice, the government department responsible for the courts and legal services, has also become more significant. Until 2003, it was known as the Lord Chancellor's Department and had traditionally been one of the less important departments. In 2003, its increasing budget and workload was recognized by the creation of a new select committee of the House of Commons set up specifically to scrutinize the Department's work. It changed its name in 2003 to the Department of Constitutional Affairs, which was an indication of the Department's wider remit. Then in May 2007 it changed its name again to the Ministry of Justice and acquired some of the Home Office's functions, bringing together, for the first time, responsibility for the entire justice system – the courts, prisons, and probation services.

1.8 This increase in the size and economic importance of the legal system has been accompanied by the accumulation of more political power within the courts. For most of the twentieth century the senior judiciary in England and Wales generally sought a very limited political role, stressing the need to maintain a strict division between the law-making role of elected politicians and the more restricted role of judges in interpreting and applying the law. The expansion by the higher courts of the law of judicial review over the last 40 years and the introduction of the Human Rights Act in 1998 have both eroded that distinction and given judges a greater input in decision-making in politically sensitive areas. In addition, the increasing domination of the legislative process by the Government and the reduced role of backbenchers in Parliament has led the judiciary to be described, at times, as an unofficial opposition. During the 1980s, the Conservative Government faced more successful challenges to its policies in the courts than in Parliament and the tension between the judicial and executive branches of government was particularly acute. Nor did this tension significantly reduce under the Labour administration. Since 1997 the courts have ruled against the Government in a number of judicial review cases which challenged official policy in the areas of immigration, asylum, and counter-terrorism.

1.9 The growth of judicial power nationally has been paralleled by the increasing influence of judges in international affairs through the growing importance of international law. Judges from England and Wales participate in a wide range of international courts such as the International Court of Justice, the European Court of Justice, the European Court of Human Rights, and various international tribunals such as the International Criminal Tribunal for the Former Yugoslavia in The Hague. In addition to an expanding role abroad, the increasing legal authority of international law and legal institutions in England and Wales has drawn the judiciary beyond the narrow confines of domestic common law and statutes. The traditional isolationism of judges is disappearing and the judiciary increasingly sees itself as part of an international legal order applying and adapting recognized legal principles to the particular conditions of England and Wales.

1.10   One effect of this increasing importance of the judiciary both nationally and internationally is the growing support for constitutional change both to protect judicial independence and to secure greater judicial accountability. The need for a stricter separation of powers between the executive and the legislature on the one hand and the judiciary on the other has become a more pressing concern. The role of the Lord Chancellor and the organization of the Appellate Committee of the House of Lords became the subject of root and branch reform with the passing of the Constitutional Reform Act in 2005, discussed in more detail in chapter 2 and chapter 16. The Act provided for the removal or reform of many of the functions of the Lord Chancellor, including transferring the role of head of the judiciary to the Lord Chief Justice. The Act also provided for the creation of a separate Supreme Court in order to remove the Law Lords from the House of Lords and set up a judicial appointments commission to select the judges.

The pace of change in the legal system

1.11   Despite the traditionally slow pace of change in England and Wales, the general trend in relation to reforming the legal system has been one of acceleration. This change is most marked in the area of criminal justice. Forty years ago the subject barely received a mention in the election manifestos of the main political parties. Now it is a key issue on which governments are judged by the media and voters, and there is pressure for the main parties to vie with each other to demonstrate that they are the 'toughest' on crime and the most successful at reducing the crime rate and tackling offenders. The search for improved justice policies has given rise to a greater willingness to scrutinize the system. At any one time there are a number of official reports and inquiries being conducted into some aspect of the legal system. In 2000, for example, a Court of Appeal Judge, Sir Robin Auld, was asked by the Government to conduct a thorough review of the criminal justice process less than 10 years after the Royal Commission on Criminal Justice carried out a full investigation lasting three years. Both reports recommended a huge array of changes, many of which have been implemented.

1.12 This changing attitude to the legal system has required the Government to make available the parliamentary time to bring about the necessary legislative changes. In particular, it has become common for the Government to introduce in Parliament at least one new Bill in the area of criminal justice every year. The concern of the judiciary about the increasing quantity of criminal justice legislation is reflected in the following comment by Lord Justice Rose, Vice President of the Court of Appeal (Criminal Division):

> It is more than a decade since the late Lord Taylor of Gosforth CJ called for a reduction in the torrent of legislation affecting criminal justice. Regrettably, that call has gone unheeded by successive governments. Indeed, the quantity of such legislation has increased and its quality has, if anything, diminished. (*R v Bradley*, 2005)

The diminishing quality of criminal justice legislation has also provoked stinging criticism from Mr Justice Mitting in a recent case:

> Section 174(1)(b)(i) of the Criminal Justice Act 2003 requires a court passing sentence to explain to an offender in ordinary language the effect of the sentence. This requirement has been in place since 1991. These proceedings show that, in relation to perfectly ordinary consecutive sentences imposed since the coming into force of much of the Criminal Justice Act 2003, this task is impossible. Indeed, so impossible that it has taken from 12 noon until 12 minutes to five, with a slightly lengthier short adjournment than usual for reading purposes, to explain the relevant statutory provisions to me, a professional judge.

> The position at which I have arrived and which I will explain in detail in a moment is one of which I despair. It is simply unacceptable in a society governed by the rule of law for it to be well nigh impossible to discern from statutory provisions what a sentence means in practice. That is the effect here... (*R v HMP Drake Hall and Minister of State for Justice*, 2008)

1.13 Nor is the increasing pace of change restricted to the criminal justice system. In the last decade the civil justice system has undergone a complete overhaul in the reforms proposed by Lord Woolf with the aim of increasing the speed and fairness of the system and reducing its cost. Similarly, the legal profession has experienced an unprecedented number of reforms in recent years. Internal pressure for change within the profession has been driven by the need to adapt to new working practices, fast-changing markets, and more international competition. External pressure has come from the attempts by successive governments to increase competition, reduce restrictive practices, and strengthen consumer power in the legal system.

1.14 This process has also affected the judiciary. Having expanded rapidly in size and significance in the last few decades, it has been forced to professionalize its practices, increase the amount of training offered to judges, and adopt better methods for communicating its work through the media. At the same time, the pressure to increase openness in the way judges are selected and to ensure a sufficiently diverse background of judges on the bench in the light of its growing political power has led to the complete reform of the judicial appointments.

Efficiency versus quality of justice

1.15 The common goal underlying many of these changes is a drive for a more cost-effective and efficient legal system. Since 1979, when Margaret Thatcher became Prime Minister, the search for cheaper ways of running the legal system has become endemic, as it has in almost all areas of publicly funded services. The Labour Government since its first election victory in 1997 pursued this goal as enthusiastically as the Conservative administration before it.

1.16 The introduction of new ways to fund the legal system and attempts to encourage competition in the legal profession has led to reforms such as the introduction of American-style no-win no-fee conditional fee arrangements; the reduction of cases eligible for legal aid and the abolition of the solicitors' monopoly on conveyancing; and the barristers' monopoly on advocacy in the higher courts.

1.17 The introduction of these reforms has led to fierce debate about whether such changes save money at an unacceptable cost in terms of their effect on the quality of justice. The tension between the competing goals of efficiency versus justice can be seen in all areas. Does replacing legal aid with conditional fees increase access to justice or reduce it? Does cutting the rate of legal aid fees save money on overpaid 'fat cat' lawyers or drive hardworking firms and chambers away from publicly funded work?

Access to justice versus litigation reduction

1.18 One clear example of the prioritization of the needs of efficiency in the legal system has been the introduction of changes designed to discourage the use of the courts, and to ensure that where they are used, cases are decided in the lower courts at less cost. In one sense, this policy merely reinforces the traditional distribution of work in the courts. The popular image of the legal system is a courtroom presided over by a High Court judge in wig and red gown listening to arguments put forward by rows of barristers. This is not surprising since trials for serious offences such as rape and murder, or libel cases involving the rich and famous, attract more media attention than any other aspect of the legal system. This focus, however, contributes to a common misconception that the law is found in the higher courts. In fact, very few legal problems ever reach the courts at all, let alone come to be argued in court by highly paid lawyers and decided by a senior judge. Most instances in which the civil or criminal law has been broken are not pursued by the people involved, or are resolved informally between the parties without the participation of legal professionals. Where lawyers do become involved in a legal dispute, particularly where it concerns a civil rather than criminal case, their first function is usually to help to settle the problem by negotiation in order to avoid the time, cost and uncertainty of a court case.

1.19 In addition, much of the work undertaken by lawyers takes place before any legal problem has arisen and is intended to avoid the risk of a court case. By advising people on the legal implications of their actions and drafting legal documents such as contracts or wills, future legal disputes are prevented. Where such disputes have already arisen, and a court action is begun, the vast majority are resolved without a full court hearing. Similarly, the great majority of criminal cases end with the defendant pleading guilty before the trial, leaving only a short court hearing to determine the sentence. In addition, most cases which are heard in full are dealt with relatively quickly and cheaply in tribunals and the lower courts – the county court or the magistrates' courts.

1.20 The legal system can therefore be seen as a pyramid. Although overall it has expanded significantly, only very few cases ever reach the upper echelons of the system. The vast majority of legal problems are dealt with privately, with or without the help of lawyers, leaving the court system serving the function of a relatively expensive and time-consuming last resort. Most cases that do reach the courts are heard in the lower courts and processed quickly through the system, with a full trial in the higher courts being statistically an unusual outcome for a case and making up only a tiny fraction of the legal system at the top of the pyramid. These cases may be very significant for the people concerned, since they often involve large sums of money or allegations of very serious wrongdoing. They may also serve a very important symbolic function. The way the legal system functions in such high-profile cases which attract intensive media coverage can have a lasting influence on public confidence in the courts. But in order to understand the nature of the system it is important to keep in mind the relationship between the totality of legal problems and the very limited role played by the courts in resolving them.

1.21 The description of the legal system as a pyramid is now more accurate than ever before. The idea that access to justice means the availability of a full court hearing has been widely rejected. Instead, it has been reconceptualized to mean access to advice and assistance which helps promote alternative means of settling disputes so that the court system represents a last resort for the small minority of cases that cannot be resolved in any other way. This change in attitude towards the role of litigation and the anxiety which the prospect of the development of a more litigious society generally promotes reveals an interesting paradox at the heart of the justice system. On the one hand, the rule of law is considered a keystone of a democratic society; yet on the other, the legal system is regarded as a costly, time-consuming, and often destructive way to deal with social or economic problems. This tension runs through the legal system. Access to justice is recognized as a measure of the effectiveness of the legal system, yet rising caseloads in the court are viewed with alarm. It seems that we are not sure whether we want more justice or less. What we have become clearer about, or at least what politicians have agreed upon, is that it should cost less.

Private versus public justice

1.22 In common with so many other areas of public life, one way in which many of the recent reforms have sought to cut costs and improve efficiency has been to import the practices and values of the private sector. This has given rise to a debate about the purpose of the legal system. Is it a part of the welfare state which, like the health service and education, should be freely available for all at the point of delivery on the basis of need? Or is it a consumer service which should be purchased by users and self-financing like any other business? Unlike the health service, the legal system narrowly missed a full nationalization process after the Second World War. During the time of the post-war Labour Government there were many who supported the construction of a national legal system in which legal services would be provided by publicly employed lawyers. Instead, it was decided that private solicitors' firms and barristers' chambers should retain their right to continue as businesses, with the Government paying for their services on a case-by-case basis through the legal aid system which was set up in 1949.

1.23 Gradually, however, there has been an expansion in the proportion of lawyers employed in the public sector. In 1986, the Crown Prosecution Service was set up, employing solicitors and barristers to prepare criminal cases for court independently of the police. In 2000, the first pilot schemes for a public defender scheme were set up, employing salaried lawyers to defend those charged with offences. There are now four Public Defender Service Offices in Cheltenham, Darlington, Pontypridd, and Swansea. In 2007–8 the Public Defender Service dealt with 3,703 cases. While the Government insists that most criminal defence work will still be carried out by independent lawyers working in private practice, it is likely that the public defender scheme will expand in coming years.

1.24 The result of this historical development has been the creation of a mixed public and private legal system with a growing divide between the civil and criminal justice system. While criminal cases are increasingly both paid for out of public funds and handled by employed lawyers, civil justice is expected to be largely self-funded and provided by private practitioners. Since the late 1990s, court fees charged for bringing a case to court have been set at levels which will cover the full court costs of the case. This particularly radical change, the effective privatization of a key feature of the justice process, has come about with little attention outside the legal world and very little public debate.

Lay versus professional justice

1.25 In contrast, one area in which there has been a high level of public debate in recent years has been the role of lay personnel in the legal system, in particular the jury system. Unlike most other countries in the world, the legal system in England and Wales relies heavily on the use of lay participants in the form of magistrates and juries. Approximately 28,000 lay magistrates are responsible for hearing over 97 per cent of criminal cases and a substantial amount of family work such as proceedings concerning the care of children. Only a small proportion of cases are heard by professional magistrates, now called District Judges (Magistrates' Court), without any lay involvement, whilst under 4 per cent of criminal cases are heard in the Crown Court by a judge and lay jury. This extensive use of untrained lay people in the criminal justice process is regarded by many lawyers in England and Wales as a valuable form of direct participation which keeps the justice system firmly tied to public values. The jury system, in particular, is often claimed to be a cornerstone of the democratic system and a protection against state oppression through political prosecutions.

1.26 Despite the strength of feeling in support of the jury, in 1999 the Government introduced a Bill to curb the right of the defendant to choose to be heard by a jury in certain cases. This was the latest in a long line of reforms designed to reduce the use of the jury. The legislation was intended to speed up the justice system by reducing the workload of the Crown Court and save over £100m a year in cases which the Government claimed were not serious enough to warrant a jury trial and could be heard more cheaply in the magistrates' courts. However, objections led to two defeats for the Bill in the House of Lords and the decision by the Government not to use its statutory powers to override the decisions of the Lords and force it through a third time. Attempts to remove jury trial in serious and complex fraud have been equally unsuccessful to date. Although provision was made in the Criminal Justice Act 2003 for such cases to be tried by judge alone, repeated attempts to bring these provisions into force between 2005 and 2007 were abandoned as a result of parliamentary opposition. The provisions of the 2003 Act which allow a case to be heard by a judge alone in the case of jury tampering are, however, in force. A case can be heard without a jury if the judge is satisfied that there is 'evidence of a real and present danger that jury tampering would take place', and 'notwithstanding any steps (including the provision of police protection) which might reasonably be taken to prevent jury tampering, the likelihood that it would take place would be so substantial as to make it necessary in the interests of justice for the trial to be conducted without a jury'. Applying this provision, on 18 June 2009, the Court of Appeal allowed the first ever Crown Court trial to be held without a jury. The case in question involved four men accused of an armed robbery at Heathrow Airport in February 2004. It was the fourth time the case has been tried, but this time in front of only a single judge (*R v T, B, C, H*, 2009).

1.27 The lay magistracy has also been the subject of recent scrutiny, with Government proposals to transfer some of its workload to the professional District Judges (Magistrates' Court). However, this too appears to have been shelved in the light of the findings of a report on its workings commissioned by the Lord Chancellor's Department (as was) which concluded that it was a cost-effective system and that the quality of justice provided by lay magistrates was generally good. Although the numbers of District Judges (Magistrates' Court) has increased from 91 to 136 since 1997, they are still a relatively small part of the magistrates' courts system. While the jury system and lay magistracy may have won a temporary reprieve, the debate about whether lay decision-makers are more or less consistent, fair, competent, and cost-effective than professional judges is likely to continue.

Inquisitorial versus adversarial justice

1.28 Another way in which cost-saving has been pursued is through the reduction in the use of adversarial methods. The involvement of lay personnel is not the only feature of the system in England and Wales which is very different from other legal systems, particularly in the rest of Europe. The use of an adversarial or accusatorial system is found in few other European countries, most of which use some form of inquisitorial system.

1.29 A key feature of the distinction between the two is that the adversarial system is based on a contest model whereas the inquisitorial system can be described as a form of inquiry. In the adversarial system the lawyers play a central role in presenting each side's case. Ideally, both sides should be equally well resourced and should strive to present their case in the best possible light. They do this by examining witnesses called by their side and cross-examining witnesses called by the other side according to relatively strict rules of evidence. The role of the judge in the adversarial system is traditionally a passive one; acting as a neutral umpire ensuring that both sides comply with the rules of court and deciding which of the two versions is most credible. In a criminal case the burden of proving the case rests with the prosecution, which must satisfy the court that the defendant is guilty 'beyond reasonable doubt'. In a civil case, the equivalent burden of proof is that of a 'balance of probabilities'.

1.30 In contrast, in an inquisitorial system the judges play a more active and central role. They decide which witnesses to call and ask them and the parties in the case questions in order to piece together the facts. Because the lawyers play a more secondary role, there is less need for the kind of formal rules of evidence which are used in an adversarial system to ensure that each side plays by the same rules. In addition, the judges in an inquisitorial system are involved in the investigation of the case as examining magistrates. In the more serious cases they direct the police, gather evidence, interview the defendant, and pass the material gathered to the trial judge for hearing if and when enough evidence is accumulated. In France, for example, an examining magistrate called the *juge d'instruction* directs the criminal investigation in more serious cases and prepares a file of evidence, called the *dossier*, for use at the trial.

1.31 It is often inaccurately claimed that the adversarial system is a contest and the inquisitorial system is a search for truth. In fact, both are different ways of exposing the truth and each has strengths and weaknesses. One limitation of the adversarial system is that if some facts are not in either party's interest to bring out, they may never be heard. A common criticism of the inquisitorial system is that the rights of the defendant are given insufficient weight.

1.32 Each system has its supporters and there is a tendency for critics of the system in England and Wales to look to the inquisitorial processes for answers. In the early 1990s, in the wake of the high-profile miscarriages of justice cases such as the *Guildford Four*, *Birmingham Six* and *Judith Ward*, there was considerable media interest in the adoption of more inquisitorial systems as a way of guarding against the wrongful conviction of the innocent. Some prominent lawyers, such as Michael Mansfield QC, argued for the adoption of an examining magistrate system in England and Wales. However, more recently concerns about long delays before trial and inefficiencies in the investigation process have led to a less uncritical view of the inquisitorial system used in much of the rest of Europe.

1.33 Although the two systems are often presented by supporters and detractors as being completely distinct, in fact most jurisdictions contain elements of both. The inquest system in England and Wales, for example, is, as its name suggests, a strongly inquisitorial procedure. This has, indeed, been one of the reasons for its unpopularity. The lack of legal representation for families of the dead and the absence of cross-examination of witnesses have been the subject of public criticism. As well as examples of the mixed use of adversarial and inquisitorial processes, there is a tendency as European states work more closely together both politically and legally, for the systems in different countries to draw closer.

1.34 France, for example, reformed its pre-trial detention rules in the 1990s to include the right of a suspect to see a lawyer on arrest, while the courts in England and Wales have introduced a more inquisitorial-style control of cases by judges in the civil justice system and greater pre-trial disclosure of evidence in both the civil and criminal courts (RCCJ 1993; Lord Woolf, 1996). In addition, there is a greater tendency for the courts in England and Wales to move away from long oral presentation of evidence and to require counsel to present their cases in writing through 'skeleton' arguments which cut down the length of time needed in the hearing. Time limits on oral argument have also started to be introduced in some parts of the court system and this practice is likely to become more common.

1.35 Despite this trend towards convergence, real differences remain between the adversarial and inquisitorial processes which are a product of the different historical development of each particular country and remind us that each legal system must be considered in the light of its own particular legal and political background.

FURTHER READING

Judicial Statistics 2005 (http://www.official-documents.co.uk/document/cm67/6799/6799.asp).

Information on the Criminal Justice System in England and Wales (1999, Home Office publication) (http://www.homeoffice.gov.uk/rds/digest41.html).

The Runciman Royal Commission on Criminal Justice (Cmnd 2263, London: HMSO, 1993), ch 1, paras 11–16.

Jacqueline Hodgson 'Reforming French Criminal Justice' (November 2001) Legal Action 6.

Lord Justice Leggatt 'The Future of the Oral Tradition in the Court of Appeal' (1995) 14 Civil Justice Quarterly 11.

Professor Hazel Genn *Paths to Justice: What People Do and Think about Going to Law* (1999, Oxford: Hart Publishing).

Rod Morgan and Neil Russell *The Judiciary in the Magistrates' Courts* (2000) (http://www.homeoffice.gov.uk/rds/pdfs/occ-judiciary.pdf).

John Spencer, The Drafting of Criminal Legislation: Need it be so Impenetrable?, 2008 Annual Judicial Studies Board Lecture (available at the JSB website http://www.jsboard. co.uk/downloads/Annual_Lecture_2008.doc).

SELF-TEST QUESTIONS

1 What are the main differences between the adversarial and the inquisitorial systems of trial? Which is the better system?

2 List three reasons why so few legal problems end up in court.

3 What are the advantages and disadvantages of the increasing privatization of the civil justice system?

4 'There is nothing systematic about the English legal system.' Discuss.

2

The organization of the courts

SUMMARY

This chapter describes the main courts and tribunals and outlines the hierarchical and bottom-heavy distribution of work in the system. It highlights the fact that the work of the top appellate courts is very different from that of the trial courts where large numbers of cases are processed quickly and cheaply. It concludes that the growing political importance of the caseload of the top courts has widened this divide between the upper and lower courts.

2.1 Many of the themes identified in the introductory chapter can be seen clearly in the structure of the courts. The pyramid shape of the system, in particular, is evident in the sharp division between the workload of the upper and lower courts. Almost all the work of the courts is carried out in the lower tiers – the magistrates' courts, the county court and the tribunals. Most of the day-to-day work there involves fact-finding and applying settled law to disputed facts. At all levels, however, judges, magistrates and tribunal members may be asked to decide on conflicting or uncertain questions of law. The higher up the court system one goes, the more time is spent dealing with such questions of law. The Justices of the Supreme Court do almost nothing else since permission for a case to be heard by the Supreme Court is only granted in cases involving a question of law of 'general public importance'. With the exception of the specialized courts such as the patents courts or tribunals, most courts have a wide-ranging jurisdiction, sometimes covering both civil and criminal work and hearing appeals as well as trials. In the High Court and above, judges are expected to be able to get to grips with law in all areas, even if they have had little experience of these as practising lawyers. This tradition is nicely illustrated by the comment of Lord Parker, a former Lord Chief Justice, that the first summing up in a criminal trial which he ever heard was the first one he gave as a judge.

Although it is unlikely that today a full-time judge would be appointed to sit in the Crown Court who had no experience as a lawyer in the criminal courts, the principle of generalization remains and it is common for civil law practitioners to be appointed as Recorders (part-time judges, on which see chapter 16) to try criminal cases in the Crown Court.

Tribunals

2.2 Tribunals are not formally part of the court system, although they are increasingly integrated in terms of training, procedures, personnel and appeals. The tribunal system was set up to provide a cheaper, faster and less formal process for challenging official administrative decisions concerning such matters as welfare benefits and tax and for settling private disputes such as between employers and employees. Many were established in the early part of the last century as a way of easing the burden of the increasing caseload of the courts. Support for the use of tribunals was not, however, universal. In the 1920s and 1930s a number of senior judges publicly criticized tribunals as bodies lacking the due process and constitutional safeguards of the courts.

2.3 Despite these concerns, the pragmatic need to relieve the pressure on the courts led to an acceptance of the place of tribunals in the legal system. Since the 1950s the tribunal system has expanded greatly in size and scope. Tribunals deal with vast numbers of cases each year. Between 2006 and 2007, 655,430 cases were decided by tribunals under the supervision of the Council on Tribunals. The workload of tribunals is diverse, covering matters such as social security, asylum and immigration, employment, tax, mental health, freedom of information and leasehold valuation. Many tribunal decisions affect people's liberty, livelihood and even their lives. For example, the Immigration Appeal Tribunal (which hears appeals from the immigration adjudicators) will decide whether or not a person claiming asylum on the grounds that they would be tortured or killed if sent home should be deported back to their country of origin.

2.4 The usual composition of a tribunal is that of a legally trained chairperson assisted by two lay members, though other permutations are also found. Lay members often have some professional expertise which is relevant to the subject-matter of the tribunal. The most important tribunals are chaired by High Court judges. In common with the civil court system the tendency in recent years has been to cut costs by reducing the numbers of members sitting on the tribunals. Whereas the norm has traditionally been three members, it is now much more common for cases to be heard by one person alone.

2.5 Some of the problems raised by tribunals are the flip-side of their advantages. The flexibility, speed and low cost which were the main reasons for creating them have been criticized as giving rise to inconsistency, rushed decision-making, and poor quality representation as a result of the absence of legal aid for those bringing cases. In the light of these concerns and the growing expansion of the system, the whole tribunal system was reviewed by a Court of Appeal judge, Sir Andrew Leggatt, in 2000.

2.6 The Lord Chancellor asked Sir Andrew to undertake the review in order to ensure a more coherent development of the currently haphazard growth of the system. The background of the incorporation of the European Convention on Human Rights into domestic law and the need to ensure that the tribunal system complied with the Convention was a particularly important part of the review and included in its terms of reference. The requirement that tribunals should be independent and impartial as required by Article 6 of the Convention is, for example, a particularly pressing issue.

2.7 The Leggatt report, produced in 2001, contained 361 recommendations for change. The key reform which was proposed was the unification of the system under the charge of a Senior President, who would be a High Court judge, and administered by one Tribunals Service. The report argued that this change would ensure that tribunals were independent of their sponsoring departments to avoid the conflict of interest which could arise under the current arrangements whereby tribunals test the policies and decisions of ministers who appoint and support them:

> ... when a department of state may provide the administrative support for a tribunal, may pay the fees and expenses of tribunal members, may appoint some of them, may provide IT support ... and may promote legislation proscribing the procedures which it is to follow, the tribunal neither appears to be independent, nor is it independent in fact (Leggatt, para 3).

2.8 Sir Andrew also noted that many tribunals were losing their original user-friendly style which was intended to be a defining feature of the system, and he proposed to remedy this through a number of changes designed to ensure that tribunals were more accessible to users and to encourage people to feel confident in presenting a case without legal assistance. Controversially, the report argued against the extension of legal aid for this reason. Instead, it proposed better provision of information to users on how to prepare and present a case (including such assistance as telephone helplines and the availability of translators) and fuller feedback to users on the progress and decision-making in their case. More generally, the report argued the need for a change of culture which recognized 'just how daunting the tribunal experience usually is for first-time users'. This change of culture would prioritize the watchwords of informality, simplicity, efficiency and proportionality (para 31).

2.9 Sir Andrew's recommendations have largely been adopted by the Government. The Tribunals Service was launched in April 2006 and the Courts, Tribunals and

Enforcement Act 2007 created a new two-tier tribunal structure, consisting of the 'First-tier Tribunal' and the 'Upper Tribunal', into which most of the current tribunal jurisdictions were transferred. The tribunal jurisdictions within the First-tier and the Upper Tribunal are organized into 'chambers'. The intention is to preserve the expertise of tribunal members because only members of a chamber to which a case has been allocated can decide it. The five chambers of the First-tier Tribunal are social entitlement; health, education and social care; tax and finance; general regulatory; and land. The Upper Tribunal is organized into three chambers: administrative appeals, tax and finance and land. The Employment Tribunal, the Employment Appeal Tribunal and the Asylum and Immigration Tribunal remain outside this new structure and instead they form separate 'pillars' within the wider tribunal system presided over by Lord Justice Carnwarth, Senior President of Tribunals.

2.10 The tendency is for tribunals to use a more inquisitorial approach, with greater proactive intervention by the tribunal members in the process of questioning witnesses or evaluating evidence. The level of formality also varies from tribunal to tribunal, but again the tendency is towards less rigid procedural rules and a willingness to allow all parties to present their case in their own words so that, whatever the outcome, they feel that they have been given a fair hearing. In contrast to the court system, there used to be a great variety of different jurisdictions and procedures in the tribunal system depending on when and for what function they were set up. The 2007 Act aims to develop a more uniform and coherent approach to procedure. A Tribunal Procedure Committee now makes Tribunal Procedure Rules which are applicable to all tribunals in the new system. Just like the Civil Procedure Rules (discussed in chapter 9) the Tribunal Procedure Rules are also subject to an overriding objective requiring that: (i) justice is done; (ii) the system is accessible and fair; (iii) proceedings are handled quickly and efficiently; and (iv) that rules are simple and simply expressed.

2.11 Tribunals are now seen as a distinctive alternative to the courts. They were created in order to provide for the quick, cheap and expert resolution of administrative disputes. The reforms discussed above further those objectives by simplifying tribunal procedures, maintaining the expertise of each 'chamber', and cutting administration costs by creating a single Tribunal Service.

Magistrates' courts

2.12 There are over 700 magistrates' courts in England and Wales. Their jurisdiction dates back to the thirteenth century and they are rooted in the local justice system. Most of the work carried out in the magistrates' courts is criminal, but there is also a substantial civil jurisdiction including family matters. All criminal cases begin in the magistrates' courts and 95 per cent of cases are concluded at this level.

2.13 Approximately 1.9 million cases per year are heard by magistrates. Many are relatively minor such as traffic offences, possession of class B drugs and low-level criminal damage. But some more serious offences such as assault are also tried here. Approximately 90 per cent of defendants plead guilty and of those who plead not guilty, approximately 80 per cent are convicted. Therefore an acquittal following a trial is a relatively rare event in the magistrates' courts.

2.14 There are approximately 28,000 magistrates, almost all of whom are lay people who sit part-time. Only about 120 magistrates are professional lawyers sitting full-time. Originally called stipendiary magistrates, they have been renamed District Judges (Magistrates' Court) in order to bring them more overtly into the main judiciary. The District Judges sit in busy urban courts where there is a heavy workload to be processed. They hear cases alone, in contrast to lay magistrates who sit in panels of three and have a qualified Clerk to advise them on the law and their sentencing powers. An appeal against sentence or conviction on a question of fact goes to Crown Court, while an appeal against conviction on a question of law alone goes to the Divisional Court of the Queen's Bench Division in the High Court.

2.15 Magistrates play the role of the judge and jury combined, in that they apply the law and determine the facts in each case. After they have reached a verdict in criminal cases (or, more commonly, after a guilty plea by the defendant) they pass sentence. The maximum sentencing powers of magistrates are currently 12 months in custody and a £5,000 fine.

2.16 Although magistrates' sentencing powers are not as great as those of judges in the Crown Court, they have a major impact on the criminal justice system because they deal with a much larger caseload. The average custodial sentence handed down by magistrates is less than that given by judges, but the greater numbers of those convicted in the magistrates' courts means that in any one year, most people who serve custodial sentences have been sentenced by magistrates. Recent increases in the sentencing powers of magistrates from 6 months to 12 months in custody have extended still further the dominant role of the magistracy in determining the size of the prison population.

Crown Court

2.17 Whereas each magistrates' court is jurisdictionally independent, covering a certain geographical area, the Crown Court is one body, sitting in different centres covering the whole of England and Wales. There are 92 Crown Court centres, varying in size depending on the caseload of the area. The Old Bailey (the Central Criminal Court) is the Crown Court for the City of London, but it is not a typical Crown Court because it is staffed only by senior judges, and hears many of the most serious criminal cases in London.

2.18 Approximately 80,000 cases are committed for trial to the Crown Court per year – about 5 per cent of the total criminal caseload. Most of these are serious cases such as wounding, manslaughter, arson, murder and serious fraud. Appeal against conviction and sentence from the Crown Court is to the Court of Appeal (Criminal Division).

2.19 When a defendant pleads not guilty in the Crown Court, the trial is heard by a judge and a lay jury of 12 people. The judge instructs the jury on the law, sums up the evidence at the end of the case and determines sentence in the event of a guilty plea or a finding of guilt by the jury. The judge also decides on the procedure to be followed during the case, for example whether or not certain evidence can be admitted or particular questions can be put to witnesses.

2.20 The jury decides on the question of guilt based on its assessment of the credibility of the evidence heard. Approximately 60 per cent of defendants plead guilty in the Crown Court. Of those who contest their case, approximately 50 per cent are acquitted either by the jury or on the instruction of the judge where she or he considers that there is not enough evidence for the jury safely to convict. A defendant's chance of acquittal is therefore considerably higher in the Crown Court than the magistrates' courts. The reasons for this are examined in chapter 18.

County court

2.21 The county court hears the majority of civil cases, such as money claims, divorce, and negligence actions. Cases of a value up to £25,000 are nearly always heard in the county court, as are many cases of up to £50,000 or more. Approximately 1.8 million cases are started each year in the county court, the great majority of which settle before they come to court. The bulk of these cases are money claims or undefended divorces.

2.22 Many smaller cases are heard in the small claims court which is part of the county court. Here the procedures are less formal and costs will not generally be awarded to cover legal fees so that the litigants are encouraged to present the cases themselves. The rules and procedures of the small claims court are designed to ensure that ordinary people with limited resources can afford to bring an action and enforce their rights. Research by Professor John Baldwin in 1999 found that litigants who had used the system were generally satisfied with it, significantly more so than those using the full county court system (Baldwin, 1999).

2.23 However, although the small claims court has achieved the aim of improving access for the less wealthy to a certain extent, many of the cases which are dealt with there are brought by companies such as gas and electricity suppliers who wish to recover outstanding debts from consumers. These cases will either be processed in bulk or, if contested, presented by lawyers whose costs are paid for by the claimants company. Moreover, Baldwin's research also found that most individual claimants who used the system were from professional or managerial backgrounds. This suggests that financial resources are not the only factor in seeking redress in the courts and that knowledge and confidence may also be required, so reducing the accessibility of the system to those without these attributes.

2.24 In recent years the Civil Procedure Rules have been changed to encourage more cases to be heard more quickly and cheaply in the county court rather than the High Court, with the result that the volume, complexity and value of the cases heard at the lower level has increased significantly. There has also been a drive to reduce the number of appeals heard from county court decisions. Appeals against the decision of the county court on a question of law or fact lie to the Court of Appeal (Civil Division) and permission to appeal is now almost always required from the Court of Appeal. These changes are in line with the general trend to ensure that, where possible, cases are heard cheaply, quickly and finally in the lower courts.

High Court

2.25 The most serious civil cases are heard in the High Court which is based in the Royal Courts of Justice in London. High Court cases are also heard around the country by High Court judges who travel 'on circuit' sitting at different court centres to hear the most serious civil cases outside London. The High Court is divided into the following three divisions:

Queen's Bench Division (QBD)

2.26 The QBD hears general civil cases such as breaches of contract claims and actions for torts (civil wrongs). It includes the Administrative Court which hears judicial review cases, which are challenges to the actions and decisions of government and officials. These cases were previously heard in the Divisional Court of the QBD, which is a court of review and hears appeal cases such as appeals on a point of law from the magistrates' courts. The Commercial Court is a specialized part of the QBD which hears commercial disputes.

Chancery Division

2.27 The Chancery Division originally heard cases developed as part of the law of Equity. Cases involve areas of the law such as trusts, wills, intellectual property and bankruptcies.

Family Division

2.28 The Family Division hears matters concerning children and families such as adoption, wardship and complex divorce cases. It will also decide on sensitive cases relating to medical treatment such as whether a person can be forced to undergo life-saving treatment against their will or whether a life-support system of a person in a persistent vegetative state can lawfully be turned off.

Court of Appeal

2.29 Like the High Court, the Court of Appeal is based in the Royal Courts of Justice in London. It is divided into criminal and civil divisions and hears appeals from the High Court, the county court and Crown Court. The Court of Appeal is the engine room of the law, in that the great majority of decisions which shape the law and the legal system are decided here. Almost all cases require the permission of the court to be heard and those that are will be decided by judges sitting in panels of three in the criminal division and two or three in the civil division.

2.30 The Court of Appeal is under considerable pressure of workload and is struggling to cut backlogs, particularly in relation to criminal appeals where the appellant is likely to be in custody awaiting a hearing. One way in which the work of the court has been speeded up in recent years has been to allow High Court judges and Circuit judges to sit with a Lord Justice in the criminal division so that each hearing does not require three Court of Appeal-level judges. This pragmatic approach to the problems of delay is another example of an attempt to strike an appropriate balance between the competing demands of efficiency and quality of justice.

Appellate Committee of the House of Lords

2.31 Although the House of Lords is the upper chamber of the legislature, until July 2009, its membership also included an Appellate Committee which constituted the highest court in the country. Under the provisions of the Constitutional Reform Act

2005 the Appellate Committee was replaced by a new Supreme Court (see chapter 16 below). Prior to the creation of the UK Supreme Court, there were 24 Law Lords, whose formal title was Lords of Appeal. Those 24 consisted of two groups of peers. First, there were 12 Lords of Appeal in Ordinary who constituted the main body of Law Lords. They were salaried and held office until the age of 70. Those professional judges were nearly always appointed from the Court of Appeal in England and Wales or from the higher courts in Northern Ireland and Scotland. The Lords of Appeal in Ordinary were supplemented by other peers who held or had held high judicial office, such as retired Lords of Appeal in Ordinary and current and former Lords Chancellor, Lords Chief Justice and Masters of the Rolls. Those other Lords of Appeal (previously 12 in number) could also have been invited to sit as members of the Appellate Committee until the age of 75. From 75 onwards they continued to be members of the House of Lords and so could speak in debate and vote, but they did not carry out a judicial role.

2.32 The Law Lords have the same rights as any other members of the House of Lords to speak in debate and vote, but usually they refrain from doing so except on matters of relevance to the justice system. Recently, Law Lords have spoken on topics such as the Proceeds of Crime Bill, the European Union arrest warrants, and European asylum procedure. Some, however, have also spoken on topics not related to the legal system such as the legislation banning fox-hunting and the Culture and Recreation Bill.

2.33 From 2000, the Appellate Committee was required to hear more politically and socially sensitive cases involving human rights issues as a result of the Human Rights Act 1998, which incorporated the European Convention of Human Rights into domestic law and which came into force in October 2000 (see chapter 4 below). Under the Act, the decisions of all public authorities, including the courts, must comply with the Convention. As the final appeal body in most cases, the House of Lords had the job of deciding whether or not important and often competing Convention rights have been breached, such as freedom of expression and the right to respect for family life.

2.34 In 2001, for example, the Law Lords were required to consider an appeal brought by Dianne Pretty, a woman dying of Motor Neurone Disease (*R (Pretty) v DPP (Secretary of State for the Home Department intervening)* (2001)). She was almost completely paralysed by the disease and faced a slow and painful death. She wished her husband to be able to help her to commit suicide if necessary and the couple had sought an undertaking from the Director of Public Prosecutions that he would not prosecute Mr Pretty in such an event. The DPP held that it was not within his power to give such an undertaking not to prosecute, and Dianne Pretty challenged that decision on the basis that it breached her human rights under the Convention – in particular her right to life, to respect for family life and the right not to be subjected to inhuman treatment. The House of Lords considered each of the relevant convention rights in turn with reference to the European case law in the area and academic writings on the subject and concluded that her rights had not been breached. That decision was later upheld in the European Court of Human Rights. The final judgment delivered by the House of Lords in July 2009 also concerned assisted suicide. In *R (on the application of Debbie Purdy) v DPP* (2009), their Lordships held that the Code of Crown Prosecutors breached Article 8 of the Convention because it gave insufficient guidance regarding the circumstances in which a prosecution for assisting another's suicide would be in the public interest. This case was deliberately picked to be the last, historic judgment by the Appellate Committee because it was a case to which the public could relate which did not involve dry legal issues.

The UK Supreme Court

2.35 The increasing role of the Appellate Committee in determining sensitive human rights cases was an important factor in the decision to establish a new Supreme Court independent from the House of Lords. The inclusion of the highest court of appeal in the legislature is an unusual breach of the concept of the separation of powers. Most other countries, particularly those in which the judges are required to interpret a Bill of Rights of some kind, such as the US or Canada, have a Constitutional Court or a Supreme Court which is given the task of deciding human rights questions. As the work undertaken by the House of Lords grew more like that of Supreme Courts around the world, the case for major reform strengthened. In June 2003, the Government announced unexpectedly that a new Supreme Court, with the same powers as the Appellate Committee, would be set up and the Law Lords would be taken out of the House of Lords. The Bill was highly controversial and there were strong arguments advanced for and against the proposal to set up a new court. Defenders of the traditional arrangements argued that the Law Lords contributed a valuable pool of expertise to the legislature. They also said that the convention that Law Lords did not engage in debate or voting on political issues maintained a clear separation, in practice, between the judicial and legislative functions of the House.

2.36 Against this, supporters of the change argued that the top court must not only be independent of the legislature, it must also be seen to be so. The establishment of a separate court in its own building would, they claimed, ensure this separation and enhance confidence in the court. Moreover, it was said that the convention that Law Lords should not engage in debate was not always observed. The retired Law Lords in particular often participated in the legislative process despite the fact that they regularly sat as members of the Appellate Committee.

2.37 The intensity of the debate over the appropriateness of the Law Lords continuing to sit in the House of Lords is a reflection of the fact that in England and Wales there is a surprising lack of agreement about the role which the separation of powers plays in the constitution. In 1991, Lord Mackay, then Lord Chancellor, declared that:

> Our constitution, unlike that of, for example, the United States, is not built on the principle that the legislative, the executive and the judicial powers should be separate and equal (Lord Mackay, 1991, p 258).

However, in 1996, Lord Irvine, shortly before replacing Lord Mackay as Lord Chancellor, stated during a parliamentary debate on the constitutional role of the judiciary that: 'it is time to return to first principles. The British Constitution, largely unwritten, is firmly based on the separation of powers.' The provisions of the Constitutional Reform Act represent the most significant statutory attempt to establish a clearer separation of powers between the judiciary and the other branches of government.

2.38 In October 2009 the 12 Lords of Appeal in Ordinary became the first members of the Supreme Court (called Justices of the Supreme Court). The new court is located in its newly refurbished building in Middlesex Guildhall, opposite Parliament. Unlike many supreme courts around the world, the UK Supreme Court will not have the power to strike down Acts of Parliament. Whether this will inhibit the Justices in their work as constitutional watchdogs and whether they will seek such a power in the future remains to be seen.

Judicial Committee of the Privy Council

2.39 The Privy Council is an ancient body, the original function of which was to advise the monarch. The Judicial Committee is made up of senior judges who are members of the Privy Council. All Court of Appeal judges and Law Lords are automatically members of the Privy Council. In practice, most cases in the Judicial Committee are heard by the Justices of the Supreme Court (formerly the Law Lords).

2.40 Historically the Judicial Committee fulfilled an important function hearing appeals from Commonwealth countries. Gradually most of these countries have abolished the right of appeal to the Privy Council so that this aspect of its role has reduced. However, some Caribbean countries which still use the death penalty have retained this right and many of the criminal appeals which are heard involve defendants who have been sentenced to death. The decisions of the Privy Council as the last court of appeal in these cases are therefore extremely important.

2.41 Opinion differs about the record of the Judicial Committee in these Caribbean criminal appeals. The judges have sometimes ruled that it would be unlawful for a person to be executed and sometimes not. Since the UK has now signed the protocol to the European Convention of Human Rights which abolishes the death penalty there is a question mark over the legitimacy of the Judicial Committee upholding the use of a punishment that breaches the Convention, albeit in another country. In practice, this problem will soon be academic as a result of the establishment of the Caribbean Court of Justice in 2005 which will take over the role of the Privy Council in hearing these final appeal cases. It is anticipated that the new court is less likely to challenge the use of the death penalty.

2.42 In 1998, the decline in the importance of the Privy Council was temporarily reversed when it was made the final court of appeal in relation to devolution appeals from Scotland, Wales and Northern Ireland. Because the devolution legislation also incorporated the provisions of the Human Rights Act 1998 in relation to the devolved regions, these appeals can raise human rights issues as well as questions about the statutory limits of the division of power between the different devolved regions and Westminster. However, this new lease of life for the Judicial Committee was short-lived, since under the provisions of the Constitutional Reform Act 2005 its devolution jurisdiction was given to the new Supreme Court when it began work in October 2009, leaving the Privy Council with only a very limited domestic jurisdiction in a number of rather peripheral areas such as hearing appeals from the Disciplinary Committee of the Royal College of Veterinary Surgeons, and of the General Medical Council.

FURTHER READING

Lord Mackay 'The Lord Chancellor in the 1990s' (1991) 44 Current Legal Problems 241.

Michael Zander *Cases and Material on the English Legal System* (1999, London: Butterworths), ch 1.

Sir Robin Auld *Review of the Criminal Courts,* ch 3 'The Criminal Courts and their Management' (http://www.criminal-courts-review.org.uk/chpt3.pdf).

The Wakeham Royal Commission on the Reform of the House of Lords *A House for the Future* (Cmnd 4534) (2000, London: HMSO) (http://www.archive.official-documents. co.uk/document/cm45/4534/4534.htm).

The Judicial Work of the House of Lords. Parliament Fact Sheet (http://www.publications. parliament.uk/pa/ld199697/ldinfo/ld08judg/ld08judg.htm#introduction).

Sir Andrew Leggatt *Report of the Review of Tribunals* (http://www.tribunals-review. org.uk).

John Baldwin 'Litigants' experiences of Adjudication in the county courts' (1999) 18 Civil Quarterly Review 12.

Andrew Le Sueur and Richard Cornes *The Future of the United Kingdom's Highest Courts* (2001, London: Constitution Unit, University College).

USEFUL WEBSITES

Expenditure and costs of the criminal justice system

http://www.homeoffice.gov.uk/rds/digest4/chapter9.pdf

Department for Constitutional Affairs home page

http://www.dca.gov.uk/

Ministry of Justice

http://www.justice.gov.uk/

Judicial Committee of the Privy Council home page. Includes history and judgments of the Privy Council

http://www.privy-council.org.uk/judicial-committee/

Tribunal Service home page

http://www.dca.gov.uk/legalsys/tribunals.htm

Court Service home page

http://www.courtservice.gov.uk/

Judicial business of the House of Lords

http://www.parliament.uk/judicial_work/judicial_work.cfm

Annual judicial statistics

http://www.justice.gov.uk/publications/6012.htm

SELF-TEST QUESTIONS

1   In what ways do the tribunals differ from courts?

2   List three factors which encourage cases in the civil and criminal courts to be dealt with at the lower levels.

3   What were the arguments in favour of transferring the judicial functions of the House of Lords and Privy Council to a new Supreme Court?

3

Sources of law

SUMMARY

This chapter explains the different meanings of the term 'common law' and examines the relationship between the common law and statute. It argues that despite the constitutional sovereignty of Parliament, the current trend is towards the erosion of the law-making powers of Parliament through the combined impact of the growth of delegated legislation, devolution, and international law.

3.1 In contrast to the civil law jurisdictions found in other European countries, the common law system in England and Wales has not been set down in written codes. Instead, the law is drawn from a variety of different sources. The judgments of past cases, primary legislation, secondary legislation, European law, and international treaties all make up the different sources of law in England and Wales.

Case law

3.2 The term 'common law', which is used to describe the system of law in England and Wales and all those jurisdictions which derive their system from the English, is confusing because it can be used in three different senses. First, it can be applied in contrast to the term 'local law' to describe the law which is common to all the country rather than being applicable only in one area. This distinction is really only of historical interest now since local law has little relevance today.

3.3 Second, the term is used to distinguish law created in the common law courts from that made in the equity courts (the Courts of Chancery). These courts developed rules which were intended to bring greater fairness to the strict application of the common law (hence the term equity). For example, under the common law, if a person gave property to another person to look after on behalf of someone else (such as a child), that property belonged completely to the recipient. The child had no rights to it and could not seek the help of the courts if the recipient kept it for himself. The law of trusts developed through the courts of equity to fill this obvious gap in the law and allow property to be held by trustees on behalf of others who had legal rights to it. Today the distinction between common law and equity is mostly of historical relevance and only occasionally matters for practical purposes.

3.4 The third, and most important, use of the term 'common law' is to refer to the law which is created in the courts as opposed to legislation created by Parliament. This is the primary meaning of common law today. Common law in this sense could include equity and local law. It is this aspect of the system that is markedly different from the civil law countries. In the UK, the decisions of the courts are written down in law reports and these decisions themselves become the law. Some of our most important laws are still found in very old decisions of the courts. For example, the original definition of murder is that set down by Lord Coke in 1797:

> Murder is when a man of sound memory and the age of discretion, unlawfully killeth within any county of the Realm any reasonable creature *in rerum natura* under the King's peace with malice aforethought, either expressed by the party or implied by law, as the party wounded, or hurt etc die of the wound or hurt, etc within a year and a day after the same.

3.5 Some aspects have been modified by statute, eg the 'year and a day rule' has now been abolished and a killing by a British citizen is now murder even if it takes place abroad. Some of the language is modernized when used in court, but the definition remains essentially the same and it is the interpretation of that definition by the Court of Appeal and House of Lords that determines the crime of murder today.

Legislation

3.6 Although England and Wales is described as a common law system, this description is in one sense misleading because it gives the impression that case law is the most important source of law. Quantitatively this was indeed once the case. Traditionally, almost all the law was found in past cases. However, as the years have gone by, most law is now covered by legislation passed by Parliament. The law of murder, cited above, is now one of the relatively few serious offences not set out in a statute.

3.7 Moreover, case law has always been secondary to legislation in the sense that where statute and case law conflict, the former takes precedence. This is because of the principle of parliamentary sovereignty which demands that Parliament can make or repeal any law it chooses. Therefore Parliament cannot be bound by the decisions of the courts nor, indeed, by any of its own earlier decisions. As discussed below, the application of this principle has been modified by the role of European legislation, and, to a lesser extent, by the Human Rights Act 1998.

3.8 We think of legislation as the statutes passed by Parliament, often described as primary legislation. But in fact the majority of legislation is secondary or delegated legislation which is passed by the executive under authority set out in statutes. That authority can give the executive wide discretionary powers to determine what the law should be, and this may require little or no scrutiny by Parliament. The increasing quantitative and qualitative importance of secondary legislation is often cited as an example of the growing power of the executive and the corresponding weakening of Parliament in the law-making process.

3.9 A striking attempt to extend the power of the executive to pass secondary legislation was found in the provisions of the Legislative and Regulatory Reform Bill 2006. This unexciting sounding piece of legislation had, in reality, very serious implications for the power of the executive in Parliament. The Bill proposed giving the executive wide powers to amend legislation which it considered 'outdated, unnecessary or over-complicated'. Opposition to the proposals in Parliament was very strong and eventually the Government was forced to introduce amendments reducing its scope.

3.10 In addition to the growing legislative power of the Executive, it is important to note that under the devolution legislation of 1998, the Scottish Parliament and Northern Ireland Assembly have been given law-making powers in certain areas of policy such as education. The Welsh Assembly currently has less power, only being entitled to pass secondary legislation under authority from Westminster (the Government of Wales Act 2006 does, however, allow greater legislative power to be devolved in the future following a referendum). These changes have transferred some law-making power from Westminster to the regions. At the same time as its role is being eroded from below, the UK Parliament is also under pressure from above, at the international level.

European law

3.11 European law passed by the European Parliament in Brussels and applied by the European Court of Justice in Luxembourg is increasingly important in those areas in which the European Union is working towards common policies and practices, such as employment law. Since the enactment of the European Communities Act 1972, European law takes precedence over domestic law (Horspool, 2003).

3.12 Thus, if the courts are faced with a conflict between a European statutory provision and a statute passed by Westminster, they must prefer the former. This has happened on a number of occasions since 1972. One example concerned the statutory provisions for part-time employees which were held by the House of Lords in *R v Secretary of State for Employment, ex p Equal Opportunities Commission* (1995) to be inconsistent with European legislation which was more generous to part-timers. As a result, the domestic statute was, effectively, struck down by the courts and was then modified by Parliament to bring it into line with European law.

3.13 Most European law comes into force in the UK through delegated legislation which is scrutinized by a committee in Parliament. This law must then be interpreted and applied by the domestic courts in the same way as any other secondary legislation. At the time the ECA 1972 was passed there was strong criticism, particularly from the political right, that this law undermined the sovereignty of Parliament by allowing the statute of an external assembly to take precedence over legislation passed by Westminster. The counter-argument put forward by the Act's supporters was that the provision was a simple Act of Parliament which could be repealed like any other by a future Parliament on a simply majority.

3.14 The ECA 1972 did not enjoy any entrenched constitutional status, for example, by requiring a greater majority for its repeal as is often found in other jurisdictions which have a written constitution. However, in *Thoburn v Sunderland City Council* (2002) Lord Justice Laws suggested that the 1972 Act was a 'constitutional statute' and as such it could not be impliedly repealed. Although the Act can be expressly repealed, in practice this is very unlikely to happen in the foreseeable future and therefore can be seen as a reduction, if not removal, of parliamentary sovereignty. To date this change has had relatively little practical effect, but it may become more significant if and when the UK's union with Europe grows stronger and covers a wider range of social, economic and political activities.

3.15 In practice, the fierce opposition to the Act's provisions has become less vocal in the last 20 years or so as a result of the relative rarity with which provisions of Parliament have been held to be in conflict with European law. In addition, more pressing European issues such as monetary and political union have emerged to occupy those who fear the loss of national sovereignty to Europe.

The Human Rights Act 1998

3.16 More recently, fresh fears about the threat to parliamentary sovereignty have been raised by the passing of the Human Rights Act (HRA 1998). The effect of the Act has been to incorporate the main provisions of the European Convention on Human

Rights and Fundamental Freedoms (ECHR) into domestic law. Before the Act, the Convention could only be enforced in the European Court of Human Rights in Strasbourg (ECtHR). The ECtHR is quite separate from the European law system described above. It was created by the Council of Europe which was set up by the leading European countries after the Second World War. Its aim was to help prevent the atrocities of the war ever happening again by committing each country to the provisions of a Bill of Rights.

3.17 The UK was one of the states which played a leading role in drafting the ECHR and was also one of the first countries to ratify it. However, until the Human Rights Act 1998 was passed, the provisions of the Convention were not enforceable in the UK courts and citizens who wanted to claim that their rights had been infringed had to go to Strasbourg to the ECtHR to do so. The provisions of the Act are considered in more detail in chapter 4 below.

3.18 The decisions of the ECtHR, in contrast to the European Court of Justice, are not binding in the UK so that victory in Strasbourg does not guarantee that the wrong will be put right in the UK. In practice, however, when there has been an adverse finding in Strasbourg against the UK Government, it has been willing to introduce the necessary legislative changes to ensure that the domestic law is brought into line with the decision. If it refused to do so it could, ultimately, be expelled from the Council of Europe.

3.19 There are a number of provisions under the HRA 1998 which give the Convention a greater role than would normally be given to international treaties in the UK courts. First, the courts in the UK are obliged to take account of the case law of the ECtHR. They are therefore not bound by the decisions of that court, but must allow litigants to refer to relevant decisions reached in Strasbourg.

3.20 The courts must also interpret legislation in a way which is compatible with the Convention 'in so far as it is possible to do so'. If they cannot do so, ie if the law is simply too clearly in breach of the Convention to be interpreted in such a way as to bring it into line, the higher courts can make a 'declaration of incompatibility'. This does not affect the continuing validity of the law, so that parliamentary sovereignty is retained, but it is expected that Parliament will normally amend legislation which has been declared by the courts to be incompatible with the Convention.

3.21 Through these provisions the HRA 1998 was designed to achieve the difficult task of enhancing the status of an external legal document in the UK, while retaining the right of Parliament to make and unmake the law. Supporters and critics of the Act will disagree about whether or not the right balance has been struck between the promotion of human rights and the principle of parliamentary sovereignty, but they would generally agree that the Human Rights Act 1998 represents a significant constitutional change which is likely to have long-term effects on the legal system.

Other international treaties

3.22 In addition to the ECHR, the UK is a signatory to many different international conventions and, although their provisions do not have the force of law in the domestic courts in the same way as statutes or case law, they are increasingly recognized as forming a body of international law which should be taken into account in the courts in England and Wales. Furthermore, many of the provisions have been incorporated into domestic law and so are binding on the courts. A good example of the changing role of international law was the *Pinochet* case (2000).

3.23 In 1998, the former dictator of Chile, General Pinochet, was arrested while visiting the UK for medical treatment. His extradition was sought by Spain to stand trial there for war crimes allegedly committed against Spanish citizens while in power in Chile in the 1970s. The decision as to whether General Pinochet could lawfully be extradited from the UK to Spain went all the way through the courts to the House of Lords. The key question concerned the interpretation of the Extradition Act 1989 which had incorporated the provisions of the International Convention against Torture. Finally the Law Lords decided that he could be extradited for crimes allegedly committed after the Act came into force in December 1988. However, in the end the Home Secretary determined that General Pinochet was too ill to be sent back to trial and exercised his discretion under the Extradition Act to allow him to return to Chile.

3.24 Although the *Pinochet* case did not change the role of international treaties generally, the hearing of such a high-profile case which attracted international attention was indicative of the increasingly global perspective of the legal system. The traditional national borders which in the past strictly divided legal actions have become less and less meaningful throughout the world, and we can expect to see many more cases being decided in the courts of England and Wales in the future which draw on international law in one form or another.

3.25 It is an unenforceable constitutional convention that international treaties will be laid before Parliament for 28 days before being ratified by the executive. In an important change, which enhances the ability of Parliament to control the executive, the Constitutional Reform and Governance Bill will turn this into a legal obligation.

FURTHER READING

Margot Horspool and Matthew Humphreys, *European Union Law* (2008, Oxford: Oxford University Press).

Khawar Qureshi 'International Law and the English Courts' (2001) 151 New Law Journal 787.

JR Spencer 'The Case for a Code of Criminal Procedure' (2000) Criminal Law Review 519.

USEFUL WEBSITES

United Kingdom Parliament home page

http://www.parliament.uk/index.cfm

European Court of Justice home page

http://curia.europa.eu/jcms/jcms/j_6/

European Court of Human Rights home page

http://www.echr.coe.int/

Welsh assembly home page

http://www.wales.gov.uk

Scottish Parliament home page

http://www.scottish.parliament.uk

SELF-TEST QUESTIONS

1   List three definitions of the common law.

2   What is the difference between primary and secondary legislation?

3   What changes were brought about to the legal system in England and Wales by the European Communities Act 1972?

4   What role is played by the European Convention on Human Rights in English courts as a result of the Human Rights Act 1998?

5   In the light of the growing importance of statutory provisions, is it any longer meaningful to describe England and Wales as a common law legal system?

4

The Human Rights Act 1998

SUMMARY

This chapter outlines the effects of the Human Rights Act 1998 on the legal system and summarizes the long political process which led to its enactment. It argues that the Act has given the judges a new role in determining human rights standards and measuring both public and private actions against those standards. It concludes that although parliamentary sovereignty is retained by the HRA 1998, its provisions have changed the traditional relationship between the courts and Parliament.

4.1 In 1998 the Human Rights Act was passed, incorporating the European Convention on Human Rights into domestic law. It was introduced by the Labour Government as part of a wider programme of constitutional reform covering devolution and reform of the House of Lords. The Act was not brought into force until October 2000 in order to give the judges and other public bodies time to undertake training on its provisions. £5m was set aside by the Government for the Judicial Studies Board to run day-long training sessions for all the full-time and part-time judges. The scale of this operation gives an indication of the significance of the Act. It may, in time, come to be seen as the most radical change introduced by the 1997 Labour administration.

The traditional English approach to human rights

4.2 The HRA 1998 represents an important change in the legal system of England and Wales because it is the first time that a written Bill of Rights has been made enforceable in the courts since 1689. Moreover, that early Bill of Rights is not a human rights document in the sense that we usually mean, setting out the rights of individual citizens, but rather was intended primarily to restrict the power of the monarch to control Parliament.

4.3 The absence, until 1998, of a written Bill of Rights of the kind found in many other countries such as the US does not mean that the UK has no tradition of legal rights. Rather, rights have been understood as part of the unwritten constitution – conventions and principles which have guided the common law over hundreds of years. Most importantly, the bedrock of the legal system has been the assumption that all citizens enjoy complete freedom except where that is specifically and lawfully taken away. This is often called a 'negative' concept of rights. Provided Parliament has not legislated to prevent a certain act or behaviour, nor has such a prohibition been developed by the courts under the common law, the courts will, in principle, uphold a person's right to do what she or he wishes however objectionable or inconvenient. This 'negative rights' approach has historically served the UK reasonably well in the sense that compared to many other equivalent democratic countries, its record of respect for rights has been relatively good.

The European Convention on Human Rights

4.4 The Convention was drafted after the Second World War by a body called the Council of Europe (not to be confused with the institutions of the European Union). Its aim was to help prevent a recurrence of the atrocities committed before and during the war by ensuring that all European states signed a declaration to abide by common standards of human rights. The UK played a central role in drafting the Convention and setting up the European Court of Human Rights in Strasbourg (not to be confused with the European Court of Justice in Luxembourg). The UK was also the first state to sign the Convention.

4.5 The main provisions of the Convention are:

Article 2.	The right to life
Article 3.	Freedom from torture, inhuman or degrading treatment or punishment
Article 4.	Freedom for slavery, servitude or slave labour
Article 5.	Freedom from arbitrary detention
Article 6.	The right to a fair trial
Article 7.	Prohibition on retrospective legislation
Article 8.	Right to respect for family life
Article 9.	Freedom of thought, conscience and religion
Article 10.	Freedom of expression
Article 11.	Freedom of association and assembly
Article 12.	The right to marry and found a family

| Article 13. | The right to an effective remedy against a breach |
| Article 14. | The right to enjoyment of the rights without discrimination |

4.6 In addition to the main rights a number of later additions (known as protocols) have been signed by the UK. These include the right to enjoyment of one's possessions, the right to vote, and more recently, the abolition of the death penalty.

4.7 Most of the rights in the Convention are qualified. That is, they allow for the rights to be breached provided the breach is in accordance with the law and is necessary in a democratic society to protect and promote certain other goals such as the rights of others, public safety or public order. Thus, one right must sometimes be balanced against another such as the right of freedom of expression against the right of privacy.

4.8 Because the Convention rights are broad and general in nature, the job of interpreting the Convention is rather a different exercise from the interpretation of more particular and detailed statutory provisions. Judges, either in Strasbourg or the domestic courts, must weigh up the competing interests of individuals and society in determining how the rights are to be applied in practice.

4.9 In interpreting the Convention, the ECtHR in Strasbourg has applied two important principles. The first is that it allows each country a 'margin of appreciation'. That is, it accepts that the particular historical, cultural, political and legal conditions in each state must allow for some differences in individual approach, provided the fundamental rights are complied with. Thus, for example, the different legal systems of a civil and common law country have led to wide differences in the type of trial and pre-trial procedure, such as the use of juries in the UK and the close constitutional connection between prosecutors and judges in many civil law countries.

4.10 The second principle is that of proportionality. This holds that where a right is breached, the extent of that breach must be no greater than is absolutely necessary to achieve the legitimate ends intended. The response of the state to a problem which necessitates breaching a right must be proportionate to the problem being addressed. The notion of proportionality was defined by Lord Clyde in *De Freitas* in 1999 as being whether:

(i) the legislative objective is sufficiently important to justify limiting a fundamental human right;

(ii) the measures designed to meet the legislative objective are rationally connected to it; and

(iii) the means used to impair the right or freedom are no more than is necessary to accomplish the objective.

Political history of the Human Rights Act 1998

4.11 Having played such a central role in the creation of the Convention, it might be expected that the UK would have been one of the first states to incorporate its provisions into domestic law, so allowing its citizens to rely on the rights set out in the Convention in the UK courts rather than having to seek redress at the Court in Strasbourg. In fact, successive UK Governments, both Conservative and Labour, showed themselves to be surprisingly reluctant to allow citizens the advantages which have been regarded as so important for citizens of other states. Indeed, it was not until 1966 that individuals were given the right to bring a case against the UK Government in the European Court. Before then, the UK could only be brought to court by other states.

4.12 The justification for this limitation was that it was felt that the citizens of the UK did not need the protection of the ECtHR because the rights enjoyed under the common law were greater than those of any other European country. This continued to be the dominant official approach to the question until the 1990s and was the main reason for the widespread opposition to incorporating the Convention into domestic law as almost all the other signatory states had done.

4.13 Nevertheless, the pressure for incorporation slowly grew. The increasing number of adverse findings against the UK in Strasbourg gradually weakened the argument that its record of rights protection was second to none. By the early 1990s, the UK had been held to be in breach of the Convention by the ECtHR more times than any other country except Turkey.

4.14 In 1995, the campaign for incorporation moved a step closer when the Labour Party adopted incorporation as its policy. After it came to power in 1997, the drafting of the HRA 1998 was one of the new Labour Government's first actions.

The structure and provisions of the HRA 1998

4.15 One of the strongest objections to incorporation had been the fear that if judges were given special powers to hold that laws passed by Parliament were in breach of the Convention and so invalid, the principle of parliamentary sovereignty would be undermined. The British constitution is founded on the idea that Parliament can make or repeal any law it wishes and that the courts have no power to strike down a law as being unconstitutional or in breach of fundamental rights. In trying to retain this principle without undermining the impact of the Convention, various constitutional models were considered.

4.16 These ranged from the US system in which the Supreme Court has full powers to strike down legislation as unconstitutional, to the New Zealand model, where the courts have no power to declare legislation which breaches their Bill of Rights invalid and can only apply the Bill of Rights in cases where there is an ambiguity in the meaning of a statute. Hybrid alternatives were also reviewed, such as Canada, where the court has US-style powers but where Parliament can apply a 'notwithstanding' clause and pass legislation notwithstanding the fact that it may be in breach of the Charter of Rights. Each of these different models, as well as other variations, had their supporters, but they were all ultimately rejected in favour of the construction of a unique and imaginative statutory formula.

HRA 1998, ss 3 and 4

4.17 Under HRA 1998, s 3 the judges are required to interpret legislation 'in so far as it is possible' in a way which is compatible with the Convention. If a compatible interpretation is not possible, the higher courts have the right to make a 'declaration of incompatibility'. HRA 1998, s 4 states that such a declaration does not affect the continuing validity of the legislation.

4.18 The effect of these two sections is that the courts have no power to strike down an Act, thereby retaining parliamentary sovereignty. But the White Paper which preceded the HRA 1998, 'Bringing Rights Home', made clear that if a statute is declared incompatible it would be expected that Parliament would move quickly to amend it, and to this end the Act makes provision for a fast-track parliamentary amendment process by which a minister can seek a speedy amendment through the use of a Remedial Order, if necessary.

4.19 This unique device is a typically British constitutional compromise. Its strength is that it allows the formal retention of parliamentary sovereignty, but opens the way for a new political reality to develop whereby the protection of rights becomes a joint enterprise between Parliament and the courts. Its weakness is that it has the potential to leave legislation (and litigants) in a vacuum, with legislation having been declared to be in breach of fundamental human rights by the courts and yet still valid and enforceable. The danger is that legitimacy and legality part company, with citizens obliged to obey, and courts to uphold, laws which have been declared fundamentally flawed. Exactly how the courts and Parliament should approach HRA 1998, s 3 and s 4 is still being worked through by judges and politicians and it will take some time before the full implications of these radical provisions become clear.

HRA 1998, s 2

4.20 HRA 1998, s 2 applies where courts are considering a Convention point. The provision states that they must 'take into account' decisions of the ECtHR. This means that Strasbourg case law is not binding on the courts but cannot be rejected out of hand. In practice, this provision has a major impact on the role of the jurisprudence of the ECtHR in the domestic courts. In *Alconbury* (2001), in which the House of Lords overturned the first declaration of incompatibility under the HRA made in the High Court, Lord Slynn stated:

> In the absence of some special circumstances it seems to me that the court should follow any clear and constant jurisprudence of the European Court of Human Rights. If it does not do so there is at least a possibility that the case will go to that court which is likely in the ordinary case to follow its own constant jurisprudence.

4.21 It appears that the courts have generally adopted Lord Slynn's approach and have sought to follow the decisions of the ECtHR where possible. However, one concern which has been expressed by human rights lawyers and interest groups is that s 2 may lead the courts to apply the Convention as a 'ceiling' rather than a 'floor'. Indeed in *R (Ullah) v Special Adjudicator* (2004), Lord Bingham held that '[t]he duty of the national courts is to keep pace with the Strasbourg jurisprudence as it evolves over time: no more, but certainly no less'. This is, however, a sensible approach for the domestic courts to take. The Convention is an international treaty which must be applied uniformly by the ECtHR to 47 countries and 800 million people. It would be inappropriate for the domestic courts to develop their own distinctive interpretation of the Convention. Nevertheless, the English courts should remain alive to the scope for developing the common law to provide a greater measure of human rights protection where appropriate.

HRA 1998, s 6

4.22 Perhaps the most far-reaching provision of the HRA 1998 in terms of its effect on the courts is found in s 6. This states that it is unlawful for a public authority to act in a way which is incompatible with a Convention right. Courts are explicitly included in the definition of a public authority. This means that every decision reached by every court must comply with the Convention.

4.23 One implication of this provision is to expand the scope of the HRA 1998 to include private bodies and individuals. On the face of it, the Convention is only concerned with the protection of individuals against the action of the state rather than against other individuals or private institutions. However, it is clear that since the courts are included in the term public authorities, they are obliged to ensure that all law, whether private or public, is in conformity with the Convention. Thus, the Act is said to have a 'horizontal effect', drawing in private law and litigation. There are, however, limits to this 'horizontal effect'. Although the courts can gradually develop existing causes of action so as to protect Convention rights, they cannot create new causes of action such as a tort of privacy.

Key Human Rights Act cases

4.24 Since the HRA has only been in force since October 2000, it is relatively early days to draw conclusions about its effect. Quantitatively, its impact has been much less dramatic than many commentators predicted. Some important cases, however, have already been decided which give an indication of what approach the judges are taking to the Act.

4.25 The early HRA cases were decided in Scotland. That is because the HRA was partially implemented there 18 months before England and Wales and Northern Ireland through the devolution legislation which required that all devolved institutions should act in a way which is compatible with the Convention. Two early cases led to much controversy and the claims that, for better or worse, the courts were going to use the Act to sweep aside many established rules and institutional arrangements.

4.26 *Brown* (2000) concerned a woman who was arrested outside a car and found to be over the legal alcohol limit for driving. She was obliged under the Road Traffic Act to declare whether or not she had been driving the car. In the Scottish appeal court, it was held that her right to a fair trial was breached because of the compulsion to answer questions. This decision, if followed in England and Wales, would have undermined the provisions of the Criminal Justice and Public Order Act 1994 which removed a defendant's right to remain silent when questioned by the police or in court. In the event, the case went to the Privy Council on appeal and was overturned on the grounds that the public policy interest of preventing death through drink-driving accidents was sufficiently important that the removal of the absolute right to silence was a legitimate and proportionate response to the problem and did not breach the right to a fair trial.

4.27 In *Starrs* (2000), the Scottish Courts held that the use of part-time judges (sheriffs) was a breach of the right to trial by an independent and impartial tribunal because part-time judges are dependent on the executive for the continuation of their contracts and have no security of tenure. As a result of the decision in *Starrs* the Lord Chancellor, anticipating a similar challenge to the use of part-time Assistant Recorders in England and Wales, changed their terms of contract, converting them to the status of Recorder with fixed five-year contracts and a guarantee of a certain number of sitting days in court each year.

4.28 In the event, neither of these cases has caused profound changes or difficulties. Similarly, predictions that there would be a great rush of cases after October 2000 which would flood the courts and cause excessive delay have proved unfounded. During the first 12 months after the enactment of the Act, the Convention was substantially considered in 167 cases before the High Court or above and affected the outcome in 98. By comparison, the Convention was raised in only 16 cases in the 21-year period between 1975 and 1996 (Klug and Starmer, 2001). Nevertheless, the practical impact of this change was not significant. The courts' workload increased only slightly and the length of cases did not increase to any significant degree. Most of the cases in which Convention points were raised did not succeed.

4.29 Some of the early Human Rights Act decisions were in unexpected areas of the law. In *Alconbury*, mentioned above, the House of Lords held that the power of the Secretary of State for the Environment to decide on planning applications was not a breach of a right to an independent and impartial tribunal. While in *Wilson* (2003), the House of Lords held that the rights of a pawnbroker to enforce his civil rights under Article 6 were not infringed by the Consumer Credit Act which prevented him from relying on a contract in court which had a technical defect. Moreover, some of the challenges which were rejected by the courts were widely expected to succeed. For example, the removal of the right of prisoners to vote was tipped for change, but was unsuccessful, the court holding that it was for Parliament, not the courts, to change the law in this regard (*Pearson* 2001). However, subsequently the ECtHR held that the blanket ban on prisoners voting was disproportionate (*Hirst* 2004). In response, the Government has recently indicated that it may allow prisoners serving sentences of less than four years the right to vote.

4.30 But a number of Human Rights Act cases in England and Wales have resulted in important changes. In particular, the law of privacy has been developed as a result of the incorporation of the Convention. Most controversially, two young men who were convicted of murdering the toddler Jamie Bulger when they were 10 and 11 were granted by the courts a lifetime right to anonymity on their release from secure local authority custody on the grounds that their rights to life would be very likely to be breached by vigilantes if the right of freedom of expression of the press was upheld and their whereabouts made public (*Thompson and Venables* 2001).

4.31 But unquestionably the most important area in which the courts have had to grapple with the implications of the Human Rights Act is that of anti-terrorism. In general the courts have been reluctant to interfere with the role of the elected politicians in determining what measures are needed in the interests of national security to prevent terrorist activity in the UK. However, in two very important decisions, the courts have applied the provisions of the Human Rights Act to rule against the Government.

4.32 The first case was heard by the House of Lords in December 2004. In *A v Secretary of State for the Home Department*, the court was asked to consider whether the provisions of the Anti-Terrorism, Crime and Security Act 2001 were in breach of the Convention. The Act allowed for the indefinite detention without trial of foreigners suspected of involvement with terrorism. It was passed after the terrorism attacks in the US in September 2001. The detention provisions, which were used when a terrorist suspect could not be deported because he or she would face persecution or threats to their life in their home country, run counter to the provisions of Article 5 of the Convention, which restrict the circumstances in which individuals can be detained by the state. The Government therefore had opted out (derogated) from the provisions of Article 5, a procedure that is allowed by the Convention 'in time of war or other public emergency threatening the life of the nation'.

4.33 The detainees had challenged the legality of the derogation and the provisions of the Act in 2002 in the Court of Appeal, which decided that they were not in breach of the Convention. When the case came to the House of Lords on appeal it was heard by nine rather than the usual five judges; a very rare event which reflected the seriousness of the case. The judges decided by a majority of 8 to 1 that the detention provisions in the Act were in breach of the Convention in that they discriminated against foreign terrorist suspects in breach of the equality provision in Article 14. The court issued a declaration of incompatibility under s 4. The effect of the judgment, therefore, was that the Act remained in force and the Government was left to determine what action to take to remedy the breach.

4.34 The Government's response was to replace the relevant part of the Act with the Prevention of Terrorism Act 2005, which was passed by Parliament in March 2005. This Act introduced 'control orders' that allow the Home Secretary to impose a variety of restrictions on the movements of terrorist suspects. In practice, these restrictions often amount to a form of house arrest. These new provisions comply with the decision of the House of Lords because they can be applied to both British and non-British suspected terrorists and so are not discriminatory. The effect of the decision, therefore, has been paradoxically to widen the range of persons who can be subject to state control without trial, albeit without being detained in custody. However, these provisions too have been successfully challenged in the courts. The House of Lords considered the legality of non-derogating control orders in October 2007. By a majority of 3–2 their Lordships held that imposing an 18-hour curfew coupled with restrictions on movement and association was incompatible with the right to liberty enshrined in Article 5 ECHR (*Secretary of State for the Home Department v JJ*). By contrast, in another case heard at the same time, they unanimously held that a 14 hour curfew with similar additional restrictions did not amount to a deprivation of liberty (*Secretary of State for the Home Department v MB & AF*).

4.35 These cases also raised an important issue of procedure: could a control order be imposed without the suspected terrorist being informed of all of the evidence against him? The only evidence revealed to the suspects had been the 'open evidence' which merely said that they had links with Islamic extremists. Further 'closed evidence' had been submitted to the judge and to a 'special advocate' who had been appointed to represent the suspects. The special advocate could not, however, reveal the closed material or discuss it with the suspects. A majority of the House of Lords held that reliance on undisclosed material would breach the right to a fair trial in Article 6 ECHR *if* the suspects had had no possibility of responding to the substance of the allegations against them.

4.36 The second important challenge in the area of anti-terrorism measures, also called *A v Secretary of State for the Home Department*, was heard in 2005. In a unanimous decision by the House of Lords it was held that evidence obtained through torture is inadmissible in court. The decision overturned a 2002 Court of Appeal decision that had decided that such evidence could be used provided it was obtained by third parties rather than interrogators from the UK.

The application of HRA 1998, s 3 and s 4

4.37 One of the key questions which observers of the HRA 1998 were asking in the first few years after it came into force was how the courts were approaching their new powers under ss 3 and 4. The judges have shown themselves ready to take an expansive approach to their duty to interpret statutes 'so far as is possible' in a way that is compatible with the Convention. They have interpreted this section as requiring them to read words and phrases into statutory provisions in order to make them compliant with the Convention. But there are limits: although s 3 imposes a strong obligation to interpret legislation compatibly, this will not be possible if a Convention-compliant interpretation would contravene a 'fundamental feature' of the legislation, or 'go against its grain' (*Ghaidan v Mendoza* 2004).

4.38 In *R v Offen* (2001) the Court of Appeal held that the 'two strikes and you're out' sentencing provisions under the Crime (Sentences) Act 1997 which provided for automatic life sentences in certain circumstances on the conviction for a second similar offence potentially breached the requirement that detention must be 'lawful' under Article 5. This is because the detention must be 'proportionate'. The Court decided that the section of the Act which allows the judges not to pass a life sentence 'in exceptional circumstances' had to be read widely to ensure compatibility by allowing the courts to decide whether or not the defendant posed a significant risk to the public. If he or she did not, this would constitute an 'exceptional circumstance' under the Act.

4.39 Similarly, in *R v A (No 2)* (2001) the House of Lords held that the removal of the power to question complainants in a rape trial about their previous sexual histories under the Youth Justice and Criminal Evidence Act 1999 was a breach of the defendant's right to a fair trial. The Court held that the prohibition against questioning complainants about their sexual history with the accused 'poses an acute problem of proportionality'. In order to ensure compatibility, the Court read into the legislation a discretion on the part of the Court to allow questions about the previous sexual conduct of the complainant where the interests of justice required. In the judgment, Lord Steyn stated that in order to apply s 3 it would sometimes be necessary to adopt an interpretation of legislation: 'which linguistically may appear strained'.

4.40 A good example of the limits of s 3 is provided by the decision of the House of Lords in *Re S* (2002). The Court of Appeal had used s 3 to read into the Children Act 1989 a range of new powers and procedures by which the courts supervise and monitor the implementation of care orders by local authorities, so as to protect children against violations of their Article 8 rights. But the House of Lords held that a fundamental feature of the Children Act 1989 was that the courts should not intervene in the way that local authorities discharged their parental responsibilities. Accordingly, it was not possible to use s 3 to read the Act compatibly and the House of Lords issued a s 4 declaration of incompatibility instead.

The Human Rights Act and judicial review

4.41 In addition to its effect on the review of legislation by the courts, the HRA has also had a significant impact on the process of judicial review, whereby the courts scrutinize the legality, fairness and procedural propriety of official decision-making. This function appears to have been extended by the introduction of the use of the test of proportionality discussed above. Initially, the approach of the courts seemed to be that they would ask themselves whether the decision-maker could reasonably have believed a decision or action which breached the Convention to be proportionate. Lord Phillips, the Master of the Rolls, stated in *Mahmood* (2001):

> When anxiously scrutinising an executive decision that interferes with human rights, the court will ask the question, applying an objective test, whether the decision-maker could reasonably have concluded that the interference was necessary to achieve one or more of the legitimate aims recognised by the Convention. When considering the test of necessity in the relevant context, the court must take into account the European jurisprudence in accordance with section 2 of the 1998 Act.

4.42 However, more recently the courts have increasingly taken the view that it is for the judges *themselves* to consider whether the decision was proportionate or not. In *Daly* (2001), Lord Steyn argued that this approach has led to a change in the courts' role which allows for a more 'intense review' of government activity which may sometimes lead to the quashing of official decisions which would previously have been allowed to stand on the more limited test of 'reasonableness' applied under the traditional judicial review test first set out in *Wednesbury* (1948). Professor Jeffrey Jowell has argued that the change to the nature of judicial review brought about by the HRA amounts to a new form of constitutional review which will profoundly affect the respective roles of government and the judiciary (Jowell, 2002).

4.43 In 2003, the first Human Rights Act decision to give rise to serious political tension between the judiciary and executive was handed down when the Administrative Court partially upheld a challenge to the way the provisions of the National Immigration and Asylum Act 2002 were being applied. In *R (Q) v Secretary of State for the Home Department* (2003) the Court held that immigration officials were breaching the Convention in the way that they were applying rules which require asylum seekers to lodge a claim for asylum on arrival in the UK or lose all social security benefits. In response to this decision it was reported in the press that the then Prime Minister, Tony Blair, and the then Home Secretary, David Blunkett, were considering amending the Human Rights Act to limit the interpretative powers of the judiciary.

4.44 The political tension around the Human Rights Act increased still further in 2006 when the High Court held that nine Afghans who had hijacked a plane in the UK could not be deported because they faced persecution or death in Afghanistan. The response of all three political parties to the decision was one of outrage. The then Prime Minister, Tony Blair, said that the decision was 'an abuse of common sense' and that consideration would be given to reforming or replacing the Human Rights Act.

4.45 The future of the Human Rights Act is uncertain. The Conservative leader, David Cameron, announced in June 2006 that if elected the Conservatives would replace the Act with a British Bill of Rights. Meanwhile, on 23 March 2009 the Labour Government published a Green Paper called 'Rights and Responsibilities: developing our constitutional framework' in which it called for a national debate on question whether Britain needs a Bill of Rights and responsibilities to supplement the Human Rights Act 1998. When announcing the Green Paper, Justice Minister, Jack Straw said that:

> This government is proud to have introduced the Human Rights Act and will not backtrack from it or repeal it. But we believe more should be done to bring out the responsibilities which accompany rights.

Quite what responsibilities we have other than to obey the law is unclear. Moreover, it doubtful that such a Bill would add anything to the existing case law of the ECtHR which already emphasizes that rights, such as the right to freedom of expression, must be exercised responsibly with due regard for the rights of others.

The Human Rights Act and the judiciary

4.46 Even before the recent anti-terrorism and asylum cases described above, it was clear that the new role which the Human Rights Act 1998 gives the judges in reviewing legislation and official decision-making is having a significant impact on the constitutional and institutional arrangements of the legal system.

4.47 One consequence of the greater power which the HRA 1998 gives to the judicial branch of government has been to focus attention on the composition of the judiciary and the judicial appointments process. Who the judges are and how they are chosen are more pressing questions when judges are required to interpret and enforce basic human rights. Whether judges should be accountable to the elect orate or representative of society in some way are questions which have not, in the past, received much attention but which have now started to attract public interest.

4.48 The judges themselves are aware of these implications and it was precisely because of the danger that the judiciary would be perceived to be a more political body that some senior judges opposed incorporation of the Convention. Lord Mackay, when Lord Chancellor in 1996, argued in a speech to the Citizenship Foundation that incorporation might lead to calls for a change in the criteria for the appointment of judges: ' ... making the political stance of each candidate a matter of importance as much as his or her ability to decide cases on their individual facts and the law applicable to those facts.'

4.49 Although there is no evidence of overt politicization of the appointments system there has been much more concern about the lack of diversity in the judiciary (discussed in more detail in chapter 16 below). In addition, it has become much more common for litigants to scrutinize carefully the background of the judges who will hear their case and to make an application that the judge should step down from hearing it if they consider that there is any possible conflict of interest which might give rise to the appearance of bias on the part of the judge.

Conclusion

4.50 The Human Rights Act has undoubtedly created a new legal regime in England and Wales and has contributed to the development of a more constitutionalized political system. How significant this change will be in practice remains to be seen. The expanded role of the judiciary in scrutinizing legislation and reviewing official decision-making clearly changes the nature of the relationship between the branches of state. But it does not, as some critics have suggested, undermine the principle of parliamentary sovereignty since the Act was passed by Parliament and could be repealed or amended by it with a simple majority vote.

4.51 Few lawyers and judges with experience of the Act would, however, have considered its repeal to be a realistic possibility at any time in the first two years of the Act's life, which is why the Government's response to such decisions as *R (Q) v Secretary of State for the Home Department* was so unexpected. In first few years of the Act the consensus which had emerged about the courts' reaction to its new role was that it was, if anything, excessively cautious (Woolf, 2002). Although there were a handful of important judgments in the early years, the overall impact on the law and policy-making was limited. Against this background, the fact that the Government could consider amending the Act to limit the interpretative powers of the judiciary in response to one unfavourable decision is evidence of the relatively fragile political foundation on which the new provisions rest. No doubt the public attacks on the Act by politicians of all parties that have become commonplace in response to unpopular court decisions in the areas of counter-terrorism and asylum are to some extent populist posturing. But there is also no doubt that the future of the Human Rights Act is much less secure than it seemed in the first few years of its life. The apparent threat to the Act's continued existence so soon after its implementation now means that the next few years will be a critical period for the survival of one of the most important changes in the legal system.

FURTHER READING

Lord Woolf *Human Rights: Have the Public Benefited?* (2002) (http://www.britac.ac.uk/index.cfm).

Michael Zander *The State of Justice* (2000, London: Sweet and Maxwell), ch 4.

John Wadham, Helen Mountfield, Caoilfhionn Gallagher, and Elizabeth Prochaska *Blackstone's Guide to the Human Rights Act 1998* (2009, Oxford: Oxford University Press).

Jeffrey Jowell 'Beyond the Rule of Law: Towards Constitutional Judicial Review' (2000) Public Law 671.

Francesca Klug and Keir Starmer 'Incorporation through the "Front Door": The First Year of the Human Rights Act' (2001) Public Law 654.

USEFUL WEBSITES

Ministry of Justice website human rights section
http://www.justice.gov.uk/about/human-rights.htm

European Court of Human Rights home page
http://www.echr.coe.int/

SELF-TEST QUESTIONS

1 Define the following terms: A 'negative' concept of rights

   'Margin of appreciation'
   'Proportionality'
   'Qualified rights'.

2 What is the effect of a 'declaration of incompatibility' under HRA 1998, s 4?

3 What approach did Lord Steyn take to HRA 1998, s 3 in *R v A*?

4 Critically evaluate the impact of the Human Rights Act 1998 on English law.

5 When is it 'possible' to interpret legislation compatibly with the ECHR?

5

The legislative process

SUMMARY

This chapter describes the process by which legislation is passed by Parliament. It highlights the dominant role played by the executive and the declining influence of backbench MPs. It outlines the advantages and disadvantages of strong governmental control and the difficulties of modernizing the parliamentary process.

5.1 Whereas in the past there were large areas of the criminal and civil law which were wholly regulated by case law, most are now covered by legislation, whether primary (passed by Parliament) or secondary (created by Government under powers delegated in primary legislation). Case law, increasingly, consists of the interpretation of legislation. The amount of new primary legislation being passed is, in practice, limited by the timetabling restraints on Parliament. Although the number of statutes passed each year only increased slightly during the twentieth century, the length of each Bill has grown enormously (Zander, 1999). Some Bills are now very large indeed. The Criminal Justice Bill 2003, for example, was introduced to the Commons with 273 clauses and left it with 307 and 32 schedules. As a result of this trend, there is strong competition for parliamentary time and it is common for legislation put forward by members of Parliament to fail to reach the statute books for lack of time.

5.2 In practice, it is only those proposals which have the strong support of the Government which will be passed. Even then, some will fail to get through the following long and time-consuming process. Most Bills must complete all their stages within one session of Parliament, which ends each year in late October/early November. However, it is also possible for the Government to circumvent the full legislative process and drive through statutes at great speed. Emergency terrorism legislation, for example, has in the past gone through all its stages in a matter of days with little debate and scrutiny.

The Whitehall stage

5.3 All Acts of Parliament start life as a Bill which must pass through Parliament. We tend to think of this stage as the main legislative process. But equally, if not more important, is what happens before a Bill reaches Parliament.

5.4 Almost all Bills are Public, that is, they affect the whole country. But a few are Private and only affect a local area or institution such as a company. These must be distinguished from Private Members' Bills which are Public Bills proposed by backbench MPs. Public Bills originate from a number of different sources. The majority are proposed by government departments in Whitehall. Surprisingly, relatively few of these have been set out in a manifesto. Most are devised by ministers and civil servants without having been put to the electorate for specific approval. Some proposed legislation originates from the findings of special commissions or official inquiries, or from reports of the Law Commission, which is a permanent body set up to review areas of the law which might need change. The Government decides whether or not to agree to these proposals and put them before Parliament.

5.5 Once a department has decided that it wishes to ask Parliament to pass legislation on a certain topic, it will undergo a consultation process with interested parties. The extent of this process will differ depending on the complexity, importance and urgency of the matter. It may take many months or a few days. The first stage is often a consultation document called a Green Paper which sets out in general terms what the Government is seeking to do and asks for views. Once these are received and taken account of (or not) the Government will produce a White Paper, which sets out the proposals decided upon and the reasons for the legislation. These two stages may be contracted into one.

5.6 These stages are not fixed by formal rules and are subject to change. For example, it is increasingly common for draft Bills to be drawn up and circulated for consultation before being formally laid before Parliament, an example being the Mental Health Bill 2002. Occasionally Bills are scrutinized by Parliamentary Committees before being formally introduced.

Drafting

5.7 At the point where a department has decided on the provisions it wishes to pass these are passed to civil servants called Parliamentary Counsel, lawyers who are experts in drafting techniques. A long or complex Bill may take many months to draft, with regular meetings between Parliamentary Counsel and the department responsible for the Bill to ensure that the wording accurately reflects what is proposed. Once the Bill is drafted it is ready to be presented to Parliament.

5.8 One effect of the need for Bills to be tightly drafted legal documents is that they are often difficult for non-lawyers to understand. In order to address this problem and so to increase the accessibility of legislation, a 'plain English' summary of the purpose and content of the Bill is now published alongside the more formal and legally drafted overview. The Coroners Bill 2006 that proposed changes to the coroners' system was the first Bill to include the new plain English section.

The Westminster stage

5.9 In order to be given time in Parliament, a Bill must have been approved by the Future Business committee. This is a cabinet committee which decides which Bills will be put before Parliament in the following session. Thus, a department wishing to pass legislation must normally seek space in the timetable from the committee the year before it will be ready to be passed. In this way, there is a rolling programme of proposals and Bills at different stages of preparation. At any one time Parliament will know what is due to come before it for the current and future session.

5.10 All Bills must be passed by both the House of Commons and the House of Lords. They can start in either, but most start in the Commons and pass through the following stages:

First reading

5.11 This is a formal stage whereby the Bill is laid before the House and is ordered to be printed. There is no debate on its content.

Second reading

5.12 At this stage, the Minister sets out the policy objectives of the Bill and a debate is held in the House on its merits in broad terms. It is rare for there to be a vote on the Bill at this stage or for a Government Bill to be defeated.

Committee stage

5.13 The detailed scrutiny of a Bill takes place in a Standing Committee, which, despite its name, is specially drawn up for each Bill. It is made up of about 18 MPs selected by another committee called the Committee of Selection. The purpose of the Committee is not to consider the desirability of the Bill in principle, since that has already been approved by the House during the Second Reading, but to scrutinize the workability of the detailed clauses.

5.14 The members of the committee must be in proportion to the representation of each party in the House overall, so that the Government will almost always have a majority. Interested parties will lobby the members and amendments will be proposed by both the opposition and government members. In practice, almost all the amendments which are successful are those which are proposed by the Government, though sometimes the members can be persuaded of the validity of a proposal for change by an opposition member.

Report stage

5.15 Once the Committee has agreed a draft Bill it goes back to the House. The Government may reject the changes carried out at Committee stage or, indeed, make further changes. One controversial development in recent years has been the growing tendency for the Government to seek to make significant changes to a Bill at this stage. A recent example being the Criminal Justice Bill 2003 in which 28 new clauses were produced by the Home Office at the report stage, including major policy issues such as restricting judicial discretion in relation to life sentences.

Third reading

5.16 The final stage is another formality, where the Bill is confirmed and is now ready to be passed to the House of Lords. No change can be made to the content of the Bill at this stage.

Process in the House of Lords

5.17 The formal stages in the Lords are broadly similar to those of the Commons, apart from the fact that the Committee stage is usually carried out in the House as a whole rather than by Committee, and this stage is less tightly controlled, with unrestricted debate allowed on amendments. In addition, changes can be made at the third reading stage. However, the culture of the Lords is rather different because there is less government control of the process. The party system which is enforced through the Whips is weakened by the presence of cross-benchers who do not belong to any party and other Lords such as the Law Lords who may contribute to debate on Bills affecting the legal system. However, the capacity of the Lords to affect legislation is also limited. It can delay the passage of most Bills for a year, but will only do so in rare cases. A recent example of the Lords exercising this power arose in relation to the legislation banning fox-hunting, which was finally passed on the second attempt.

5.18 Similarly, in 1999 the Lords twice voted against the Criminal Justice (Mode of Trial) Bill which sought to reduce the right of a defendant to elect trial by jury. As a result, the Government was forced to withdraw the Bill and decided not to reintroduce it the following session. Such a complete defeat is nowadays very rare. However, challenges to particular aspects of legislation are not. In the 2007–8 parliamentary session, for example, the Lords inflicted 29 defeats on the Government and in the 2002–2003 session the Government suffered 88 defeats at the hands of the Lords – the highest number since 1975–6. The effect of the greater willingness in the Lords to oppose Government proposals is that it is common for the content of Bills to be amended by the Government after negotiations with peers in order to avoid defeat in the Lords. The Labour Government is currently in a small minority in the Lords which means that it must work hard to obtain support for its legislation there.

5.19 At present the House of Lords is in a transitional phase. In January 2000, a Royal Commission Report on the future of the House of Lords, chaired by Lord Wakeham, was presented to Parliament which proposed that the second chamber should consist of a majority of appointed members and a minority of elected members representing regions of the UK. In 1999, most of the hereditary peers were removed as the first step in the process of reforming the composition of the Lords. This change has increased the legislative authority of the Lords, but the fact that its members continue to be appointed rather than elected means that its continuing role in the legislative process is dependent on its acceptance that the Commons, as the elected chamber, must ultimately have the power to pass laws as it sees fit.

5.20 Since 1999, debate has continued about the exact future make-up of the House, and in particular, what should be the proportion of elected to appointed members. On the one hand, supporters of the creation of an elected second chamber argue that the current arrangements are undemocratic and limit the effectiveness of a bicameral Parliament. On the other hand, defenders of an appointed House of Lords claim that its less partisan culture and more loosely structured procedures, combined with the wide-ranging expertise of its members, creates a highly effective scrutinizing chamber which can improve the quality of legislation passed. It is not yet clear, there-fore, whether the Lords will emerge from this period of change as a more account-able and powerful second chamber, or continue its historical trend of declining influence and relevance. The Constitutional Reform and Governance Bill seeks to remove the few remaining hereditary peers, but it is unsatisfactory that a decade after the House of Lords Act 1999 the shape of the House of Lords of the twenty-first century is still uncertain.

Royal Assent

5.21 This is the final stage in the legislative process whereby the Queen signs the Act of Parliament. It may come into force immediately or at a future stage, as stipulated in the Act. For example, the Human Rights Act was passed in 1998 but came into force in October 2000 once training and other preparations had been completed.

Overview of the system

5.22 The key feature of the legislative process is that it is strongly controlled by the Government, and the bigger the Government's majority the greater that control. Almost all legislation is initiated by the Government and even backbench MPs of the party in power have relatively little scope to influence its content. Through the system of Whips, MPs who enforce party discipline, they are required to support their party line on almost all important legislative decisions. Occasionally backbenchers will revolt and vote against the Government, or threaten to do so unless amendments are made. But this is a card which most MPs can only play rarely without threatening their chances of ever being asked to join the Government, or indeed, without running the risk of having the Whip withdrawn, thus being expelled from the parliamentary party.

5.23 The advantage of this system of strong Government control is that the party elected can implement the manifesto on which it was given a mandate by the electorate. The disadvantage is that those who voted for another party, who may constitute a majority of the population, have almost no effective representation in the law-making process.

5.24 In addition, the quality of legislation may be weakened by lack of meaningful debate or unwillingness to take account of valid input from those outside the Government. There are many examples of ill-thought-out and unworkable legislation which has been rushed through by the Government in response to a perceived crisis. The Dangerous Dogs Act, for example, was passed in 1991 as a result of a few cases of serious injury caused by dog attacks. In practice, as many critics warned at the time, the Act has been almost impossible to implement because of the difficulties of identifying the particular breeds of dog certified as dangerous. Failure to take account of these comments in the rushed consultation and draft stage resulted in a flawed piece of law being on the statute books and unlikely ever to be repealed.

5.25 While such examples highlight the potential lack of sufficient checks and scrutiny in the law-making process, there is an equally strong argument for saying that the system suffers from being too slow and cumbersome. For every case of ill-thought-out legislation rushed through, there is a worthwhile and overdue statute which is not passed through lack of time in the parliamentary timetable. One reason for this is that many of the procedures in Parliament are left over from a time when the legislation passed was shorter and less complex and when many MPs had other interests and occupations which needed to be attended to during long vacations. If a law-making body was being designed from scratch it is very unlikely that it would share many of the detailed arrangements of the current Parliament.

5.26 In recent years there has been a drive to modernize the procedures of Parliament to address these problems. The pressure for change has also been driven by arguments that the current working arrangements discriminate against those with family responsibilities, predominantly women, who make up only 19 per cent of MPs. For example, the fact that debates and voting are often carried out in the evenings and late at night is particularly hard for parents of young children. But resistance to change among many members is strong and one of the few areas in which backbenchers still exert some power is control over the procedures of the House. To date, although some progress has been made in reforming parliamentary procedure, there is still a long way to go in modernizing the way the law is made in Parliament to strike a better balance between scrutiny and the efficient use of its time.

5.27 One knock-on effect of the constant shortage of time available for legislation is that there is a reluctance to make time for repealing redundant legislation and passing Consolidating Acts which draw together different pieces of law on the same subject. The presence of old and overlapping law is not just untidy, it has a practical impact on the level of justice. Old Acts which have long been considered inappropriate for current conditions and so redundant have sometimes been resuscitated for questionable purposes. For example, the use of the draconian provisions of the long-dormant Vagrancy Act 1864 to stop and search black suspects on the street in Brixton in the 1980s was instrumental in leading to the inner city riots of 1981 and 1985. Periodically Parliament passes Acts to repeal obsolete legislation and to tidy up the statute books. The Statute Law (Repeals) Act 2008 repealed 260 Acts in their entirety and partially repealed a further 68 Acts. Many redundant pieces of legislation were removed from the statute books, such as twelve Acts regulating the East India Company – a company which had been dissolved in 1873!

5.28 The vast and confused state of the statute books also removes any hope that ordinary people might be able to understand the law without specialist legal help. Ignorance of the law is no defence to a criminal charge and yet most people cannot know even a tiny fraction of the law. For these reasons, the campaign for codification, at least in relation to the criminal law, has attracted considerable support. The Law Commission has been working on a draft code for many years, though there is no sign yet of time being made available in Parliament for this to be passed.

FURTHER READING

Michael Zander *The Law Making Process* (2004, Cambridge: CUP), chs 1 and 2.

The Select Committee Report on Modernisation of the House of Commons: The Legislative Process (1997–1998 HC 190) (http://www.parliament.the-stationery-office.co.uk/pa/cm199798/cmselect/cmmodern/190i/md0102.htm).

The Work of the House of Lords. Parliament Briefing Paper (http://www.parliament.uk/documents/upload/HoLwork.pdf).

The Wakeham Royal Commission on the Reform of the House of Lords *A House for the Future* (Cmnd 4534) (2000, London: HMSO) (http://www.archive.official-documents.co.uk/document/cm45/4534/4534.htm).

USEFUL WEBSITES

House of Commons home page
http://www.parliament.uk/about_commons/about_commons.cfm

House of Lords home page
http://www.parliament.uk/about_lords/about_lords.cfm

All current UK statutes since 1988
http://www.legislation.hmso.gov.uk/

DCA website section on House of Lords reform
http://www.dca.gov.uk/constitution/holref/holrefindex.htm

SELF-TEST QUESTIONS

1 What are the advantages and disadvantages of the strong executive control of the legislative process?

2 What changes might be introduced to the parliamentary procedure to improve the efficiency and effectiveness of the law-making process?

3 List three ways in which the law-making procedure in the House of Lords differs from that in the House of Commons.

4 Define the following terms:
Public Bills
Private Members' Bills
Private Bills
Consolidating Acts.

5 'The legislative process in the Westminster Parliament is deficient. Bills are subject to inadequate scrutiny.' Discuss.

6

Statutory interpretation

SUMMARY

This chapter reviews the ways in which judges undertake the task of statutory interpretation. It describes the increasing dominance of a 'purposive' approach to interpretation and compares the relative impact of the rule in *Pepper v Hart* and the provisions of the Human Rights Act 1998 on the way judges approach the interpretation of legislation.

6.1 As legislation has increased in length and scope the great majority of cases decided in the courts now involve the consideration of statutory provisions. This development might be expected to have reduced the role of the judges in developing the law, particularly since the traditional approach to drafting UK statutes has been to ensure precision in their wording so as to minimize the likelihood of disagreement about the meaning of the provision. In practice, however, it is impossible to draft a statute which covers all eventualities and which contains no potential for conflict about its application.

6.2 Where the implications of that conflict are serious enough to warrant the time and cost of a court case, it will come before the judges to decide how the wording of a statute should be interpreted. Ultimately, therefore, what a law means is what the judges say it means. Parliament can later change the law if it disagrees with the judges' interpretation, but, in practice, this will rarely happen. Thus, despite the principle of overriding parliamentary sovereignty and the increasing proportion of the law which is found in statutes, the judges still have a central role to play in shaping the law through the process of statutory interpretation.

6.3 In order to assist the judges in determining the meaning of legislation, 'rules' of statutory interpretation have been developed by the courts. These are not law, but guidelines on how to approach the task of interpreting legislation. Traditionalists would argue that these provide a coherent framework which assists judges to find the 'correct' reading of a statute. A more critical approach challenges the idea that in difficult cases (by definition those which reach the appeal courts) there is one correct meaning, or indeed one fixed parliamentary intention which the courts can 'find'. Instead, the process of statutory interpretation is seen as a creative one in which the judges themselves develop the law according to their own understandings and interpretative priorities.

6.4 The evidence to support this claim comes from the fact that interpretation differs from judge to judge and case to case, often with conflicting decisions on meaning between judges in the same court and between different levels of court as a case goes through the appeal process. According to this more critical approach, the primary function of the rules of interpretation is to provide the appearance of scientific method to what is, in practice, a largely subjective process in which judges exercise a wide degree of discretion to read statutes in the manner that seems to them most appropriate. The extent to which the interpretation of statutes is context-based is much easier to see when the reasoning in older judgments is scrutinized. For example, in 1909 the House of Lords was asked to decide whether women could vote for the old university seats in Parliament. It was required to determine whether the word 'person' included women. The Lord Chancellor concluded that:

> It is incomprehensible to me that any one acquainted with our laws or the methods by which they are ascertained can think, if, indeed, any one does think, there is room for argument on such a point. It is notorious that this right of voting has, in fact, been confined to men. (*Nairn v University of St. Andrews* [1909] AC 147 (HL))

The tone of this decision is clearly a reflection of the very different social and political context in which the case was heard. Nevertheless, the judiciary was, for many years, reluctant to accept that the interpretation of statutes was a process in which values and policy choices had any place.

Different approaches to statutory interpretation

6.5 In the early twentieth century, most judges, if asked how they interpreted statutes, would have said that their approach was to respect the authority of the words in the statute as drafted and seek to apply their plain and obvious meaning, whether or not this reading leads to a sensible outcome. This approach was epitomized by the following quote from Lord Simonds, Lord Chancellor, in 1951:

It is sufficient to say that the general proposition that it is the duty of the court to find out the intention of Parliament – and not only of Parliament but of Ministers also – cannot by any means be supported. The duty of the court is to interpret the words that the legislature has used; these words may be ambiguous, but, even if they are, the power and duty of the court to travel outside them on a voyage of discovery are strictly limited.

6.6 By adopting this literal approach the scope for the judges to apply their own pre-ferred interpretation of the law and run the risk of undermining parliamentary sovereignty is reduced. Provided the drafters are meticulous in their choice of words, supporters of the literal rule would argue that it is the best hope for ensuring that judges do not interfere inappropriately with legislation. However, the assumption that laws can and will be drafted so clearly and coherently as to avoid all gaps or ambiguities is, arguably, an unrealistic one. Moreover, by definition those cases which have reached the higher courts to be interpreted are those where there is at least an arguable case for different interpretations. The literal approach has been criticized as being 'mechanical, divorced both from the realities of the use of language and from the expectations and aspirations of the human beings concerned and, in that sense, it is irresponsible' (Zander, 2004).

6.7 In addition, the literal approach may fail quite blatantly to give expression to the intention of Parliament. As a result of these weaknesses, the courts developed a modified version of this approach; the so-called 'golden rule'. This rule states that where the application of the literal rule leads to a manifest absurdity, the judges are required to adapt the language of the statute in order to produce a sensible outcome. The golden rule therefore accepts the premise of the literal rule that, ideally, judges should look only to the words themselves, but considers that some adaptation is needed to cater for the occasions when this approach results in an outcome which Parliament has not foreseen and which clearly was not intended. The golden rule has been described as 'little more than an unpredictable safety-valve to permit courts to escape from some of the more unpalatable effects of the literal rule' (Zander, 2004).

6.8 Both these two rules prioritize what Parliament said over what it may have meant. Their weakness is that they are founded on an assumption that words have 'plain meanings'. This is contradicted by the fact that even dictionary definitions often have a number of different meanings which can only be identified in context. Moreover, judges themselves often disagree about what the 'plain meaning' of a word should be. Critics of this approach have, therefore, argued that for the judges meaningfully to apply the law as passed by Parliament requires a more proactive engagement with what the statute was intended to achieve.

6.9 In recent years, the limitations of the traditional approach to statutory interpretation have been more generally recognized by the courts and the tendency has become, increasingly, to interpret a statute in the context of the aims of the provision in order to give full expression to the intention behind the legislation. This approach seeks to identify the 'mischief' which the statute was seeking to correct or the purpose behind the provisions. Its premise is that in order for the judges to interpret the statute accurately, they need to understand why Parliament wished to pass the law in the first place. This is sometimes called a 'purposive' approach.

6.10 This approach, which was first set down as early as 1584, has only relatively recently been widely applied by the judges. For most of the twentieth century the literal rule, subsidized by the golden rule, was the dominant approach. It is only in the last few decades that the mischief rule has been widely accepted by the judges and applied in the courts. The current approach was summarized by Lord Griffiths in the important case of *Pepper v Hart* (1993) discussed below:

> The days have long passed when the courts adopted a strict constructionist view of interpretation which required them to adopt the literal meaning of the language. The courts now adopt a purposive approach which seeks to give effect to the true purpose of legislation.

6.11 A good example of such an approach is found in *R v Smith* (2001) in which the House of Lords was required to consider the interpretation of the provisions of the Criminal Justice Act 1988 relating to the confiscation of the proceeds of crime. The defendant was convicting of smuggling cigarettes, which had been intercepted and confiscated by customs. At his trial, the judge had made a confiscation order for the amount of unpaid duty on the cigarettes. The defendant appealed against the order on the grounds that the wording of the Act only applied when the offender had benefited from any relevant criminal conduct 'by obtaining a pecuniary advantage'. The Court of Appeal held that since the cigarettes had been confiscated, no pecuniary advantage had been obtained. The House of Lords disagreed with the Court of Appeal's interpretation of the term 'pecuniary advantage' and held that: 'the ordinary and natural meaning of pecuniary advantage must surely include the case where a debt is evaded or deferred'. However, Lord Rodger also went on to give a clear purposive rationale for that interpretation. He rejected the interpretation of the Court of Appeal on the grounds that:

> ... if adopted, their interpretation would go a long way to making the confiscation provisions ineffective against smugglers. After all, there will be few, if any, cases where customs officers will fail to seize contraband goods which they find in the hands of smugglers. The decision of the Court of Appeal would mean that in any such case, for the purposes of section 71(5), the smugglers would derive no pecuniary benefit from evading the excise duty and so no confiscation order could be made against them.

6.12 One of the factors which has encouraged the increasing popularity of this approach to statutory interpretation is the growth of cases involving the application of

European Law in the UK courts. In interpreting these more open-ended and concise provisions, the courts have found it necessary to adopt the more purposive approach which predominates in the European Court of Justice. Familiarity with this method of interpretation in the area of European Law has inevitably reinforced the growing popularity of the mischief rule in interpreting domestic legislation.

Aids to interpretation

6.13 One of the difficulties, in practical terms, with the application of the purposive approach is that in order for the courts to discover the original intention of Parliament it is necessary for the judges to consider evidence of the nature of the problem which the statue was intended to address. A key issue, therefore, is what resources are available to the courts to answer this question.

6.14 First, there are a number of aids within the Act itself. Most obviously, the judges can read the statute in its entirety in order to place the particular provision in context. They can look at the short and long title, the marginal notes, the section headings, the schedules and the preamble, which was often lengthy in older statutes.

6.15 More problematic is the question of whether the courts can look to external sources to determine the policy which underpinned the statute. Until recently, courts were not allowed to look at White Papers or the explanatory memoranda attached to Bills before Parliament. Since the decision in *Black-Clawson* (1975) the courts have been able to consider White Papers for the purpose of identifying the mischief, but not for the purpose of correcting that mischief.

6.16 In practice, this distinction may be more theoretical than real. The use of explanatory memoranda as an aid to interpretation has been particularly relevant since 1998 when Bills have been published with much fuller explanatory notes attached, designed to explain the background to a statute, to summarize its provisions and place them in context (Jenkins, 1999).

6.17 Despite the gradual increase in the range of material available to the judges to assist them in the task of statutory interpretation, one of the sources which the courts had, until recently, consistently refused to consult was the Hansard reports of proceedings in Parliament. This rule was based on a strict interpretation of s 9 of the 1689 Bill of Rights which prohibits the courts from scrutinizing anything said in Parliament. This rule was originally intended to preserve parliamentary authority and protect MPs from oppressive action in the courts, but came to be interpreted strictly by the courts as preventing them from reviewing parliamentary proceedings for any purpose whatsoever.

Pepper v Hart

6.18 In 1993, in *Pepper v Hart* the House of Lords decided by a 6 to 1 majority to reverse this rule and allow the statement of a Minister in Parliament as reported in Hansard to be referred to in the limited circumstances where there is an ambiguity in the legislation or the application of the literal rules leads to an absurdity and where Hansard clearly discloses the mischief aimed at.

6.19 Lord Browne-Wilkinson who gave the leading judgment argued that in the small number of cases where a ministerial statement would shed light on the intention of Parliament, it was wrong for the court to 'blind' itself to a clear indication of what Parliament intended.

6.20 Critics of the decision in *Pepper v Hart* (1993) (including the one dissenting judge, the then Lord Chancellor, Lord Mackay) claimed that it would lead to extra expense, since lawyers arguing a point of construction would feel obliged to spend time searching Hansard for ministerial statements on the law. Moreover, it was said that if the courts were then persuaded to allow such evidence to be raised, cases would inevitably take longer and so incur greater costs.

6.21 A more theoretical objection to the decision in *Pepper v Hart* (1993) was put forward by Dr David Robertson. He argued that the decision did not, in fact, liberalize the courts' practices, but rather restricted their ability to determine accurately the intention of Parliament by freezing the interpretation of a provision at one moment in the past:

> Reference to Hansard necessarily sets an interpretation within the immediate contemporary understanding of the government of the day ... It risks imposing a literalism in interpretation ... on the basis of an interchange, possibly in a nearly empty chamber late at night indicative only of what [the Government] would like the law to be. (1998, pp 171–183)

6.22 Despite the very limited terms in which the change was framed by Lord Browne-Wilkinson, the evidence suggests that, in practice, the fears that it would come to be used very regularly have proved well founded. The courts have considered ministerial statements in a relatively wide range of different circumstances, although the usefulness of such scrutiny is open to question. In 1998, one High Court judge stated that he had yet to hear a case 'where the exercise of consulting Hansard proved the slightest bit helpful and many when it proved time consuming and wasteful'. A similar view has been expressed by Lord Steyn (2000), who originally supported the decision in *Pepper v Hart* (1993), but has come to regard it as a mistake.

6.23 In a study of 60 cases in which Hansard was referred to, carried out by Professor Michael Zander in 2000, it was found that the references almost never helped to resolve an ambiguity by revealing the statutory intent behind the provision. These findings would suggest that the concerns set out in the dissenting judgment of Lord Mackay appear to have been largely borne out. At the time, however, there was much criticism of his solitary dissent, particularly in the light of his role as Lord Chancellor who therefore carried responsibility for the legal aid budget which stood to increase because of the additional time and resources which would be needed by lawyers in researching the debates. Some commentators suggested that his 'ministerial hat' might have been weighing too heavily in his decision-making process.

6.24 In opening up the range of sources available to judges in the task of statutory interpretation, the courts in the UK have followed a trend which is evident in many other commonwealth countries. Whether this change helps or hinders the process of determining accurately the intended meaning of a statutory provision is still very much open to question.

The Human Rights Act 1998

6.25 While *Pepper v Hart* (1993) seems to have had relatively little effect on the decision-making of the courts, the provisions of the Human Rights Act 1998 represent a fundamental change in the way in which judges approach the task of statutory interpretation. The provisions set out in s 3 require the courts to interpret legislation 'in so far as it is possible' in a way which is compatible with the European Convention on Human Rights. This new duty means that the rules of interpretation by which the courts have been guided to date must take second place to the requirement of compatibility.

6.26 Much discussion took place before the HRA 1998 came into force among judges, lawyers and academics as to what the phrase 'in so far as it is possible' means in practice. There is general agreement that where there are two or more possible readings of the words in a statute the courts are now obliged to choose the one which conforms to the Convention. This rule, however, already applied in relation to international treaties to which the UK was a signatory before the HRA came into force. Section 3 clearly intended the courts to go further than deciding between two alternative interpretations in favour of the Convention.

6.27 What is less clear is how far the courts are able to strain the meaning of the words in order to obtain compatibility and the extent to which they are allowed to 'read in' words to legislation which are not there in order to comply with HRA 1998, s 3. When the Human Rights Bill was going through Parliament, the Home Secretary, Jack Straw, stated that the Government did not intend that the courts in applying s 3 should 'contort' the meaning of words to produce implausible or incredible meanings.

6.28 Since the Act came into force in October 2000, senior judges have been striving to determine the limits imposed upon them by HRA 1998, s 3. The leading case on the interpretation of statutes under s 3 is *Ghaidan v Mendoza* (2004). Mr Mendoza claimed that he was entitled to succeed to a secure tenancy under the Rent Act 1977 following the death of his same-sex partner who was the original tenant. The Rent Act provided that 'a person who was living with the original tenant as his or her wife or husband' would be treated as the tenant's 'spouse' and would therefore also be entitled to a secure tenancy. On ordinary principles of statutory interpretation same-sex partners were excluded in breach of Article 8 and 14 of the Convention. But applying s 3 the House of Lords held by a majority of 4 to 1 that it was possible to read this provision so that 'spouse' included same-sex partners.

6.29 Whether it is 'possible' to interpret a statute compatibly will depend on the particular statutory context and the rights in issue, nevertheless *Ghaidan* confirms the general approach that the courts should follow:

(i) s 3 should not be used to produce a result which is contrary to a 'fundamental feature' of the legislation, nor should the judges make decisions which 'would require legislative deliberation';

(ii) the court can 'read down' statutory language, interpreting it restrictively and it can also 'read in' additional words;

(iii) the judges must ensure that any words read in 'go with the grain' of the statute;

(iv) 'reading-in' does not depend upon the number of words used to achieve a Convention compatible result and when reading-in the court does not have to emulate the precision required by the parliamentary draftsmen – it suffices if they make clear what a Convention-compatible outcome will be;

(v) it is possible to depart from the intention expressed in the language of a statutory provision, provided that the resulting interpretation accords with the *purpose* underlying the provision.

6.30 A good example of a case where s 3 could not be used because 'legislative deliberation' was required is *Bellinger v Bellinger* (2003). The House of Lords declined to interpret 'female' in the Matrimonial Causes Act 1973 to include a transsexual female with the result that Mrs Bellinger remained male in the eyes of the law and could not marry a man. The case raised important issues of social policy and, as Lord Nicholls, observed, the question of when precisely a transsexual acquires their new gender is one of immense medical and psychological complexity. Furthermore, the ramifications of altering the legal meaning of gender were far-reaching because gender is used in many other areas of the law, for example to determine entitlement to benefits and in taxation statutes. Accordingly, it was more appropriate to make a declaration of incompatibility and allow Parliament to address these issues after proper debate and consultation.

6.31 These decisions show the considerable effect that s 3 of the HRA 1998, has had in the field of statutory interpretation. This change, combined with the growing influence of European Law in the domestic courts, is resulting in the courts adopting a much less literal and formalistic approach than in the past. The political implications of this change in terms of the distribution of law-making power between Parliament and the judges may be very significant.

FURTHER READING

Michael Zander *The Law Making Process* (2004, Cambridge: Cambridge University Press), ch 3.

Michael Zander 'What Precedents and Other Source Materials Do the Courts Use?' (2000) 150 New Law Journal 1790.

Lord Steyn '*Pepper v Hart*: A Re-examination' (2001) 21(1) Oxford Journal of Legal Studies 59.

Christopher Jenkins 'Helping the Reader of Bills and Acts' (1999) 149 New Law Journal 798.

David Robertson *Judicial Discretion in the House of Lords* (1998, Oxford: Clarendon Press).

SELF-TEST QUESTIONS

1 What is meant by the 'purposive approach' to statutory interpretation?

2 'The traditional rules of statutory interpretation have been fundamentally altered by the provisions of the Human Rights Act 1998.' Discuss.

3 Summarize the decision in *Pepper v Hart* in relation to statutory interpretation. What has been the effect of that decision?

4 What is meant by the intention of Parliament? What is its role in the interpretation of statutes?

Case law, precedent, and judicial law-making

SUMMARY

This chapter explains the rules of precedent which determine when courts are bound by earlier decisions and compares the common law system with that of civil law countries. It explains how these rules have been affected by the Human Rights Act 1998 and by the increasing willingness of the judges to accept that they do not 'discover' the law, but play a role in its formation. It concludes that this acknowledgement of a law-making function raises questions about the legitimate boundaries of judicial law-making and how judges determine the social consensus on which changes to the law are based. It links this development to the emergence of a more intense debate about who the judges are and how they are appointed.

The rules of binding precedent

7.1 One of the requirements of a just legal system is that decisions of courts are consistent, in that like cases are treated alike so that litigants can, to some extent, predict the likely outcome of cases. To this end, it is normal for judges in all legal systems to seek to reach decisions which conform to earlier cases. In the common law system, however, this principle is elevated to a formal system of binding precedent which requires judges to follow the decisions of earlier courts in certain circumstances.

7.2 Cases are decided in hundreds of courts every day, but it is only cases decided in the higher courts, that is the High Court and above, which are binding on the lower courts and must be followed in subsequent cases. The system is essentially a simple hierarchy – the higher the court, the more authority its decisions have. Thus the House of Lords, as the highest court, binds all courts below it. Its judgments are therefore the most important source of case law.

7.3 Where the decisions of higher courts do not constitute binding precedent, they are often said to be persuasive. That is, the courts will take them into consideration and will follow the decision unless they think there is good reason not to. Thus, decisions of the Privy Council which are not binding on other courts (except in cases involving Scottish and Welsh devolution issues) are persuasive and will often be followed. A good example is the Privy Council's decision in an appeal from Australia which has become one of the leading decisions on the law of negligence (*The Wagon Mound* (1963)).

7.4 In order for a case to be followed by later courts it must be written down and published (reported). Historically, when only a small proportion of the cases were reported this factor was a significant limitation on the system of precedent. Today, this poses less of a problem as there are full reports (both on paper and electronic) of almost all the significant decisions of the higher courts. Interestingly, however, the process of reporting cases is not the responsibility of the courts, but is left to publishing companies, newspapers and journals, and some important cases still go unreported.

7.5 It is quite easy to state the rules of binding precedent, but in practice, it is not always easy for the courts to know how to apply them. In a typical case in the higher courts, the legal representatives of both sides will present the court with a number of different cases which each side claims supports their arguments. The court must go through a series of decisions in order to determine whether or not it is bound by a particular previous decision.

7.6 The first question the judges must ask themselves is whether the facts of the case are sufficiently similar that the earlier case constitutes a precedent. In practice, no two cases will have identical facts and a case is only applicable if the *material* facts are the same. The key question is whether the differences between the present and previous case have a bearing on the outcome of the case. If there are materially different facts, the court may *distinguish* the case from the earlier cases and so apply a different rule. To decide whether facts are material or not, the court must determine what the general rule is which was laid down by the earlier case. This is called the *ratio decidendi*, which is the combination of the rule of law and the material facts to which it applies.

7.7 For example, in *Camplin* (1978) the House of Lords held that a 15-year-old boy who killed a man by striking him with a chapati pan after the man had sexually assaulted him could claim the defence of provocation to a charge of murder. If in a later case, all the facts were the same, but the defendant had stuck his assailant with a kettle, that would not be considered a material difference in fact and the case would be a binding precedent. However, if a subsequent case involved a man of 30, would that be a material fact? To answer the question the court has to be able to determine the *ratio* of the case.

7.8 It has generally been agreed that the ratio in *Camplin* (1978) was that in deciding whether or not a person could claim the defence of provocation to a charge of murder, the court should consider the effect of the provocation on a reasonable person with the same general characteristics as the defendant. Therefore the age of the defendant in the later case would probably be considered to be a material fact. The court would still be bound by the general rule set down in *Camplin* (1978) but might distinguish the outcome on the facts. The key question in determining the *ratio* is to know what the level of generality of the rule is, and this is not always easy for the court (or anyone else) to discern.

Common law and civil law systems compared

7.9 It is possible to make too much of the difference between a common law and civil law system in terms of the role of precedent. In countries such as France judges are not bound by earlier decisions, but in practice, they too seek the benefits of consistency, certainty and finality which following earlier decisions brings.

7.10 However, one significant effect which the system of binding precedent does have is to give a greater role to the appellate courts in a common law country. It is because the decisions of senior judges make up part of the law itself that the judiciary in England and Wales has historically wielded greater authority than in most civil law systems. Moreover, this authority is not merely based on the historical function of the judges in developing the common law.

7.11 It is clear from what has been said above that judges have considerable scope for discretion in the application of the rules of precedent. Gaps, conflicting decisions and ambiguity in the decided cases leave plenty of room for the judges to leave their mark on the law today. The continuing process of developing the common law is not a mechanical one. It requires the courts to make often finely balanced choices between different decisions. Because it is an art not a science, there is room for other factors such as ethical values and policy concerns to find their way into the decision-making process. The question of where the creative application of the law becomes judicial law-making is a controversial one.

Are earlier decisions binding on the court which made them?

7.12 One important question in the system of precedent is whether higher courts are bound by their own earlier decisions. The rules differ for different courts. Trial courts are not bound by their own decisions, so the magistrates' courts, county courts and High Court are generally free to depart from their previous rulings. However, the Divisional Court of the High Court, being a court of review, is generally bound by its own decisions in the same way as the Court of Appeal. In *Young v Bristol Aeroplane Co. Ltd* (1946) the Court of Appeal set out the rule that it is bound by its own decisions except in the following circumstances:

- earlier decisions of the Court of Appeal conflict, in which case it can choose which to follow;
- an earlier decision has been overruled by the House of Lords;
- an earlier decision was reached in error because a binding precedent or statutory provision was overlooked.

7.13 In general, these rules apply to both the civil and criminal divisions of the Court of Appeal. However, in the criminal division there is also a rule that the Court can depart from a previous decision which is against the defendant if the interests of justice so require. This is usually justified on the grounds that the liberty of the person is at stake and therefore the judges need a greater measure of flexibility in order to ensure that injustice is not done in individual cases. It is also argued that because very few criminal cases reach the House of Lords, there is greater need for the Court of Appeal to put right earlier decisions which manifestly should not stand. The difficulty, however, with this approach is that in adapting the law to the requirements in particular cases the criminal law has often been left in a state of confusion with a series of conflicting decisions.

7.14 Until 1966, the House of Lords was bound by its own decisions unless they were decided in ignorance of an earlier binding case or a statutory provision. However, in that year the Lord Chancellor set out a practice direction which stated that while the House of Lords would normally regard itself as bound, it might depart from a previous decision where the earlier decision was influenced by a condition which no longer existed.

7.15 In practice, the House of Lords rarely departed from its earlier decisions. One such example was Howe in 1987, in which the court held that it was not open to a defendant to plead duress to a charge of murder, so overturning its earlier decision in *DPP of Northern Ireland v Lynch* (1975). It is expected that the Supreme Court will continue to follow the practice of the House of Lords in this area.

The scope of judicial law-making

7.16 In deciding whether or not a precedent applies to a set of facts which has not previously been considered by the court or in choosing between competing precedents or constructing the meaning of a statute, the judges can be said to be creating the law. The so-called 'rules' of precedent and statutory interpretation are simply guiding structures within which judges necessarily exercise a wide measure of discretion.

7.17 Sometimes this discretion must be exercised because new technologies throw up situations which have not occurred before. These cases sometimes involve issues around medical treatment and require judges to make highly sensitive and difficult decisions. An example of this arose in 2001 when the Court of Appeal was left to decide whether it would be lawful for surgeons to separate conjoined twins in order to save the life of one twin in an operation which would result in the certain death of the other (*Re A*).

7.18 No precedent existed for such a situation and the criminal law could not be reconciled with the facts, since it was arguable that if the surgeons did not operate they might be committing a criminal offence by failing in their duty to save the life of the stronger twin, while if they did separate the babies, they might also be said to be committing a crime by bringing about the death of the weaker twin. In practice, the judgment was forced to look beyond the law to the underlying principles on which the criminal law is based, by balancing up the interests of the two children, and in so doing, came up with a reasoning which allowed the operation legally to proceed though it was difficult to reconcile with the existing law.

7.19 Sometimes the changes which give rise to the need for judicial law-making are not technological, but social. Courts are regularly faced with precedents which are completely clear but which are no longer in step with current values. The judges are then faced with the choice of applying them or explicitly changing the law. In 1991, for example, the courts held that a husband was no longer immune from prosecution for raping his wife (*R v R*). Until then, the common law rule was that by marrying, a women effectively gave her ongoing consent to sexual intercourse with her husband. Instead of abiding by the precedent and leaving Parliament to abolish the immunity if it so wished, the court went ahead and changed the law to bring it into line with current social attitudes to rape and marriage.

7.20 Similar changes have arisen in relation to the interpretation of statutes. In *Fitzpatrick v Sterling Housing Association* (2001) the House of Lords held that the term 'family' in the Rent Act 1977 governing the rights of a member of a family of a protected tenant to inherit those rights on the tenant's death should extend to same-sex partners. Although the law had up to that time been interpreted to include only heterosexual couples, the court held that the change was 'in accordance with contemporary notions of social justice'. In *Ghaidan v Mendoza* (2004), the court completed the change of law in this area when it considered whether the provision of the Act which allowed unmarried heterosexual couples to inherit statutory tenancies should be interpreted to include same-sex couples. It held that Article 14 of the European Convention required that the wording of s 2(2) which read: '... a person who was living with the original tenant as his or her wife or husband shall be treated as the spouse of the original tenant' should be changed to '*as if they were* his or her wife or husband', so including same-sex couples.

7.21   In *White v White* (2000), which concerned the division of assets on divorce, the House of Lords held that the court should start from the assumption that the husband and wife were entitled to equal shares on divorce, rather than, as it had done up to that time, seeking to provide for the 'reasonable needs' of the non-earning partner (usually the woman). The decision of the court was explained as in keeping with contemporary understanding of equality which required that the contribution of the non-earning partner in the home should be viewed as equivalent to that of the earning partner.

The traditional approach to judicial law-making

7.22   From the description above, it is clear that judges, particularly the senior judges in the Court of Appeal and House of Lords, are widely engaged in law-making. Moreover, it can be argued that it is impossible for them to avoid doing so and the distinction between the creation and interpretation of law is so difficult to draw as to be almost meaningless. Nevertheless, until relatively recently the traditional interpretation of the judicial function was that judges do not make law. This understanding of the judicial role was founded on a fiction that 'cases do not make law, but are the best evidence of what the law is'. Judges therefore in their decisions were merely declaring what the law was. The following two quotes from senior judges in the 1940s and 1950s sum up the traditional approach to judicial law-making:

> The function of the legislature is to make the law, the function of the administration is to administer the law and the function of the judiciary is to interpret and enforce the law. The judiciary is not concerned with policy. It is not for the judiciary to decide what is in the public interest. These are the tasks of the legislature, which is put there for the purpose, and it is not right that it should shirk its responsibilities. (Lord Greene, 1944).

> We should loyally follow the earlier decisions of the House of Lords ... the problem is not to consider what social and political considerations do today require, that is to confuse the role of the lawyer with the task of the legislator. It is quite possible that the law has produced a result which does not accord with the requirements of today. If so put it right by

legislation, but do not expect every lawyer to decide what the law ought to be … do not get yourself into a frame of mind of entrusting to the judges the working out of a whole new set of principles which does accord with the requirements of modern conditions. Leave that to the legislature, and leave us to confine ourselves to trying to find out what the law is. (Lord Jowitt, Lord Chancellor from 1945 to 1951)

7.23 Exactly how the law came to exist before it was 'discovered' and 'declared' by the judges was never made very clear in these conventional explanations of the role of the judge.

7.24 By the nineteenth century, legal thinkers such as Austin and Bentham had written about the concept of 'judge-made law'. But it was not until the late twentieth century that judges themselves fully admitted their role in judicial law-making. A key moment came with the publication by a law lord, Lord Reid, of an article in 1972 called 'the Judge as Lawmaker' which included the following statement:

There was a time when it was thought almost indecent to suggest that judges make law—they only declare it. Those with the taste for fairy tales seem to have thought that in some Aladdin's Cave there is hidden the common law in all its splendour and that on a judge's appointment there descends on him knowledge of the magic words 'Open Sesame' … We do not believe in fairy tales any more (Lord Reid, 1972).

7.25 Since Lord Reid wrote, the claim that senior judges merely declare the law is no longer heard either on or off the bench. Instead, debate focuses on where the limits of judicial law-making should lie. Lord Bingham's 2005 British Academy Maccabean Lecture provides an excellent analysis of the competing viewpoints. He concludes that judicial law-making is desirable, but that the power should be exercised with restraint: 'authority in interpretation of the law naturally derives from learning combined with good judgment and discretion in its deployment'. Or, as Lord Devlin simply put it, 'The first quality of a good judge is good judgment'.

Parliamentary sovereignty

7.26 The traditional denial of a law-making role for judges may seem perverse since it is now so widely accepted that judges do make law. There are, however, sound democratic principles why judges should take a very restrictive approach to their law-making function. The notion of parliamentary sovereignty, which is one of the foundations of the British democratic system, requires that laws are made only by elected representatives. Every time judges take upon themselves the task of determining what the law should be, they risk undermining this vital principle.

7.27 In the 1990s, an interesting public debate arose about the limits of parliamentary sovereignty and the relationship between Parliament and the judiciary. In 1997,

Lord Woolf, then Master of the Rolls, borrowed Lord Reid's words when he apparently questioned the absolute nature of parliamentary sovereignty and argued that the legislature and the judiciary were engaged in a joint law-making project:

> My approach ... does involve dispensing with fairy tales once and for all. But I would suggest that this is healthy ... I see the courts and Parliament as being partners both engaged in a common enterprise involving the upholding of the rule of law. (Lord Woolf, 1997)

7.28 An even more radical claim to judicial law-making was made by Lord Justice Laws, who argued that Parliament was subject to a 'higher law' which stood above statutes and with which statutes must comply. It was, he claimed, the role of the judges to apply this higher law in the courts.

7.29 The reaction of the judiciary and the Lord Chancellor to these arguments was swift and firm. A debate was called in the House of Lords to discuss this constitutional issue and a general attempt was made by most of the senior judges to re-establish the clear message of unquestioning respect for the sovereignty of Parliament. The following comment made by Lord Steyn in 1997 is indicative of the need which some judges felt to re-establish the constitutional boundaries between the different branches of government:

> The relationship between the judiciary and the legislature is simple and straightforward. Parliament asserts sovereign legislative power. The courts acknowledge the sovereignty of Parliament. And in countless decisions the courts have declared the unqualified supremacy of Parliament. *There are no exceptions ... the judiciary unreservedly respects the will of Parliament as expressed in statutes.* [Emphasis added]

7.30 Despite such a clear rejection of Lord Justice Laws' arguments, it is arguable that through the advent of the European Communities Act 1972 and the Human Rights Act 1998, a new vision of constitutionalism has found its way into the legal and political system according to which Parliament does not wield *absolute* power. As Lord Steyn himself acknowledged in *Jackson v Attorney General* (2005):

> The classic account given by Dicey of the doctrine of the supremacy of Parliament, pure and absolute as it was, can now be seen to be out of place in the modern United Kingdom. Nevertheless, the supremacy of Parliament is still the *general* principle of our constitution. It is a construct of the common law. The judges created this principle. If that is so, it is not unthinkable that circumstances could arise where the courts may have to qualify a principle established on a different hypothesis of constitutionalism. In exceptional circumstances involving an attempt to abolish judicial review or the ordinary role of the courts, the Appellate Committee of the House of Lords or a new Supreme Court may have to consider whether this is a constitutional fundamental which even a sovereign Parliament acting at the behest of a complaisant House of Commons cannot abolish.

Problems raised by judicial law-making

7.31 If, therefore, there is clearly scope for judges to make law, whether by filling in gaps, applying the law to new circumstances, adapting it to changing conditions or ensuring it complies with human rights, a number of important questions arise.

7.32 First, where do the judges derive the rationale for their law-making? Some commentators, such as Professor Ronald Dworkin, have argued that judges find the law from the underlying principles on which society generally agrees. In the 1970s, Lord Devlin claimed that judges were entitled to make law where there was a clear social consensus on a topic:

> In a changing society ... the law acts as a valve. New policies must gather strength before they can force an entry: when they are admitted and absorbed into the consensus, the legal system should expand to hold them, as also it should contract to squeeze out old policies which have lost the consensus they once obtained. (Lord Devlin, 1976)

7.33 However, in a modern multicultural society, determining a 'consensus' is likely to be much harder than when Lord Devlin wrote over 30 years ago.

7.34 A further problem is raised by the homogeneous backgrounds of the judges in terms of such factors as class, gender, age, ethnicity and education. Judges cannot be representative in the sense of being chosen to promote the interests of a certain constituency, since this would undermine the fundamental principle of judicial impartiality. But it can be argued that they should be representative in the sense that they should reflect the make-up of society at large; or at least, that they should not be wholly unreflective of that society.

7.35 This argument is stronger the greater the law-making role of the judges. If judges are determining what the law should be, or how fundamental rights such as the right to liberty, privacy and expression should be interpreted in practice, the question of who they are and what values they hold becomes more pressing. In addition, the legitimacy of a powerful decision-making body is weakened if its composition is completely lacking in diversity. The increased law-making role of the judiciary therefore raises important questions about the way judges are appointed which are discussed in chapter 17.

The Human Rights Act 1998

7.36 One of the most significant features of the provisions of the Human Rights Act 1998 which has received relatively little attention is its potential impact on the system of precedent. Under HRA 1998, s 2, when deciding on Convention points, courts must 'take account' of the case law of the European Court of Human Rights. It is therefore explicitly not bound by those decisions, but it is under a duty to consider them. However, under s 3, courts must, so far as possible, interpret legislation in a way which is compatible with the European Convention on Human Rights and, furthermore, under s 6 it is unlawful for the courts (as public authorities) to act in a way which is incompatible with the Convention.

7.37 Taken together, these provisions mean that when any court is considering a statutory provision or the common law which raises Convention issues, the courts must look at the jurisprudence from Strasbourg and interpret the requirements of the Convention in the light of that case law.

7.38 But s 2 does not alter the established rules of precedent. Where there are contradictory rulings of the House of Lords and the European Court of Human Rights, domestic rules of precedent prevail and the Court of Appeal is obliged to follow the House of Lords (*Lambeth LBC v Kay; Price v Leeds CC* (2006)). Lord Bingham, however, allowed for one exception: in circumstances such as occurred in *D v East Berkshire Community NHS Trust* (2005) where the House of Lords' decision had been made without reference to the Human Rights Act 1998, the Court of Appeal would be free to depart from the earlier House of Lords ruling.

Summary

7.39 Although the rules of precedent limit the extent to which judges can change the law, judges clearly make law. How actively they should do so is still very much open to debate. Should they restrict themselves to filling small gaps in the law where there is clearly widespread agreement in society about the need for change? Should they leave it to Parliament to correct more important weaknesses or take the pragmatic approach that such changes simply may not happen unless they are made in the courts? Is it right to see the courts and the legislature as engaged in a joint law-making venture? The answer to these, and other similar, questions depends largely on one's view of the role of the judiciary within the political system.

7.40 Whether or not it is good for a democratic system to rely on judges to make the law, in practice it seems likely that judges in the higher courts will be called upon more frequently to shape the law in areas which have political, economic and moral significance. The following comment on the judicial law-making in the US courts, which highlights the way in which judges approach their law-making role, is probably equally applicable to the UK courts: 'Judges' decisions are a function of what they prefer to do, tempered by what they think they ought to do, but constrained by what they perceive is feasible to do.' Whether or not the right balance between preference, obligation and feasibility is being struck by the judges is an ongoing and crucial question in the legal system today.

FURTHER READING

Lord Reid 'The Judge as Lawmaker' (1972) 12 Society of Public Teachers of Law 22.

Lord Devlin *The Enforcement of Morals* (1968, Oxford: Oxford University Press).

Lord Devlin 'Judges as Lawmakers' (1976) 39 Modern Law Review 1.

Ronald Dworkin *Law's Empire* (1986, London: Fontana Press).

Lord Woolf '*Droit Public* – English Style' (1995) Public Law 57.

John Laws 'Law and Democracy' (1995) Public Law 72.

Kate Malleson *The New Judiciary* (1999, Hampshire: Ashgate Publishing), ch 2.

Michael Zander *The Law Making Process* (2004, Cambridge: Cambridge University Press), ch 7.

Lord Bingham *The Judges: Active or Passive* 2005 Maccabean Lecture in Jurisprudence (http://www.britac.ac.uk/pubs/src/maccab05/index.cfm).

SELF-TEST QUESTIONS

1 'The doctrine of precedent (binding and non-binding) unduly hinders the judges in adapting the law to changing circumstances.' Do you agree?

2 Under what circumstances is the Court of Appeal not bound by its previous decisions?

3 Summarize two cases in which the House of Lords has overruled its previous decisions.

4 Should the Court of Appeal be free to depart from House of Lords/Supreme Court authority in favour of a later decision of the European Court of Human Rights?

8

The civil justice process

SUMMARY

This chapter highlights the trend towards streamlining the civil justice system through the redeployment of cases from the higher to the lower courts, reducing the right of appeal and encouraging the use of alternative dispute resolution processes. It argues that assessing the effectiveness of the civil justice system depends on identifying what goal it is required to fulfil – whether it should be a last resort designed to encourage settlement out of court or an accessible system for processing cases quickly and cheaply. It concludes that there are tensions between the public and private nature of the system and overlap between the aims and procedures of the civil and criminal systems.

8.1 Before looking in detail at the way in which the civil justice system works, and in particular, the major procedural reforms which have been implemented in recent years as a result of the Woolf report in 1999, it is important to consider some of the general trends in the system and to ask what functions the civil justice system serves (or should serve) and how it differs from the criminal justice system.

Distribution of workload

8.2 In common with the criminal court structure, the civil court structure is pyramid-shaped. The great majority of cases are dealt with in the lower courts – the county court and tribunals – with very few ever reaching the upper levels of the High Court, Court of Appeal, and Supreme Court. Moreover, one of the most notable general trends in the civil justice system in recent years has been to redeploy cases away from the High Court. Cases which previously would have been heard by a High Court judge are now routinely dealt with by a Circuit judge or even a District Judge in the county court.

8.3 The workload of the Queen's Bench Division of the High Court declined significantly throughout the 1990s by about two-thirds, while the number of cases dealt with in the small claims court has grown as its jurisdiction has been expanded to allow more cases to be settled using the less formal and costly procedures used there. The threshold for hearing cases, other than personal injury cases, in the small claims jurisdiction has been raised from £1,000 to £3,000 and then to £5,000.

Appeals

8.4 Not only are cases being heard at a lower level of court than in the past, but there has also been a reduction in the opportunity to appeal to the higher courts against a decision in the lower courts. As a result of the Bowman report in 1996, which concluded that the Court of Appeal was dealing with too many less important cases, the civil appeal process was streamlined and reformed in the Access to Justice Act 1999. Almost all cases seeking to appeal must now obtain permission and no longer have an automatic right to do so. Moreover, there is normally now only one possible level of appeal, whereas in the past some cases could be appealed from the county court to the High Court and then on to the Court of Appeal. In addition, cases in the Court of Appeal can now be heard by one or two judges rather than the traditional three-judge court. The time taken for a case to be heard has also been reduced by the substitution of written representation for long oral argument in the form of fuller skeleton arguments produced by counsel for the judges to read before the case.

8.5 A growing problem in recent years has been the increasing numbers of unrepresented litigants in the Court of Appeal. The rise in such litigants since the 1990s can largely be attributed to the reduction in the availability of legal aid discussed in chapter 19. Without the benefit of legal advice and representation, these litigants are at a real disadvantage in presenting their case while their presence also makes extra work for the court staff and judges who must take time to ensure that the procedures are understandable to them and that the arguable points in their case are fully and fairly heard while reducing the time taken up with hopeless or irrelevant arguments.

Alternative dispute resolution

8.6 As well as encouraging cases to be dealt with in the lower courts and resolved at trial level without an appeal-level hearing, there has been an increasing emphasis on the development of alternative dispute resolution methods (ADR) which avoid the time, cost and stress of a formal court hearing. The most common forms of ADR are mediation, arbitration and conciliation.

8.7 These different processes have in common the use of an independent third party who either imposes a decision to which the parties are contractually bound, or helps them to reach a resolution to which they agree. The advantages of these systems are that they can be cheaper because they do not involve lawyers and they can be more flexible by allowing for a range of tailor-made solutions to a dispute, some of which would be outside a court's power to impose. They can also help to mitigate the conflict by using less adversarial techniques than the traditional court-based system and provide a response which is proportionate to the scale of the dispute in terms of cost, speed and complexity.

8.8 Through mediation a third party attempts to help those in dispute to reach a settlement by acting as a go-between, articulating and explaining the views of each of the parties. The mediator fulfils an intermediary role rather than being an active participant in the resolution process. In contrast, in the process of conciliation the conciliator actively seeks to promote settlement by suggesting possible options. The use of arbitration takes this process a step further, and the arbitrator has a role much closer to that of a traditional judge – hearing both sides then imposing a settlement which each side agrees in advance to abide by.

8.9 One area in which arbitration has been particularly successful is large commercial contracts. A number of city firms of solicitors deal with global arbitration cases which involve many millions of pounds. One advantage of ADR for clients of such firms is the private nature of the process. Unlike a court hearing, an arbitration process is not held in public, which may be particularly desirable for large companies who do not wish detail of their commercial activities or disagreements to be known by rivals or clients.

8.10 However, the popularity of arbitration in the field of international commerce is not matched in the area of small-scale private disputes. Despite widespread support from government and relevant interest groups for these court-avoidance methods, their use has not been as enthusiastically embraced in England and Wales as in other countries and only a very small fraction of cases are currently resolved using ADR.

8.11 In the area of divorce, where most optimism has been expressed about the potential benefits of a less confrontational and court-based system, the results of pilot schemes which introduced mediation for divorcing couples have been disappointing. Less than 10 per cent of divorcing couples chose to make use of the service, and a high proportion of those who did so still felt the need of a lawyer working on their behalf.

As a result of these and other similar findings, the introduction of compulsory mediation in the divorce process has been shelved.

8.12 In contrast, a more successful and widespread use of ADR is found in the small claims court, which adopts an arbitration-based system (Andrews, 2008). The explanation for this is that here the process is compulsory and binding. The experience of ADR to date indicates that if the parties to a dispute can choose not to use them, or can challenge the ADR decision on appeal, they are unlikely ever to form more than a small part of the system.

8.13 In order to address this problem, recent statutory regulation of arbitration procedures has reduced the circumstances in which parties using arbitration can appeal against a decision. However, by denying people a right to challenge a decision in the court system, there is a danger that such provisions may fall foul of Article 6 of the European Convention on Human Rights which guarantees access to an independent and impartial tribunal for the determination of a person's 'civil rights and obligations'. Nevertheless, in 2007 the Court of Appeal held an arbitration agreement excluding the right of appeal on a point of law did not breach Article 6 (*Sumukan Ltd v The Commonwealth Secretariat*).

8.14 An additional problem posed by ADR in the courts is the effect of the fact that the court has no power to order that the losing side pays the winning side's costs. The idea of removing cost awards in the small claims procedure was to encourage individuals with few resources to bring a case without the danger of incurring costs which might end up being more than the value of the claim. However, in practice, the removal of cost awards has often left individuals at a disadvantage when sued by companies while also deterring them from bringing cases against well-resourced defendants.

8.15 The effect of the arrangement is that unrepresented individual claimants seeking damages from a business or organization find themselves in an unequal position since such defendants are often willing and able to pay for the costs of a lawyer in order to ensure a better chance of success. In such a situation the unrepresented claimant with no experience of the court system is likely to feel intimidated into settling or dropping a case.

8.16 In practice, the majority of claimants in the small claims courts are companies for whom the small claims procedure provides a quick and cheap method of debt recovery. While this function is a perfectly valid one for the courts to perform, it was not the original purpose behind the removal of costs, which was to improve access to the justice system for less well-off individuals and to promote greater equality of arms by encouraging people to bring cases without the involvement of lawyers.

The compensation culture

8.17 The move towards the disposal of cases in the lower courts with a limited right of appeal and the growing support for ADR implies that the philosophy underlying recent trends in the civil justice system is that the courts are undesirable places for resolving disputes and that people should be discouraged from using them. It is common now to hear concern expressed that England and Wales is becoming an increasingly litigious society, following the US model. In fact, this view is something of a myth since the number of civil cases has generally fallen in recent years. The number of personal injury cases started between 2000 and 2005 went down despite the introduction of a 'no-win no-fee' system (see chapter 15). In May 2004, the Better Regulation Task Force (BRTF) produced a report which concluded that the belief that the UK is in the grip of a US-style 'compensation culture' was unfounded. It showed that for all but one of the previous 15 years the cost of civil claims as a proportion of gross domestic product had been steady at about 0.6 per cent – one of the lowest of all developed states. Moreover, the report pointed out that where damages are awarded, these are generally relatively small amounts, with over half those who are successful in the county courts receiving less than £3,000.

8.18 The BRTF findings were supported by a review of the 'compensation culture' carried out by the House of Commons Constitutional Affairs Committee in March 2006. The Committee's report concluded that the evidence did not support the view that there was such a compensation culture. However, it did find that there was a widespread mistaken belief that litigation was increasing and that this was leading to 'excessive risk aversion' in some areas of public life which had a negative effect on valuable activities such as volunteering, sports activities and educational trips for children. The report supported the conclusion of the BRTF that: 'The compensation culture is a myth; but the cost of this belief is very real.'

8.19 Fear of a compensation culture can lead to people adopting overly defensive practices to minimize the risk of being sued. The Compensation Act 2006 attempts to overcome this by making clear that when considering a claim for negligence, in deciding what is required to meet the standard of care expected of the defendant, courts are able to consider the wider social value of the activity in the context of which the damage or injury occurred. In other words if a school pupil is injured on a school trip, when deciding whether the school has been negligent the court can have regard to the wider social value of organizing school trips and the need not to discourage such activity because of a disproportionate fear of litigation.

Do we want more litigation or less?

8.20 Setting aside the question of the indirect cost of the erroneous perception that we are in the grip of a compensation culture, the recognition that litigation is not out of control does not help us to determine whether a decrease in the number of civil actions started in the courts is a good thing or a bad thing.

8.21 This question can only begin to be answered by knowing more about the nature of civil disputes and people's attitude to these problems. In 1999, a major research project conducted by Professor Hazel Genn into people's experiences of civil justice provided, for the first time, a picture of people's reactions to breaches of the civil law. Based on a large representative sample of the public, it found that of those who had experienced a justiciable civil dispute, 95 per cent took some action to resolve it. Of the 5 per cent who did not, those on low incomes and with poor educational qualifications were over-represented. Of those who sought a resolution, 34 per cent settled the matter by agreement (with or without legal advice) and 14 per cent through the use of some form of court or tribunal (with or without a hearing). In the remaining 52 per cent of cases, no resolution was reached and the case was abandoned (again, either with or without legal advice).

8.22 These findings confirm the relatively small role which courts play in resolving civil disputes. At one level this could be seen as a positive finding. All civil cases could be argued to be a societal failure. Each one is evidence of an unresolved conflict and all effort spent trying to resolve it in the courts is time and resources directed away from more productive economic or social activity. Even Lord Woolf, in his report on civil justice which aimed to make the system more accessible, efficient and fair, argued that: 'Because of the burdens which it imposes on society and on the court system [litigation] should not be too easy an option.'

8.23 However, since conflicts are inevitable, the use of the legal system to settle them is evidence that people are willing to use a forum where, in theory at least, rules and fairness override brute strength – physical or economic. Thus, it is not easy to determine the 'right' size of the civil justice system. An increase in the use made of the civil courts can be seen as evidence of the growth of an unhealthy culture of complaint and an inability to accept risk as a normal part of life or, on the other hand, as evidence that people are more willing and able to enforce their legitimate rights and to ensure fair treatment under the law.

8.24 The tension between the need for access to justice, on the one hand, and the recognition of the potentially damaging nature of litigation was recognized as long ago as 1952 by the Lord Chancellor, Lord Simonds, in debate on the new legal aid system: '... the public mind clearly rejects the idea that a man should now be debarred from justice because of a lack of means. [Yet] in mankind there is a deeply litigious spirit. This has to be guarded against.'

8.25 This tension at the heart of civil justice is just as evident today, over 50 years after Lord Simonds' comment. The civil justice system is a non-productive and costly process which can exaggerate and exacerbate conflict in society while at the same time being an essential vehicle for the promotion of justice and the avoidance of cruder methods of domination. Where the balance should be struck and what constitutes the 'right amount' of civil justice is essentially a political judgment which depends on the economic conditions and cultural values of society at any one time.

8.26 Whether or not the use of the civil justice system is an appropriate response to a dispute involving a breach of the civil law will depend on a range of factors. These include the seriousness of the harm suffered, the attitude of the individual parties to the dispute, the availability of legal advice and assistance, and the time and cost involved in pursuing the matter through the civil justice system.

8.27 The confusion over whether more litigation promotes access to justice or is just a costly and destructive conflict to be avoided is illustrated by the Woolf reforms discussed in the next chapter. Many of Lord Woolf's reforms were designed to keep cases out of the court, to use alternative dispute resolution mechanisms or to settle early, yet the title of his report was 'access to justice' and in his report he commented: 'The effect of my other proposals should be to reduce barriers to access to justice and hence potentially to increase the number of contested cases.'

8.28 At another level, whether we want more or less civil justice depends also on how well the system functions in practical terms. If it fulfils its goals then we might want to encourage its use, whereas if it is grossly inefficient and ineffective it would be better for people to stay out at all costs and find other means of settling their disputes. However, assessing whether or not the system functions well is hampered by the fact that some fundamentally different demands are made of it.

Different functions of the system

8.29 At one level, the purpose of the civil justice system is to act as an ultimate fall-back. It is a threat to be used only as a last resort in order to force those in dispute to negotiate and reach a settlement. This function is being played out in solicitors' offices and barristers' chambers every day.

8.30 Most civil cases are straightforward claims for the recovery of a debt or a claim for damages arising from negligence, and the purpose of starting an action in the court is to ensure payment without the further expense of the court case. Every time a lawyer writes a letter asking for payment or action within a certain time otherwise proceedings will be issued, she or he is hoping that it will not be necessary to use the court system. The great majority of cases which are started are never expected to reach court for a trial and the commencement of proceedings is a way of promoting settlement rather than a first step towards a court hearing (see chapter 1). To fulfil these essentially motivational purposes, the civil courts need to be cheap and easy to access, fast in issuing claims, and certain and effective in enforcing their judgments so that the threat is taken seriously. The quality of the judges' adjudicative skills and the fairness of hearing are much less important than speed and certainty.

8.31 Moreover, for these purposes an expensive trial system may actually be a benefit since in cases where there is no defence to a claim, the threat of large costs arising for the defendant if the matter goes to court will add to the incentive to pay what is owed before the case reaches court. The court therefore serves an important function as a tool for ensuring that people settle their debts or pay damages where they are clearly responsible for another person's loss.

8.32 However, not all cases fall into this category. A minority of cases involve a dispute about liability or damages or, for example, the question of who should have custody of a child, which fail to be settled through negotiation. In these cases where a trial is needed the requirements of the system can be very different. The need to keep down the costs of the trial becomes critical where the outcome of the case is less certain.

8.33 The higher the costs, the more likely that people who have suffered losses will not be willing to take the risk of losing and so will not pursue the case or will be forced to settle for inappropriately reduced damages. Different methods of funding civil justice such as 'no-win no-fee' arrangements may ameliorate some of these effects by redistributing the risks, but ultimately the link between likely cost and people's willingness to pursue a case in the courts remains.

8.34 In addition, the quality of the adjudication in terms of the need for impartial and competent judges who can apply the law consistently and fairly, which in most routine cases which will never reach court is of only limited indirect importance, becomes critical. The question of speed also becomes more complex in the small number of cases which proceed to trial. Whereas straightforward debt cases require a system which responds fast, difficult cases may need more time to prepare. Rushing these cases to trial may actually compromise the quality of the justice and add to the costs of the trial because they are not sufficiently well prepared and presented.

8.35 The difficulty which the civil justice system faces, therefore, is that it is required to perform different functions for different cases. The degree of flexibility which an ideal civil justice system would exhibit in order to meet the needs of all the different types of cases which require its services is probably beyond any system to deliver. Whatever type of system is developed, certain goals will be prioritized which will inevitably lead to winners and losers. These problems will be revisited when we consider the strengths and weaknesses of the Woolf reforms and ask which type of case has benefited and which has suffered as a result of the recent changes.

Is the civil justice system public or private?

8.36 The effectiveness and efficiency of the system is only one factor in deciding whether more or less civil justice is desirable. The answer is also partially dependent on whether the civil justice process is regarded as essentially a public or private process. Is it part of the welfare state, like the National Health Service and the education system, which should be free to citizens at the point of delivery with resources rationed according to the total need of society as a whole? Or is it a consumer service which should be self-funding and, like any other business, expand or contract to meet the needs of the people who pay for its services – the litigants?

8.37 One way to approach this question is to compare the civil justice system with the criminal justice system, which is generally regarded as being the most public aspect of the legal system. Do the two systems differ fundamentally? A key difference is often said to be that the criminal justice system is there to uphold the shared morality of society, whereas the civil justice system exists to regulate the private relations between citizens. In a criminal case, an action is generally brought by the state (technically the Queen) against an individual or company, whereas in the civil courts the parties are usually private bodies or individuals.

8.38 The subject-matter of criminal cases concerns wrongs which are perceived to be of public concern, that is having some wider moral or social implications, in contrast to the essentially private nature of civil justice involving such matters as family arrangements or money claims. The fact that juries and lay magistrates are almost exclusively used for criminal cases is an indication of the wider social concern of the subject-matter since lay personnel are intended to represent the values of society as a whole. Because the criminal law is felt to have a core moral element, the impact of a finding against a person in the criminal courts is considered to be more serious than in the civil courts. One result of this distinction is the different burden of proof. In the criminal courts a case must be proved 'beyond reasonable doubt', whereas in the civil courts the burden of proof is lower – 'a balance of probabilities'.

8.39 Leading on from this distinction is a difference in the consequences which flow from a finding of guilt in the criminal courts or liability in the civil courts. Criminal sanctions are intended to exact retribution or to reduce crime. It is hoped that crime reduction will be achieved by deterring the convicted person and other potential offenders from committing similar offences or through the incapacitation and/or rehabilitation of the offender. In contrast, civil damages and orders are designed, so far as possible, to put claimants back in the position they would have been had the civil wrong not happened, eg if the contract had not been broken or the negligent act not committed.

8.40 These differences would appear to highlight the essentially private nature of the civil justice system in contrast to the public criminal justice system. However, a closer look at the two systems suggests that the differences between them can be overstated. Although most civil cases do involve two private parties, whether individuals or corporations, in many others the state is a party to the action. In particular, the growing number of judicial review cases and negligence claims brought by individuals against government departments and agencies blurs the boundary between public and private actions. These cases can raise important issues about the conduct of government, policy choices and the relationship between the state and the individual. Moreover, the cost of negligence claims now has a significant impact on some departmental budgets. In relation to the penalties of the court, civil courts can also award 'punitive' damages to express disapproval of the defendant's behaviour and discourage others from following it, thus effectively adopting the rationale behind criminal sanctions. In addition, the criminal courts have the power to order that a convicted person pays compensation to the victim for his or her loss, thereby fulfilling the role traditionally allocated to the civil courts. Moreover, these compensation orders take priority over fines so that a criminal court is required, where appropriate, to impose a compensation order in preference to a fine.

8.41 In addition, the breach of certain orders imposed by the civil courts can lead to criminal sanctions and imprisonment. Recent examples are orders made under the Protection from Harassment Act 1997, which was introduced in response to concerns over 'stalking', and Anti-Social Behaviour Orders, which were intended to tackle the problems caused to local areas of persistent low-level criminality and 'neighbours from hell'. Both provisions allow for the imposition of restrictions on a civil burden of proof leading to criminal sanctions if breached so further blurring the distinction between civil and criminal penalties.

8.42 Another common feature of the two systems is found in the overlap of personnel. Many advocates and judges undertake both civil and criminal work. In addition, the distinction between the parties who can bring cases in the two systems is not as clear-cut as is sometimes suggested. Prosecutions can be brought by individuals and private bodies as well as the state. Thus a large department store may choose between bringing a private prosecution or a civil action against those it believes to have stolen goods. Nor are private prosecutions confined to less serious offences, an example being the prosecution for murder of five youths brought by the family of the murdered teenager Stephen Lawrence in 1994.

8.43 Equally, the subject-matter being litigated in the two systems is not necessarily different. Many criminal offences such as assault, theft, careless driving, manslaughter and murder are also civil wrongs, even if they are known by a different name in the civil courts. People can be prosecuted in the criminal courts and sued in the civil courts for the same illegal behaviour. Just as the Lawrence family could bring a private prosecution in the criminal courts, so they could have sued the alleged killers in the civil courts.

8.44 In 1998, Tony Dierdrick was sued by the family of a murdered woman and held to be responsible for her death although he had never been prosecuted in the criminal courts because the Crown Prosecution Service had concluded that there was insufficient evidence to bring a prosecution against him. In that case, the defendant was found liable on the civil burden of proof. However, it is more usual in civil cases which have a criminal element such as serious assault or fraud for the judge to decide the case on a criminal burden of proof, thus reducing still further the distinction between the two types of process.

8.45 These sorts of cases highlight the overlap between civil and criminal actions. But equally there are many civil cases which do not have a criminal equivalent and yet cannot be said to be concerned only with the regulation of people's private affairs. For example, many family law cases which relate to the most personal matters raise issues of wider social importance. In recent years the civil courts have had to decide whether a couple should be allowed to adopt a child obtained through the Internet; whether a patient in a persistent vegetative state can be denied food and medication; and whether a wife can claim that her work in the home entitles her to an equal share of her husband's business assets on divorce. While these sorts of cases are clearly private in the sense that they involve highly sensitive personal issues for the parties, they also concern difficult matters of public interest which attract a great deal of media attention and public debate.

8.46 The mix of public and private found in the civil justice system which these examples illustrate is reflected in the different philosophies which underpin the civil procedure reforms. The introduction in the 1990s of increased court fees was intended to ensure that the civil court system was self-financing, in line with a vision of the system as a private enterprise. The justification for higher fees was that the civil courts provided a service to the consumer which could and should be paid for by litigants. On the other hand, an underlying rationale for the Woolf reforms was to ensure that the civil justice system functioned well for all those who needed to use it. To this end, judges were empowered and encouraged to ration the resources of the court system so as to ensure the fair distribution of court time.

8.47 The goal of 'dealing justly with cases' which is stated to be the overriding objective of the Civil Procedure Rules explicitly requires judges to allocate to each case an appropriate share of the court's resources: 'while taking into account the needs of others'. The exercise of this function through, for example, enforcing strict time limits and reducing the number of witnesses who can be called at trial can be carried out even against the wishes of both parties. These aspects of the system are clearly founded on a view of civil justice as an essentially public service provided for the benefit of society as a whole. In the light of this, it is not surprising that Lord Woolf has been a strong critic of the policy of full costs recovery. In July 2002, speaking at the annual Judges' Dinner, he described it as 'self-evidently nonsense'. He went on to argue that: ' While it is not wrong to require the citizen to pay court fees, access to the civil courts must be seen as providing a social and collective benefit, as well as a service to the individual.'

8.48 The result of these different approaches and practices is that civil justice remains a mixed public and private system in which some areas which were previously public have been privatized and vice versa. These changes have produced a paradox. In the past, litigation was more likely to be paid for out of public funds yet litigants and their representatives were much freer to conduct their litigation as they considered best suited their needs with relatively little interference by the court. Under the current system, litigants are required to pay full court fees and are more likely to be funding the litigation privately yet they now find that the service they are purchasing may be tailored not to their requirements but to those of the civil justice system and other court users.

Fault

8.49 The confusion over the private/public nature of the civil justice system is matched by a growing uncertainty over the role which fault should play in the system. In the expanding area of negligence the law is based upon the principle that damages are payable only if the claimant can prove that their loss was caused by carelessness on the part of the defendant. Where the person who caused the loss cannot be found, or the fault cannot be proved for lack of evidence, or, indeed, where there was no fault and the loss was caused by a simple accident, the case will fail.

8.50 In this respect the civil justice system shares the same moral foundation as the criminal justice system since it is based upon the concept of blame. Yet if one way in which the civil and criminal justice systems are distinguished from each other is the fact that the aim of civil justice is not to censure but to make reparation, the centrality of fault is difficult to justify. If, for example, a person is injured in a car accident and cannot work again, she or he will need financial support to compensate for the loss of future earnings whether or not someone can be found who can be proved to have caused the accident through their negligence. From society's point of view, the civil justice system can be an unfair, unreliable and expensive way of supporting and compensating those who have suffered loss.

8.51 For this reason, the use of alternative 'no fault' systems is being explored in some areas such as medical negligence, which costs the National Health Service many millions of pounds each year in legal fees. A new system is being proposed whereby all those who suffer loss or damage which can be shown to be caused by the treatment will receive a payment without needing to prove the fault of the medical staff involved. The total payment in each case will usually be less than under the current system, but the victims will receive the money without the stress, uncertainty and delay of litigation. Supporters of the change argue that because much less money will be spent on legal fees, there will be more money to compensate those who suffer loss according to their need regardless of whether anyone is to blame for that loss. Another advantage of this approach is that it may reduce the tendency for doctors to practise 'defensive medicine' whereby their decisions are driven by the need to avoid litigation rather than patient well-being. A good example of this is the growing number of babies born through Caesarean deliveries, a trend which has been attributed to an over-cautious approach to the process of labour on the part of hospitals.

8.52 However, removing the element of fault and blame may remove the stigma of a finding of liability by a civil court and so weaken the incentive to take sufficient care. Again, this suggests that the civil system is being used to act as a deterrent in the same way as the criminal courts rather than a mechanism for dispute resolution. The debate over no-fault liability is therefore another example of the uncertainty over what function we want the civil justice system to perform.

Enforcement

8.53 Whichever of the various aims of the civil justice system is prioritized, each is premised on the assumption that the system has the capacity to enforce its decisions. In practice, this assumption is often hard to justify and the difficulties which claimants face in obtaining enforcement of the courts' judgments have become an increasing source of concern. In 2000, the Lord Chancellor's Department (as was) carried out a review of civil court judgments and identified enforcement as a particular problem. It estimated that £600 m per year is lost to creditors through unpaid civil judgment debts (LCD, 2000). In order to determine the nature of this problem the department had previously set up an Enforcement Review to examine, among other things, the methods available for enforcement of county court and High Court judgments and to assess their effectiveness.

8.54 The Review found that only 35 per cent of all warrants of execution were paid, while a study of small claims judgments found that 35 per cent of successful claimants had received no part of the sum awarded to them several months after judgment (Baldwin, 1997). The Review also found that the issue of unpaid judgments was not the only problem associated with enforcement. It drew attention to a report by the National Association of Citizens Advice Bureaux which found evidence of the abuse of power on the part of bailiffs; primarily among private bailiffs acting on behalf of the local authority or magistrates. This abuse took the form of intimidation, misrepresentation, and acting beyond their powers. The report identified problems arising out of the seizure of goods and an absence of effective independent monitoring, complaints and redress mechanisms. It suggested that bailiff action is overused compared to the rest of the European Community (NACAB, 2000).

8.55 In March 2003, the Government produced a White Paper setting out significant changes to the enforcement process. It announced that a new regulatory regime was to be set up for bailiffs (who were renamed Enforcement Agents) and a new Data Disclosure Order brought in which would authorize those holding personal and financial data on debtors to release it to allow for the more effective recovery of the debt. The White Paper stated that its aim was to ensure a balance between the needs of those with a claim to obtain fast and effective recovery, and the need to protect debtors who genuinely do not have the means to pay from oppressive pursuit of a debt. However, press coverage of the White Paper focused almost exclusively on the new right to be given to Enforcement Agents to enter premises by force to recover goods rather than measures to protect the vulnerable, such as removing the power to seize the belongings of tenants who owe rent.

8.56 In 2005, the House of Commons Constitutional Affairs Committee reviewed the county court small claims procedure. It found that the issue of enforcement was identified as a serious problem by almost all the witnesses who gave evidence. The Committee's report concluded that there was an urgent need for reform:

> It is time for the Department [of Constitutional Affairs] to implement much sought after improvements to the system of enforcing judgments. It is unacceptable that litigants, who at the conclusion of a case are led to believe that they have been successful, often find that the judgment that they have obtained is in a practical sense unenforceable.

8.57 Following these criticisms, the law of enforcement has been modified by Parts 3 and 5 of the Tribunals, Courts and Enforcement Act 2007. The Act introduces a new regime for 'taking control of goods', replacing the old system of 'seizure of goods', it creates new methods of obtaining information concerning a debtor's assets and indebtedness, and it 'introduces a package of measures to help those who are willing and able to pay off their debts over time'.

FURTHER READING

Constitutional Affairs Committee *The Courts: Small Claims* (December 2005, HC 519) (http://www.publications.parliament.uk/pa/cm200506/cmselect/cmconst/519/51902.htm).

Constitutional Affairs Committee *Compensation Culture* (March 2006, HC 754-I) (http://www.publications.parliament.uk/pa/cm200506/cmselect/cmconst/754/75402.htm).

Michael Zander *The State of Justice* (2000, London: Sweet and Maxwell), ch 2.

Professor Hazel Genn *Paths to Justice: What People Do and Think about Going to Law* (1999, Oxford: Hart Publishing).

John Baldwin *Small Claims in the County Courts in England and Wales: The Bargain Basement of Civil Justice* (1998, Oxford: Oxford University Press).

John Baldwin *Monitoring the Rise of the Small Claims Limit* (LCD Research Series 1/97).

Lord Chancellor's Department *First Phase of the Enforcement Review* (July 2000) (http://www.dca.gov.uk/civil/cjustfr.htm).

National Association of Citizen's Advice Bureaux *Undue Distress: CAB Clients' Experience of Bailiffs* (May 2000).

Neil Andrews, *The Modern Civil Process* (2008, Tübingen, Mohr Siebeck)

USEFUL WEBSITES

Ministry of Justice website section on civil justice
http://www.justice.gov.uk/civil/procrules_fin/index.htm

SELF-TEST QUESTIONS

1 What lessons can be drawn from the fact that in the past hundred years there have been over 60 official reports on reform of civil procedure? Why is the problem of reducing cost and delay in civil litigation so difficult?

2 What are the differences between mediation, arbitration and conciliation?

3   List three differences and three similarities between the civil and criminal justice systems.

4   What are the advantages and disadvantages of a no-fault system of civil justice in the area of medical negligence?

5   'Following the Woolf reforms with their emphasis on modes of Alternative Dispute Resolution such as mediation and settlement, civil litigation is now the "alternative" form of dispute resolution.' Discuss.

9

The Woolf reforms to civil justice

SUMMARY

This chapter summarizes the changes introduced by the Woolf reforms to civil justice. It outlines the criticisms made of the reforms when introduced, in particular that they would result in 'front-loading' of costs in the early stages of a case. It reviews the effects of the reforms and concludes that the evidence suggests that more cases are settling earlier but that there has been an increase in costs.

9.1 In 1994, Lord Woolf was asked to conduct an inquiry into the civil justice system and make proposals for its modernization. The request was prompted by growing criticism from lawyers, the judiciary and litigants that the system had become unacceptably inefficient and ineffective, to the point where it was in a state of crisis. Lord Woolf undertook consultations with those who worked in the civil justice system as well as reviewing the systems in other countries. In 1995, he produced an interim report followed by a final report entitled *Access to Justice* in 1996.

9.2 The main problems with the civil justice system which he identified were cost, delay, complexity and uncertainty of outcome. He argued that these were interrelated and stemmed from the fact that the litigation process was controlled by lawyers. Since they set the pace, it was in their interests to draw out the process and so increase costs. Because there was very little judicial management the process often degenerated into an excessively adversarial contest.

9.3 *Access to Justice* stated that the overriding objective of the civil justice system was to deal with cases fairly. To achieve this, the report determined that it was necessary to ensure that, as far as possible, the parties to the litigation are on an equal footing and that the amount of time and money spent on each case was proportionate to the amount of the claim and the complexity of the issues.

Lord Woolf's proposals

9.4 In order to address the problems which he identified, Lord Woolf recommended that the following key changes should be made:

- Cases should be dealt with through different procedures according to the amount of money involved and their complexity.

- Stricter timetables by which different stages of the litigation should be completed should be imposed by the court.

- Judges should actively manage cases from the point at which a claim is made.

- Unified and simpler procedural rules should be drawn up for the county court and the High Court.

- There should be a reduction in adversarial techniques, eg there should be full disclosure of evidence by both sides and use of agreed expert witnesses where possible.

- Information technology should be developed to manage and track cases.

- One senior judge should be appointed to head the civil justice system.

9.5 Not all these changes were completely new to the civil justice system. For example, rules to encourage a more co-operative approach between the parties and the more active involvement of judges in managing cases had been used in the family courts for some years. In relation to the problem of increasing delays and growing costs, a number of earlier reforms had paved the way for more active judicial intervention in the court process.

9.6 In 1995, for example, a practice direction to judges issued by the Lord Chief Justice, Lord Taylor, and the Vice Chancellor, Sir Richard Scott, encouraged judges to limit the time taken by lawyers in court when presenting their case or cross-examining witnesses. To some extent, therefore, the Woolf reforms built on existing reforms. Nevertheless, the range and ambition of the changes went far further than any previous developments. They were intended to represent a complete change of litigation culture which would operate throughout the system.

9.7 Almost all Lord Woolf's recommendations were accepted by the Government and implemented. Because the changes amounted to such a root and branch reform of the system, it was recognized that their success was largely dependent on comprehensive training for judges and lawyers to prepare them for the new system. The Judicial Studies Board was therefore provided with an extra budget so as to ensure that all judges would be trained, while the Law Society and the Bar Council offered equivalent training sessions for solicitors and barristers.

The civil procedure rules

9.8 The key to the changes was the creation of a new set of written rules governing the civil justice process. These were implemented through the Civil Procedure Act 1999 which gave authority for the creation of Civil Procedure Rules drawn up by the Civil Procedure Rules Committee (CPRC). The CPRC is headed by the Master of the Rolls as head of civil justice. The rules are supplemented by detailed practice directions which are guidance notes drawn up by the senior judges to help lawyers and judges interpret and apply the rules. In addition, pre-action protocols have been drawn up for different areas of civil justice which guide practitioners on how they should be conducting litigation in a particular field. These have been created by specialist practitioner groups such the Association of Personal Injury Lawyers.

9.9 Lord Woolf recognized that if the reforms were to work, they would require a change not just in the formal rules which governed the system, but also in the culture which influenced the interpretation and application of those rules. Judges and lawyers would need to accept the goals of the system and implement the rules, directions and protocols in the light of this. To this end, the rules explicitly confirm Lord Woolf's view that the overriding objective of the system is to enable the court to deal with cases justly, for example by ensuring that the parties are on an equal footing and that costs are kept down. The purpose of the overriding objective is to ensure that all discussion and disagreement about the interpretation and application of the rules are informed by this principle so that the ultimate goal of the civil justice system is not lost sight of in the detail of the litigation process.

9.10 An important feature of the rules is that they apply equally to both the county court and High Court. In the past, a different set of practices applied in the two levels of courts adding to the complexity and confusion of the system. Lord Woolf considered the possibility of a complete merger of the two courts, but decided that the best solution was for the formal distinction to remain while reducing the practical differences between them. By creating a set of unified rules, Lord Woolf intended that the question of whether a case began in the county court or High Court would matter less than it had in the past.

Costs

9.11 Lord Woolf identified high costs as the most serious problem besetting the litigation system. He argued that it deterred litigants and led to unacceptably low levels of settlement even when a party had a sound case to pursue. In this way richer litigants could take unfair advantage of poorer opponents. He emphasized that costs were often out of all proportion to the amount in dispute. Quite apart from the unfair distribution of costs, he stressed that the economy suffered from excessive costs. The uncertainty of costs also prevented litigants from predicting the likely liability which they might face and made the civil justice system less attractive as a forum for dispute settlement for parties to overseas commercial contracts.

9.12 His response to these problems was to propose fixed and determinate cost regimes. Predictability and transparency were the goals. However, this is one aspect of the reforms which has proved difficult to implement. In 2003, some progress was made in this area when a system of fixed pre-trial costs in less serious road accident cases was established, but the implementation of fixed costs in all fast-track cases as Lord Woolf intended has not materialized.

9.13 In 2002, Lord Phillips, then Master of the Rolls, stated that the current costs regimes were failing and needed root and branch change. He argued that: 'Questions over what costs can be recovered are poisoning the relationship between the two sides of the litigation industry.' As a result of these concerns, Lord Justice Jackson has been appointed to conduct a major review of costs in civil litigation. His brief is to review the rules and principles governing the costs of civil litigation and to make recommendations in order to promote access to justice at proportionate cost. His interim report was published in May 2009 and it calls for far-reaching reforms. Lord Justice Jackson questions the government's policy of making the courts self-financing. His report says that court fees now account for about 80 per cent of the £650 million a year cost of running the civil and family courts in England and Wales, yet such fees have risen 'substantially' above the rate of inflation. He also calls for a review of the 'sacred cow' principle in English civil litigation that the loser pays the winner's costs. That principle is aimed at deterring unmeritorious claimants, but as the report notes, it does not apply to all disputes: for instance in tribunals each side bears its own costs. Lord Justice Jackson has ruled out complete abolition of the 'loser pays' rule as not 'realistic', but he suggests that it could be modified or abolished in certain areas because:

> We have arguably reached the position in this jurisdiction where the level of costs is so high that facing a full adverse costs order is likely to be a disaster for most ordinary citizens.

Allocation of cases

9.14 In addition to a set of unified rules, the new system reduces the relevance of where the case commences by allowing for greater flexibility in transferring between the two tiers of the court. Whereas in the past it was largely up to the parties to decide where a case was heard, it is now the job of the judges to determine whether a case is more appropriately dealt with in one court or the other and to allocate it accordingly on the basis of the value of the claim and its complexity.

9.15 In line with the general trend to ensure that more cases are dealt with in the lower courts, the rules restrict personal injury claims in the High Court to those with a value of over £50,000 and other money claims to the value of more than £25,000. All cases below those limits are now normally started in the county court. On receipt by the court, each case is allocated to one of three types of procedure, or 'tracks':

9.16 For claims of up to £5,000 the case is dealt with through the small claims process in which the hearing is based upon an arbitration process. The process can be conducted on paper if both parties agree, no orders for costs will normally be made, the procedure itself is relatively informal and the grounds for appeal are limited.

9.17 Cases valued at between £5,000 and £25,000 are allocated to the fast-track procedure. The main feature of the fast track is the use of standard directions which are intended to facilitate a speedier and less costly process for claims in the medium range of cases.

9.18 Remaining cases valued at over £25,000 or those raising more complex issues are usually allocated to the multi-track procedure. Here there is greater scope for the judge to intervene and impose whatever directions are appropriate to dispose of the case fairly and efficiently.

Time limits

9.19 One of the most notable features of the new system is the role played by timetables. This is particularly the case for the fast track where a trial date must be set down within 30 weeks and the hearing will normally be expected to be completed within one day. There are fixed times for serving a defence and disclosing evidence and sanctions for breaches of these time limits can be imposed in the form of cost penalties.

9.20 While similar inducements to speed existed in the old system, they were relatively rarely enforced and time limits were commonly set aside if the judge agreed to the delay. In contrast, the new rules limit the circumstances in which judges may exercise their discretion to extend deadlines. Moreover, because the changes were premised on the belief that lawyers often collude to increase delay in order to drive up their costs, the new system allows very little scope for setting aside the timetable by mutual consent.

Case management

9.21 The introduction of a system of active case management by judges represents a significant change in the litigation culture. Under the old system the civil justice process operated along traditional adversarial principles and left the control of the litigation to the parties and their representatives. Judges generally saw their function as that of neutral arbiters or referees whose procedural role was largely restricted to resolving disputes between the parties about how the case should proceed. Indeed, in his book *The Due Process of Law* Lord Denning recounts the story of a High Court judge being removed for asking too many questions when trying the case of *Jones v NCB* (1957).

9.22 Provided the parties could agree on the pace and nature of the process, most of the issues arising in relation to the pre-trial preparation and the handling of the case at trial were left to the lawyers. What material should be disclosed to the other side, which witnesses should be called and how the case should be conducted were not generally the concern of the judge. Over the years, a number of rules had been introduced to increase the speed and fairness of the proceedings, to encourage greater openness and observe certain time limits, but these reforms had been piecemeal and largely discretionary so that their impact was limited.

9.23 By contrast, the Woolf reforms were intended to involve the judges in the decision-making process from the moment that a claim is made. As the case proceeds to trial, there will normally be at least one case management conference in which the judge can assess progress and make any necessary orders to facilitate the process of preparation for trial.

9.24 The aim of this active case management is to encourage the parties to settle or to use an alternative dispute resolution process, to identify the real issues in dispute at an early stage and to fix dates and give directions so that the case can be dealt with speedily. All judicial decisions are to be taken bearing in mind the likely costs and benefits of any particular course of action in order to ensure that the process adopted is proportionate to the complexity of the dispute and the amount of the claim.

9.25 One example of the different approach of the new rules concerns the role of expert evidence. Many cases call for professionals such as doctors or accountants to give evidence about the nature or causes of a claimant's injuries or losses. In the past it would be usual for each side to call their own expert witness or witnesses who would present contradicting opinions. This typically adversarial approach was criticized by Lord Woolf as being costly and time-consuming, since it often involved the duplication of work. It was also criticized for detracting from the real issues and for often forcing professionals to give evidence in inappropriately black and white terms rather than to present a more balanced and accurate opinion.

9.26 To tackle these weaknesses the new rules give the judges power to order that the parties should agree on a joint expert witness. If such agreement is not possible, the court can limit the number of witnesses each side can call, usually to one. This process is supplemented by the pre-action protocols. For example, in relation to personal injury cases, a framework is set out which assists the parties to agree on a joint expert. In addition the rules envisage that expert evidence will normally be provided in writing and that oral evidence will only be given with the permission of the court.

Information technology

9.27 The civil procedure reforms were implemented at a time when courts had begun to take seriously the potential of information technology to improve efficiency, access and speed in the justice system. Lord Woolf considered that the introduction of a high-quality computer system for recording and tracking the progress of cases was an essential element of his reforms. In the event, the system which was adopted took much longer to put in place than had been anticipated and had serious teething problems. It is too early, therefore, to assess whether the new IT system is proving cost-effective.

9.28 In addition to the role played by IT in managing cases, the reforms also recognized that there is considerable scope within the new system for greater efficiency through the use of new forms of communication. For example, the rules allow for evidence to be taken by telephone or video link and it is anticipated that conference calls will become a common way of holding a pre-trial hearing so that parties and their lawyers are not required to travel to court.

The use of plain English

9.29 As the title of Lord Woolf's report suggests, one goal of the reforms was to make the system more user-friendly both to lawyers and lay people. One way in which he sought to promote this goal was by introducing a requirement that all rules and procedures should be written in plain English. To this end, the use of many Latin phrases has been replaced by common English words. For example, the term '*ex parte*' to describe an application by one party in the absence of the other party was replaced by 'without notice'. The word 'claimant' replaced 'plaintiff' and the 'writ' was discarded in favour of the 'claim form', which is the term applied to the start of proceedings in both the county court and High Court.

9.30 Inevitably the old words and phrases linger on so that it is now common to hear a rather confusing mix of the old and the new. No doubt, the new terms will ultimately replace the old and will probably make life easier for law students grappling with the system for the first time. Whether these changes of terminology in themselves will significantly benefit lay people is less certain. For an unrepresented litigant struggling to master a completely unknown process, the use of some unfamiliar terms is probably the least of their worries. The civil justice system will only become truly accessible to the lay person if the use of plain English signals the move to a more general culture of prioritizing simplification and accessibility throughout the system.

Problems with the reforms

9.31 Although the Woolf reforms were generally well received within government, the judiciary and the legal profession, there were a number of critics who argued that the changes could actually aggravate problems within the system, or simply replace old difficulties with new ones. In one respect, the prospects for success of the reforms were not good. *Access to Justice* was the latest in a long series of inquiries and proposals for reform, all of which had achieved very little. Lord Woolf argued that past attempts at change had been unsuccessful because they had been piecemeal and had not managed to address the interrelated nature of the key problems. In contrast, his proposals constituted a root and branch attempt at modernization. Nevertheless, a number of potential problems have been identified with the reforms.

Front-loading

9.32 One of the most persuasive concerns to be voiced by critics of the reforms was the argument that they would have the effect of 'front-loading' the system by requiring much more time and money to be spent by lawyers and judges on a case before it came to court (see Zander, 2000). In the case of those actions which eventually came to court, this effort might be worthwhile since it could potentially save time and cost at trial. However, the fact that approximately 97 per cent of cases settle before trial raises real doubts about the cost-effectiveness of imposing greater pre-trial burdens.

9.33　For the great majority of cases which settle before trial, time and effort spent in preparation will be wasted. The new system imposes a regime which benefits the very small proportion of cases which come to court at a cost to the vast majority which settle. Moreover, since there is no reliable method of distinguishing between those cases which will go to trial and so would benefit from pre-trial intervention in the form of case management and those that would have settled satisfactorily without, there is no effective way to reduce this costly front-loading.

9.34　Similar arguments were made in relation to the time spent by judges reading papers at the pre-trial stage. Under the new system, the assumption is that time spent by judges on pre-trial reading will reduce the length of the trial because less time need be spent in court familiarizing the judge with the case. However, in the majority of cases much of this effort will prove to be unnecessary since the case will not come to court.

9.35　In addition, the problem arises that even in the small proportion of cases which do come to trial, effort spent in pre-trial preparation might be a waste of time if the trial judge and the judge who has case-managed it before trial are different. In practice, the logistical difficulties of listing cases means that this outcome will often occur with the result that more than one judge will have spent time reading the papers, leading to a duplication in work.

Speed

9.36　The problem of front-loading arises because different cases have different needs. The same difficulties affect the issue of time limits. While some cases may indeed have been inappropriately drawn-out by lawyers and so would probably benefit from strict limits, others may actually need a longer time in which to negotiate a settlement. Tight deadlines may simply drive such cases to court for lack of time in which to resolve them by agreement.

9.37　In addition, there is an important ethical question raised by the imposition of strict sanctions for breaching time limits. Ultimately the cost of these is borne by litigants. Yet in many cases, as Lord Woolf acknowledged, the slow pace is set by lawyers for their own interests. Is it legitimate to penalize litigants for the failings of their legal representatives?

9.38　Some more fundamental criticisms were also raised about the new approach to delay. First, that the reforms were premised on assumptions about the role of delay in the system when there was no reliable empirical evidence as to whether or not delay was a serious problem. Comparative research evidence from the US suggested that litigants were more concerned about fairness than delay. Even if it could be shown that ways ought to be found to reduce delay, there was equally no sound evidence to support the claim that active case management was the answer. Indeed, empirical evidence from the US also indicated that active pre-trial intervention had not been effective in reducing delay.

9.39 A further problem is the relationship between costs and delay. An empirical study carried out in 1999 on the impact of sources of finance of personal injury litigation found that reduced costs could actually increase delay:

> Speedier transfer of information between the parties should aid settlement and reduce delays ... However, lower costs may reduce the cost pressure faced by litigants and thereby increase delays, unless tighter case management by judges is realised in practice. (Fenn, Gray and Rickman, 2002)

Case management

9.40 The Fenn research recognized the role of case management as a key factor in the Woolf reforms. Yet even among those commentators who supported the reforms generally, and the idea of case management in principle, there was concern about the workability of the changes. In particular, not everyone was convinced that judges and lawyers were ready or willing to adopt a new approach to civil litigation. There were also practical worries, for example that creating teams of judges to manage cases will be an administrative nightmare and that the use of part-time judges would make the whole process more difficult to institute.

Evidence to date

9.41 Since the reforms came into force in April 1999, evidence has gradually been gathered about their effects. Discounting the inevitable confusion and teething problems of the first few months, there has now been time for the reforms to settle in to some extent. To date, a rather mixed message has emerged.

9.42 On the whole, fears that judges would not respond to the call to adopt the new case management culture have proved unfounded. Research carried out on case management conferences in 2005 concluded that these were regarded as one of the major successes of the new system and that the culture of litigation had changed for the better with more co-operation between the parties and between the parties and the courts (Peysner and Seneviratne, 2005).

9.43 Whether the goal of providing a more user-friendly system has been achieved is not clear. It is generally agreed that the new rules are written in more comprehensible language than was usually the case in the past. However, the fact that the rules, practice directions and pre-action protocols have expanded to many thousands of pages somewhat undermines the goal of creating a new system which is more accessible than the old.

9.44 Perhaps the most positive sign for supporters of the reforms is that the number of actions started in the courts dropped significantly in the post-reform period. The fall was particularly marked in the High Court. In 2003, the number of claims being issued in the Queen's Bench Division (QBD) fell by 24 per cent from 2002. Mediation appeared to be used more often and there is evidence that the pre-action protocols have encouraged more cases to settle and to do so faster.

9.45 On the other hand, there is evidence that front-loading has indeed increased costs incurred at the early stages. The picture which emerged one year after the reforms in 2000 led the former President of the Law Society, Michael Mears, to conclude that: 'The present auguries suggest that in the long as well as the short term, the net effect of Woolf will be speedier but more expensive justice.' If this is the case, the increase in the rate of settlement may just be a reflection of the fact that more litigants are being forced to abandon their claims because of the escalating costs being incurred at early stages.

9.46 Mears' prediction appears to be confirmed by the early research findings into the changes. A review of the impact of the reforms on pre-action behaviour commissioned by the Civil Justice Council and the Law Society found that the reforms had changed the culture of litigation for the better with a less adversarial approach being taken (Goriely et al, 2002). Cases were settling earlier and there was a reduction in the use of 'hired gun' experts. Less encouragingly, costs had generally gone up because of the front-loading of work, though this increase was not uniform; in housing disrepair cases, for example, the research found that costs had decreased.

9.47 Nor are the more positive findings concerning delay without their difficulties. The apparent increase in speed may simply be the effect of lawyers spending more time conducting negotiations before proceedings are issued because of the increased costs which they will be forced to incur once the claim form has been issued. The effect of this trend may be that the overall time taken to resolve a dispute is the same, or indeed has increased, but that the court stage of the process is being pushed further down the line, thus presenting a distorted picture of a much faster process. Evidence of such a redistribution of the length of pre-and post-claim periods was found in the Goriely research. In addition, the more recent research by Pesyner and Seneviratne found that the evidence was mixed as to whether or not delay had been reduced.

Summary

9.48 There can be little doubt that in the period since the civil procedure rules were introduced they have, unlike so many reforms before them, had a significant effect on the process. The exact nature of that effect, however, is difficult to assess, partly because the empirical evidence which we had on the civil justice system before the changes was so limited and patchy. Much of the evidence of the changes is therefore anecdotal and partial. Nevertheless, the picture which seems to be emerging is that the changes may have led to faster but more expensive civil justice.

9.49 Whether or not this change is a good or bad thing brings us back to the question raised earlier of whether we want more or less litigation, and whether it should be faster or slower, or more or less expensive. The assumptions upon which the Woolf reforms were based were that in all cases accessible, fair, fast and cheap litigation is the goal of the system. The problem with this one-dimensional approach is that it ignores the dilemma raised by the varied and often contradictory functions of the civil justice system.

FURTHER READING

Lord Woolf *Access to Justice, Final Report* (http://www.dca.gov.uk/civil/final/index.htm).

John Peysner and Mary Seneviratne *The Management of Civil Cases: The Courts and Post-Woolf Landscape* (2005, Department for Constitutional Affairs, DCA 9/05) (http://www.dca.gov.uk/research/2005/9_2005_full.pdf).

Tamara Goriely, Richard Moorhead and Pamela Abrams *More Civil Justice? The Impact of the Woolf Reforms on Pre-Action Behaviour* (2002) (http://siteresources.worldbank.org/INTLAWJUSTINST/Resources/MoreCivilJustice_R43Report_v1.pdf).

Michael Zander *The State of Justice* (2000, London: Sweet and Maxwell), ch 2.

Neil Andrews *The Modern Civil Process: Judicial and Alternative Forms of Dispute Resolution in England* (2007, Türbingen, Mohr Siebeck).

Hazel Genn *Hamlyn Lectures 2008: Judging Civil Justice*.

Lord Justice Jackson *Civil Litigation Costs Review: Preliminary Report* (2008) (http://www.judiciary.gov.uk/about_judiciary/cost-review/preliminary-report.htm).

USEFUL WEBSITES

Home site of the Civil Justice Council
http://www.civiljusticecouncil.gov.uk

Ministry of Justice website section on civil justice
http://www.justice.gov.uk/civil/procrules_fin/index.htm

SELF-TEST QUESTIONS

1 What four main problems in the civil justice system were identified by Lord Woolf in his report Access to Justice?

2 What is meant by 'front-loading' of costs and what evidence do we have of such 'front-loading'?

3 'The Woolf reforms have joined the long list of failed attempts to reform the civil justice system.' Discuss.

4 Critically evaluate the aims of the overriding objective in Part 1 of the CPR 1998. Can the various objectives be satisfactorily reconciled with each other?

10

Recent trends in the criminal justice system

SUMMARY

This chapter highlights the growing political importance of the criminal justice system and identifies a number of key issues which currently dominate the debate on criminal justice. These include the 'rebalancing' of the system away from the defendant towards the victim and the control of crime, the problem of racial discrimination and the approach to illegal drug use and the criminal justice system. It argues that the tension between the goals of efficiency and justice, identified at the start of the book as a recurring theme in the legal system, is acutely evident in the area of criminal justice. The pressure for greater efficiency is manifested in reforms designed to streamline the system, for example by encouraging earlier guilty pleas, fewer court hearings and the disposal of more cases in the magistrates' court rather than the Crown Court. The quality of justice arguments against such changes are that they lead to summary justice, undermine due process and increase the risk of miscarriages of justice.

The politicization of criminal justice

10.1 Criminal justice is a central feature of the political landscape in England and Wales. Rarely a day goes by when the news does not carry at least one major item on crime or the criminal justice system. Likewise, every political party annual conference can be expected to devote a considerable amount of time to its criminal justice policy.

10.2 Yet this phenomenon is relatively recent. Forty years ago crime barely received a mention in the manifestos of the main parties and legislation concerning criminal justice was considered necessary once a decade or so. In contrast, criminal justice statutory provisions of some kind are now passed annually. Since the Labour Party came to power in 1997, more than 20 major criminal justice statutes have been passed. In 2003, for example, four major pieces of criminal justice legislation were introduced in Parliament – the Criminal Justice Bill, the Anti-Social Behaviour Bill, the Sexual Offences Bill and Courts Bill. And in 2008 the Criminal Justice and Immigration Act dealt with matters as diverse as clarifying the law on self-defence, creating a new crime of inciting hatred on grounds of sexual orientation, abolition of the common law offence of blasphemy, and the creation of a new offence of causing a nuisance or disturbance on NHS premises. The speed and quantity of new criminal justice legislation is now such that major changes to the system are sometimes introduced without being properly scrutinized or debated. In 2005, for example, the Serious Organised Crime and Police Act gave the police extensive new powers to arrest citizens without warrant for minor offences. This provision went through in a little-noticed section of the Act with almost no comment. In addition, the criminal justice system is currently subject to an almost constant stream of official reviews. In 1993, the Runciman Royal Commission on Criminal Justice produced a wide-ranging review of the system after two years spent commissioning research and formulating proposals for reform, many of which were implemented.

10.3 Within seven years of this complete overhaul, the Government had asked Lord Justice Auld to carry out another review of the whole process. In between these two, other inquiries were commissioned on various aspects of the system, such as the Narey report on delay in the criminal justice system and Sir Iain Glidewell's review of the Crown Prosecution Service in 1999. Despite the large amount of research which has been conducted on the criminal justice system in recent years, the policies which shape the system are largely driven by political forces.

10.4 One area which has risen very quickly up the political agenda is sentencing. Traditionally, sentencing powers were generally very wide and judges had considerable discretion to determine appropriate sentences. While Parliament laid down the basic sentencing framework, judges were left to determine the correct sentence in individual cases. Today, a vast array of statutory provisions constrain judicial decision-making and determine the sentencing options so that the sentencing process has become highly technical in many cases. At the same time, however, it has also become a far more politicized process, with politicians and the media regularly criticizing judges for their sentencing decisions. In 2006, for example, a trial judge was widely condemned in the press and by a minister in the DCA for having sentenced a man convicted of a serious sexual offence against a child to a sentence that would allow him to be eligible for release after five years. In the event, it transpired that the judge had been doing no more than following the statutory rules that obliged him to calculate the sentence in a certain way (for example, by allowing an automatic reduction of sentence because the defendant had pleaded guilty). Such cases led the Lord Chief Justice, Lord Phillips, to speak out against incorrect media reporting of allegedly lenient sentences and to warn that they risked undermining confidence in the criminal justice system.

Getting tough on crime

10.5 In the 1970s and 1980s, the Labour Party broadly pursued a liberal line in relation to criminal justice which emphasized the need to reduce the prison population by finding alternative methods for dealing with crime and protecting the rights of suspects from abuse by the police. As the political profile of criminal justice rose in the 1990s, a new consensus emerged between the political left and right that crime could only be dealt with by a faster, more effective and more punitive criminal justice system.

10.6 In 1997 when the Labour Party was elected to power, its soundbite on criminal justice was 'tough on crime, tough on the causes of crime'. The background to this new approach was the rising crime figures during the 1990s and the growing awareness of the 'justice gap'– the discrepancy between the number of crimes committed and the number of successful prosecutions. The New Labour philosophy acknowledged that many of the causes of crime were outside the control of the criminal justice system, such as poverty, lack of education and opportunity, and poor parenting. The twin approach was, therefore, intended to reduce the root causes of offending while also introducing measures to improve the effectiveness of the criminal justice system in dealing with crime.

10.7 The Government intended that these problems would be tackled by a number of different government departments and non-governmental agencies working together in a new form of 'joined-up' government to address the underlying causes of crime with long-term solutions. In contrast, the criminal justice system was expected to provide short-term 'tough' solutions which primarily meant higher detection, prosecution and conviction rates followed by more punitive sentences. The latter, at least, appears to have been achieved, with a steady increase in the use of custody and a significant rise in the prison population to an all-time high in August 2009 of 84,150.

10.8 A recent example of the Government's commitment to being tough on crime was the decision to introduce measures to criminalize begging, noisy neighbours, and other perceived anti-social behaviour. The effect of such measures has been to increase the size of the prison population still further. In 2007, the Ministry of Justice was forced to introduce a controversial early release scheme, where prisoners are let out up to 18 days earlier than they would have done, as overcrowding hit a crisis point. On average 2,500 prisoners per month have benefited from this early release scheme, but it has done little to halt the increase in the growth of the prison population which in August 2009 passed 84,000 for the first time.

10.9 Despite the huge increase in spending on the criminal justice system and the comprehensive reform programme which has been pursued, affecting all criminal justice agencies it is questionable whether the official approach adopted in recent years has worked. A 2009 report published by the Centre for Crime and Justice Studies concludes that:

> Despite a decade of reform, crime and victimization levels remain high and the proportion of crimes dealt with is extremely low. Questions remain about whether the government is placing too much emphasis on finding criminal justice solutions to complex social and economic problems. Should the government continue to place such heavy expectations on the criminal justice system or should it be clearer about its limitations? The time is right for the government to take stock and reflect on what the criminal justice agencies can realistically achieve in reducing crime and increasing public safety and on what the appropriate level of resourcing should be.

The rise of the victim and the decline of the offender

10.10 One distinct feature of this new politics of criminal justice has been a shift away from the rights of the defendant to those of the victim. The high-profile miscarriages of justice cases such as the Guildford Four, the Birmingham Six and the Maguire Seven, which commanded so much attention in the early 1990s, have faded from public memory and there is now relatively little general interest in police malpractice or suspects' rights. In contrast, the victim has moved centre stage.

10.11 Traditionally, criminal justice has been envisaged as a conflict between the individual (the defendant) and the state in which the only official function of the victim is to give evidence in court as a witness if necessary. He or she may attend a trial as a member of the public but has no influence on the decision of the court. During the 1980s, victim support groups developed which fought to reverse the marginalization of the victim in the justice process. One result of their lobbying was the production of a Victims' Charter which sets out the role of the victim in the justice system and the treatment which they can expect. In particular, the Charter emphasizes the need for better information on the decision-making process and the progress of cases so that victims know what is happening, when and why.

10.12 In the US this process of victim-centred justice has gone much further, and some state courts allow the victim to provide a written 'impact' statement which will be considered when the defendant is sentenced. A variation on this system was adopted in England and Wales in October 2001, when the Home Office introduced the Victim Personal Statement Scheme as set out in the 1996 Victims' Charter. Victims can submit a statement to the police and can also submit a further statement prior to the trial describing the effect the crime has had on them. However, these statements have only a limited (and rather unclear) role to play in the sentencing process. The Home Office Guidance states that it is judges and magistrates who decide how an offender is punished and that the court will not consider the victim's opinion when they reach a decision. It can, however, take the statement into account in identifying how the offence has affected the victim. Similarly, a Practice Direction issued by the Lord Chief Justice, Lord Woolf, states that the opinions of the victim or the victim's close relatives as to what the sentence should be are not relevant, although the consequence of the offence on the victim is. In Perks (2001), the Court of Appeal issued guidelines for the use of victim impact statements. Garland J stated:

> The opinions of the victim and the victim's close relatives on the appropriate level of sentence should not be taken into account. The court must pass what it judges to be the appropriate sentence having regard to the circumstances of the offence and of the offender subject to two exceptions: (i) where the sentence passed to the offender is aggravating the victim's distress, the sentence may be moderated to some degree (ii) where the victim's forgiveness or unwillingness to press charges provide evidence that his or her psychological or mental suffering must be very much less than would normally be the case.

10.13 One important development in this area is the suggestion that the victim should have legal representation in court in certain cases, such as sexual offences, where the complainant must give evidence and may find his or her credibility and personal life questioned as thoroughly as that of the defendant. In 2005, the Government published a consultation paper *Hearing the relatives of victims of murder and manslaughter*. This proposed that the relatives of the victim in such cases could make a statement in court before the defendant is sentenced or, if they preferred, could instruct a publicly funded advocate to help them make such a statement. The aim of these changes was stated by the Lord Chancellor, Lord Falconer, as being to 'rebalance' the criminal justice system by placing the victim at its centre and allowing the voice of the victim to be heard. The Victims Advocate Scheme enables a pre-trial meeting to take place between the prosecutor and the victim's family to explain the processes and assist in making a victim personal statement. These statements include the impact the crime committed had on the victim's family. Research published by the Ministry of Justice in March 2009 found that the scheme has been a success and that families welcomed it as an opportunity to have their voice heard in court and felt a sense of positive and active involvement in the trial. They reported the process of preparing and delivering the statement to be therapeutic. A variety of different reasons were given to the researchers for families wanting to have a personal statement read out in court. These included a desire to give the court a better appreciation of the victim's character and to make the defendant understand the gravity of what he or she had done.

10.14   One particularly explicit example of the reorientation of the system away from the rights of defendants to those of victims was the 2003 Criminal Justice Act. The White Paper which set out the measures to be included in the legislation stated that its purpose was to: 'rebalance the system in favour of victims, witnesses and communities'. Speaking in 2002 in support of the proposed legislation, the Prime Minister, Tony Blair, argued that: 'Justice is weighted towards the criminal and is in need of rebalancing towards the victim ... we will rebalance the system emphatically in favour of the victims of crime. Offenders get away too easily.' The range of measures proposed to achieve this included restricting the right to bail for defendants accused of committing an offence while on bail; encouraging early guilty pleas by giving defendants an indication of likely sentence if they plead guilty; expanding the circumstances in which the previous convictions of a defendant would be disclosed in court; creating a new commissioner for victims supported by a National Victims' Advisory Panel and a new victims' code of practice setting out the protection and information that all victims would be entitled to receive.

10.15   Not all of these proposals were incorporated into the Criminal Justice Bill 2002. For example, the victims' commissioner and the statutory code of practice backed by an independent ombudsman were both dropped. Nevertheless, the range of measures included in the Bill represented a significant change in priorities on the part of the Government. Evidence in support of the need for a better deal for victims came from a research study carried out for the Lord Chancellor's Department in 2003 which looked at the perceptions of witnesses about their treatment in the courts. It found that about one-third of witnesses in the Crown Court and one-quarter of those in the magistrates' courts felt that their treatment had been unfair (Hood, Shute and Seemungal, 2003).

10.16   The goal of reducing these figures is a laudable one. However, the current official victim-centred approach is problematic for a number of reasons. First, it is based on the assumption that there is always a clear victim who is separate and distinguishable from the offender. In the case of some offences, such as possession of drugs, there is no obvious victim, except perhaps the offender themselves. Second, victims may often be friends or relations of the offender (for example, in the case of domestic violence or child abuse) who have ambivalent feelings about the case or may suffer economically or emotionally if the offender is prosecuted. Third, many victims have also been offenders and vice versa. Members of vulnerable or marginalized groups such as teenagers excluded from school, drug or alcohol addicts, street sleepers or the mentally ill may find themselves involved in the criminal justice system as offenders one day and victims the next. The introduction of provisions to criminalize activities such as begging is likely to compound this problem. Lastly, the current approach assumes that victims' rights can only be advanced through the reduction in the rights and protections of suspects and defendants. In practice, many of the changes which improve the experience of victims such as keeping witnesses informed of the progress of their case and explaining why decisions have been taken by the police or CPS are unrelated to the treatment of the defendant. Moreover, provisions which reduce defendants' safeguards almost always increase the danger that innocent people will be convicted, leaving offenders undetected and unpunished; an outcome that cannot be said to be in the interests of the victims of crime or the security of society as a whole.

The growing importance of race

10.17 One particular area in which the rights of victims have attracted a great deal of public debate is the treatment of members of minority ethnic groups. The murder of the black teenager Stephen Lawrence in 1993 and the subsequent inquiry by Sir William MacPherson into the police investigation of the case has had a profound and lasting effect on the whole of the criminal justice system far beyond its original focus. The effect of the report has been to widen the debate on race and justice to encompass the treatment of minorities as suspects and of those who work in the criminal justice system. Issues around discrimination which had been festering have finally come to the surface in a whole range of areas. The MacPherson report was the first to identify 'institutional racism' in the police – the claim that the institutions and practices of the police service are racist irrespective of the views and attitudes of individuals within it. This has been followed by a similar finding of an inquiry into the Crown Prosecution Service. In 2001, the United Nations Human Rights Committee highlighted a number of areas of concern in the UK. Among these was the issue of racial bias within the criminal justice system (Concluding Observations of the Committee on the Elimination of Racial Discrimination: Great Britain and Northern Ireland, 1 May 2001). Most recently, in 2009, the Equality and Human Right Commission produced a report entitled *Police and Racism: What has been achieved 10 years after the Stephen Lawrence inquiry report?*. The Commission found that progress had been made in the past ten years on recruitment, training, and employment of ethnic minority police staff. However, the report argued that the police must do more to tackle the poor retention of new ethnic minority officers and it revealed evidence of a 'canteen culture' among some specialist units which are still seen as a 'closed shop' to some ethnic minority recruits.

10.18 The cumulative effect of these reports is that all institutions in the criminal justice system have now been put on notice of the need to scrutinize their practices and cultures for racial bias and put in place policies to address this issue. One area in particular which has attracted considerable attention has been the high proportion of black people among suspects who have died in custody. The failure to date of attempts to bring legal action against the police and the prison service in a number of these cases has been the subject of growing public criticism. The decision of the CPS not to prosecute in one such case has been successfully challenged by the courts (*Shiji Lapite* 2001).

10.19 Two practical reforms have resulted from this new awareness of race discrimination in the criminal justice system. The first is the change in policy in relation to the investigation, prosecution and sentencing of racially motivated crimes. The police have committed themselves to prioritizing the investigation of all cases which involve racism, and the CPS now include this as an additional factor in deciding whether it is in the public interest to proceed with a case. Similarly, the courts have powers to increase sentences where the offence is racially motivated (Powers of Criminal Courts (Sentencing) Act 2000, s 153).

10.20 The second practical reform is the creation of racially aggravated criminal offences in the Crime and Disorder Act 1998 (ss 28–32). These consist of existing criminal offences with the additional factor that they are racially motivated. The statute has therefore created nine new offences of violence, public order, harassment and criminal damage with new maximum sentences. Research has shown that, although the number of racist incidents recorded by the police trebled in two years, largely due to more reporting and recording, the numbers of racially aggravated offences sentenced by the courts was comparatively small; 1,150 in 1999 compared with nearly 48,000 incidents reported in 1999–2000. One suggested reason for this discrepancy is that the CPS is accepting guilty pleas to the underlying substantive offence in exchange for dropping the racial motivation element.

10.21 But although the numbers of those sentenced are small, the research has shown that where they do reach the magistrates for sentencing, they are treated very seriously. Guidelines for sentencing racially aggravated crimes were laid down by the Court of Appeal in *Kelly and Donnelly* (2001). The figures show that adult offenders are

85 per cent more likely to receive a custodial sentence for a racially aggravated offence than for the equivalent basic offence and that the average fine is 50 per cent higher. This is in contrast to Crown Court statistics which show that in relation to the 293 racially aggravated offences sentenced in the Crown Court in 2000, the sentencing patterns were very similar to those of the equivalent basic offences (Burney and Rose, 2002).

10.22 In view of the deep-seated social causes of such offences, it is doubtful whether these changes can themselves lead to a significant reduction in racially motivated crimes, but if they are vigorously pursued they may have an important positive impact by raising confidence in the criminal justice system among members of minority ethnic groups. The relationship between confidence in the courts and ethnic background has recently been addressed by research conducted by Roger Hood, Stephen Shute and Florence Seemungal (2003). This study investigated the extent to which defendants and witnesses from minority ethnic groups in Crown Courts and magistrates' courts perceived their treatment to have been unfair because of their ethnic background. It also took into account the views of court staff, judges, magistrates and lawyers.

10.23 The study found that one in five black defendants in the Crown Court, one in ten in the magistrates' courts, and one in eight Asian defendants in both types of court believed that they had been treated unfairly because of their ethnicity. Most of these complaints concerned sentences perceived to be more severe than those imposed on a similar white defendant. Only 3 per cent in the Crown Court and 1 per cent in the magistrates' courts identified racist conduct or attitudes on the part of judges or magistrates. The study also found very little evidence of perceptions among witnesses of unfair treatment because of their ethnicity. The authors argued that these findings were better than they had expected on the basis of previous research and led them to conclude that there had been: 'a substantial change for the better in perceptions of ethnic minorities of racial impartiality in the courts'. Nevertheless, they cautioned against complacency. One finding which they highlighted as giving cause for concern was the fact that black lawyers and court staff were much more likely than their white counterparts to consider that there was unfair treatment in the courts on the basis of ethnicity.

Drugs and the criminal justice system

10.24 One aspect of the race and criminal justice debate which has been the subject of concern for many years has been the disproportionate targeting of young black men in the policing of drug-related offences. As part of the 'tough-on-crime' approach, politicians from across the political spectrum have, until recently, been keen to reaffirm the war on drugs. In the light of the consensus that abuse of drugs is directly or indirectly responsible for much criminal behaviour, police forces and the courts were for many years urged to clamp down on illegal drug use.

10.25 This hardline message has, however, been increasingly at odds with awareness of the complexity of drug issues and the growing public debate about the need to rethink the criminalization of drugs. In recent years, senior police officers have, for the first time, publicly objected to the time spent policing the possession of class B drugs, particularly cannabis, so diverting scarce policing resources away from more serious crime.

10.26 A more fundamental objection to the current policy towards drugs and criminal justice is that it is criminalization rather than the drugs themselves that cause the most harm. It is now increasingly common for professionals in the criminal justice system to express the view that regulation and control, as exists in relation to alcohol and tobacco, is preferable and would cause less crime, economic cost and social damage overall.

10.27 These arguments are not unique to the UK, but are now heard throughout Europe, as evidenced by the recent total decriminalization of narcotics in Austria and Portugal and partial decriminalization in Switzerland and Belgium. The adoption by police in Lambeth, South London, in 2001 of a policy of taking no action against those found in possession of cannabis represented the first decriminalization by a police service in England and Wales. In 2002, the Government decided to downgrade cannabis from a class B to a class C drug, which will mean that its possession is of itself no longer an arrestable offence. However, in 2005 concerns about the growing evidence of a causal link between heavy cannabis use and the development of psychotic illness led to a debate within Government about whether the class B categorization should be reinstated. At the same time, the growing evidence of the beneficial use of cannabis for those suffering from illnesses such as multiple sclerosis has led to pressure to allow it to be provided on prescription for these medical purposes.

10.28 What we are seeing is a growing diversity of views and policies in the criminal justice system over the issue of drugs and crime, with police, prosecutors, magistrates, judges and juries all struggling to reconcile these conflicting arguments about the best way to tackle the problem. The result is that whether a person is arrested, charged, prosecuted, convicted, sent to custody or provided with treatment for addiction in relation to a drug-related offence has become something of a lottery based on geography and the attitudes, policies and resources of the particular legal institutions in that area.

Different aims of the criminal justice system

10.29　The current confusion over drugs and criminal justice policy is a reflection of the fact that the criminal justice system is required to fulfil a number of conflicting goals. Just as the civil justice system seeks to deter, blame and make reparation, so too criminal justice promotes the moral goals of upholding social standards and exacting retribution on the one hand and the functional goals of preventing future harm and compensating victims on the other.

10.30　The wide range of disposal options available to the police, the CPS and courts reflect these different aims. Cautioning, binding over, discharges (conditional or unconditional), compensation orders, community service orders, fines, confiscation orders and custody are just some of the choices open to decision-makers. The courts and criminal justice agencies who must select from this menu are inevitably making choices between different underlying goals. Their choices will be driven by ideological, economic and practical considerations and may or may not be consistent and rational. Likewise, politicians who construct different legislative or policy initiatives in criminal justice will favour one set of disposal options or another as different responses to crime come in and out of favour.

Streamlining criminal justice

10.31　One of the effects of the contradictory and confused goals of the criminal justice system and the increasing recognition of the very limited role which it plays in reducing crime has been a tendency to focus on the more achievable practical goal of improving efficiency. In the absence of a consensus about the underlying rationale for criminal justice there has been a growing acceptance that speeding up the system and reducing cost should be prioritized.

10.32　A dominant trend in recent years has been the streamlining of pre-trial and trial procedures, for example by reducing time-consuming oral hearings in favour of paper applications, expediting the disposal of guilty pleas, setting time limits for the prosecution and defence and reducing the use of more expensive jury trials. One significant example of this trend is the increasing use by the Crown Prosecution Service of designated case-workers for handling less serious matters in the magistrates' courts such as uncontested traffic cases. These case-workers are not lawyers and therefore are cheaper than using Crown Prosecutors or self-employed barristers. The Crown Prosecution Service has plans to extend the use of these workers to a wider range of cases which are currently handled by lawyers.

10.33 Despite these changes, the costs of the system are still attracting considerable attention. In 2002, the Audit Commission reported that delays and inefficiencies were occurring throughout the system and that cases were dropping out unnecessarily, allowing offenders to evade justice. It concluded that over £80 million was wasted each year through adjournments and cancellations. Its proposed solution to this problem was greater co-operation between the different criminal justice agencies and the imposition of clearer shared targets.

10.34 These proposals for a more 'joined-up' criminal justice system are the latest in a long line of similar recommendations. No doubt some of the detailed proposals in the Audit Commission report, as in those which preceded it, would reduce delays and improve efficiency. But many of the problems are not resolvable without the imposition of procedures, rules and sanctions which would raise serious questions about the quality of justice of the system.

10.35 For example, if witnesses fail to turn up to court, cases must be adjourned. If they change their mind about giving evidence or give contradictory evidence then cases must be dropped at the last minute. The draconian use of contempt of court powers to punish errant witnesses would be expensive and cause public outcry. Similarly, defendants may be encouraged to enter early guilty pleas through reduced sentences, but the right not to plead guilty until the last minute must remain in a system in which the presumption of innocence is valued. Criminal trials rely on the orchestration of a number of different people and the presence of a degree of delay and inefficiency are unavoidable consequences of such a system.

10.36 The development of changes to ensure faster, cheaper justice is taking place against a background debate about the overall levels of funding for the criminal justice system. Although some areas, such as policing, have received increased funding in recent years, others, such as the courts, have not. In 2002, the Lord Chief Justice, Lord Woolf, joined this debate when he commented that the drive to save money had caused the quality of justice to suffer:

> I'm afraid we are in a situation where, so far as the criminal justice system is concerned, we are facing the same problems as the health service, the education system and the transport system. We have been under-resourced. (*The Times*, 9 July 2002)

10.37 The Government, however, argues that the remedy for the failings of the system lies in tackling the 'justice gap', which it has identified as a 'key measure of the success of the criminal justice system'. Its strategy for achieving this result is to overcome weaknesses in the system by targeting particular offences and particular offenders (CPS inspectorate, 2002).

10.38 Many of the reforms introduced in recent years were designed with this in mind. These included closer working arrangements between the police and the Crown Prosecution Service; increased emphasis on pre-trial case management; improvements to the case listing system in court; improvements in the degree of compliance, with pre-trial disclosure obligations by both prosecution and defence and greater incentives and sanctions for good preparation by defence lawyers. Whether such changes can be successfully introduced without an increase in spending or a reduction in the quality of justice remains to be seen.

FURTHER READING

Home Office *Guide To the Criminal Justice System of England and Wales* (http://www.homeoffice.gov.uk/rds/pdfs/cjs2000.pdf).

Andrew Ashworth and Mike Redmayne *The Criminal Process* (2005, Oxford: Oxford University Press).

Lord Woolf *Tools for the Job*, Keynote Address to Modernising Criminal Justice Conference, London (20 June 2002) (http://www.judiciary.gov.uk/publications_media/speeches/pre_2004/lcj200602.htm).

Sir Robin Auld *A Review of the Criminal Courts of England and Wales* (2000) (http://www.criminal-courts-review.org.uk/).

Michael Zander 'What on Earth is Lord Justice Auld Supposed to Do?' (2000) Criminal Law Review 419.

Justice for All White Paper (July 2002) (http://www.cjsonline.gov.uk/downloads/application/pdf/CJS%20White%20Paper%20-%20Justice%20For%20All.pdf).

Burney and Rose *Racist Offences – How is the Law Working?* (2002, Home Office Research Study) 244.

Crown Prosecution Service Inspectorate *Thematic Review of Attrition in the Prosecution Process (the Justice Gap)* (2002).

Solomon, E, Eades, Garside, and Rutherford, *Ten Years of Criminal Justice under Labour: An Independent Audit* (2007) (http://www.crimeandjustice.org.uk/opus55/ten-years-of-labour-2007.pdf).

Ministry of Justice *Evaluation of Victim Advocates Scheme Pilots* (2009).

Bennetto, *Police and Racism: What has been Achieved 10 Years after the Stephen Lawrence Inquiry Report?* (2009) available on the Equality and Human Rights Commission website at (http://www.equalityhumanrights.com/uploaded_files/raceinbritain/policeandracism.pdf).

USEFUL WEBSITES

Home Office website listing publications, links, and news on the criminal justice system
http://www.homeoffice.gov.uk

Criminal Justice System online home page
http://www.cjsonline.org/home.html

Prison service home page. Includes daily update on numbers of people in custody
http://www.hmprisonservice.gov.uk

Victim Support home page
http://www.victimsupport.org.uk

SELF-TEST QUESTIONS

1   What is meant by a 'victim impact statement'? What are the objections to their introduction in England and Wales?

2   In what ways have racially motivated crimes been given greater priority in recent years?

3   List three mechanisms for reducing delay in the criminal justice system which have been introduced in recent years.

4   'Effective and lasting reform to the English criminal justice system is precluded by the politicization of the issue.' Discuss.

5   'Victims have no place in the criminal justice system other than as witnesses. The criminal trial is a contest between the state and the defendant.' Discuss.

11

Police powers

SUMMARY

This chapter reviews police powers under the Police and Criminal Evidence Act (PACE) 1984. It sets out the powers of the police on the street and in the police station, highlighting the politically controversial nature of the use of powers against people from minority ethnic groups. It contrasts the relatively limited effectiveness of PACE in regulating stop and search powers on the street with the better-regulated detention regime in the police station. It reviews the impact of the Human Rights Act (HRA) 1998 on police powers and argues that although PACE in general complies with the European Convention on Human Rights many claims of breaches of PACE now rely on s 6 HRA 1998. It emphasizes the role of police discretion and concludes that the ways in which this discretion is exercised is a key factor in determining the degree of fairness, effectiveness and legitimacy of police powers. It identifies the recent strengthening of police powers as further evidence of the general trend to 'rebalance' the criminal justice process away from the rights of the suspect and defendant in favour of the victim and the goal of increasing the conviction rate.

Recent trends

11.1 In deciding whether or not to grant the police extra powers in order to prevent and detect crime, Parliament and the courts have tried to strike a balance between the needs of the community to be protected from crime and the rights of the suspect to be treated fairly. Exactly where that balance has been struck has depended on the political mood of the time. In recent years, the increasing political importance of crime as an election issue has led to a greater willingness among politicians to extend police powers and to place less importance on the rights of suspects. Examples are the abolition of the right to remain silent when questioned by the police, restrictions on the right to bail and the development of electronic police surveillance techniques.

11.2 This trend towards a general extension of police powers may, however, be countered by the effects of the Human Rights Act 1998, which incorporates the European Convention on Human Rights into domestic law. The right to a fair trial (Article 6), freedom from arbitrary detention (Article 5), freedom from inhuman and degrading treatment (Article 3) and the right to privacy (Article 8) all have the potential to impact upon the exercise of police powers.

11.3 Under the Act, the police, as a public authority, are obliged to comply with the provisions of the Convention. Citizens who claim that their rights have been breached by the police may bring a civil action against them or may seek to have evidence obtained in breach of the rules excluded by the judge at trial (PACE, s 78). Whether or not the provisions of the HRA 1998 will have a significant effect on the use of police powers depends on the attitude of the courts to such claims. To date, many human rights arguments which have been raised in court involve claims of a breach of Article 6, some of which relate to the alleged abuse of police powers.

11.4 The Human Rights Act represents an important potential external influence on police practice. An equally important development in recent years has come from within the police. In the 1990s, the 43 police forces were renamed police services as part of a reconstruction of the police as an institution providing a service to the community as consumers rather than a force imposing order on citizens. Some critics have dismissed this change as a public relations exercise, but it should also be understood as part of a wider political trend which recognizes that those in authority can no longer expect to command automatic respect from the public but must demonstrate some degree of commitment to accountability and quality control.

11.5 The reconstruction which has taken place in the police services is the result of a growing awareness that public confidence is essential for effective policing and that without the co-operation of the public, the police cannot do their job. In particular, there is a new willingness within the police to acknowledge that certain sections of the public, minority ethnic groups in particular, feel that they have not received the same treatment by the police as other groups in society either as victims or suspects.

11.6 The highly critical report in 1999 by Sir William MacPherson into the investigation by the police of the murder of the South London black teenager Stephen Lawrence played a significant part in this process of self-scrutiny. Whether or not the rhetoric has been matched by practice in the attempt to tackle illegal behaviour by the police or to address the 'institutional racism' which MacPherson identified is more difficult to assess. Widespread criticism remains about the ineffectiveness of the police disciplinary process and the very low rate of convictions of officers for criminal behaviour in the exercise of their powers. As a result of these concerns, the police complaints and disciplinary system has recently undergone a complete overhaul in an attempt to ensure that it operates in a more independent and proactive manner.

The statutory framework – the Police and Criminal Evidence Act 1984

11.7 Before 1984, police powers were not uniform throughout the country and were derived from a variety of different statutory and common law sources. It was widely recognized that this situation led to inconsistencies in police practices and the potential for injustice to occur as a result of the absence of clear rules about how the police should exercise their powers.

11.8 PACE was passed in 1984 and implemented in 1986 in order to allow time for police training. Its provisions were based on the recommendations of the Royal Commission on Criminal Procedure (the Philips Royal Commission) which reported in 1981. The Commission's aims were to produce powers which were 'fair, workable and open'.

11.9 The report was strongly attacked by the civil liberties lobby as unfair and lacking in transparency, arguing that it gave unacceptably wide discretion to the police to interfere with citizens' civil liberties. The police were reasonably happy with the balance struck by the provisions, but were more concerned about the 'workability' of the proposals, arguing that they would be hampered in their duties by the need to ensure that everything was done according to formal rules.

11.10 A year later the Conservative Government introduced an amended version of the report in a Bill which aroused fierce debate in Parliament. After a number of amendments, the Bill was finally passed in 1984 (having been delayed by the general election of May 1983). At the time there continued to be a wide difference of opinion as to whether the Act had extended or restricted police powers. Some members of the police described it as a 'villain's charter', while some defence lawyers saw it as a licence for police abuse.

11.11 Two decades after PACE came into force it can be concluded that neither of these predictions were accurate. Within a few years most of the procedures became standard police practice and were relatively unproblematic. Most defence lawyers and police officers today would say that overall the provisions have proved to be 'fair, workable and open'. Criticisms remain, however, from different quarters about particular aspects of the provisions. In general terms it can be said that they have been more successful at regulating practice in the police station than on the street. What is without doubt is that few would wish to return to the time of uncertainty, inconsistent and loosely regulated policing of pre-1986.

The structure of the Act

11.12 The provisions of PACE cover the following areas: stop and search in the street; entry search and seizure; arrest; detention; questioning and treatment of persons; evidence at trial; and complaints against the police and disciplinary proceedings. In addition, the Act includes codes of practice which give guidance to the police on how the main provisions should be interpreted and applied. The codes are drawn up by the Home Secretary and are periodically revised. Unlike the Act itself, the codes are not law, so that breaches of their provisions cannot lead to criminal or civil proceedings. When the codes were first drawn up, a breach led automatically to disciplinary proceedings. This provision has since been removed.

11.13 In contrast, a breach of the main sections of the Act might constitute a civil wrong or a criminal offence. The judge at trial might also exclude evidence which was obtained in breach of the provisions. The judge is not generally obliged to exclude illegally obtained evidence, but has the discretionary power to do so if: 'having regard to all the circumstances, including the circumstances in which the evidence was obtained, the admission of the evidence would have such an adverse effect on the fairness of the proceedings that the court ought not to admit it' (PACE, s 78). However, an exception to this discretionary approach is found in s 76. This *requires* a judge to exclude a confession when it has been obtained through oppression or in circumstances which make it unreliable. In practice, the provisions of s 76 are used relatively rarely, whereas the discretionary power under s 78 is quite frequently exercised by magistrates and judges.

Police powers on the street – stop and search provisions

11.14 One of the most common situations in which people, particularly young people, find themselves on the receiving end of the exercise of police powers is when they are stopped in the street and asked by the police to open their bags or turn out their pockets. A study of the use of the power in London in 1983 carried out by the Policy Studies Institute found that about 1.5 million stops and searches were carried out each year in London. However, the total number of stops and searches officially recorded for the whole country each year is far below that figure.

11.15 The under-recording of stops and searches by the police suggests that most stops are considered to be 'voluntarily' and therefore are not regarded by the police as falling within the provisions of PACE. The police, like any other citizens, can ask someone to stop and be searched and if they consent to such a 'voluntary search' the statutory provisions regarding police powers are largely irrelevant. However, research by Dixon et al (1990) suggests that many searches are not genuinely voluntary in that the person agrees to the search because they feel under pressure to consent or are ignorant of their right to refuse. The consent to the search is therefore often not fully informed. In response to concerns about the under-reporting of voluntary stops and searches, the Home Office issued a draft revised PACE Code of Practice A in 2002 which required that the police should make a record of every incident in which a police officer 'requests a person in a public place to account for themselves'. This provision was, however, dropped from the final draft which was put forward in November 2002. Instead, the Home Office has instituted a similar recording scheme on a pilot basis in seven police services before deciding whether or not to implement it nationally. One significant change which has, however, been implemented in the 2003 revised codes is that a search must not normally be conducted unless there is a legal power to do so, even if the person gives their consent. If heeded, this provision may have an impact on the numbers of 'voluntary' stops and searches carried out.

11.16 Before PACE was passed a variety of laws were in force which gave the police power to stop and search, such as the Misuse of Drugs Act 1971 and the Vagrancy Act 1864. Now PACE provides a uniform regime throughout the country, but the pre-PACE laws still exist and are still used by the police.

11.17 PACE gives the police the power to search 'any person or vehicle … for stolen or prohibited Articles' (s 1(2)). The officer must have 'reasonable grounds' for suspecting that the person has these articles in his or her possession. An article is 'prohibited' if it is an offensive weapon or is made or adapted for use in the course or in connection with burglary, theft, taking a motor vehicle or obtaining property by deception. An offensive weapon is defined as an article made or adapted for use for causing injury to persons. Everyone searched has a right to be told of the reason for the search and the officer is obliged to make a record of the search. The person searched can request a copy of that record.

11.18 Code A sets out guidelines on what constitutes 'reasonable grounds for suspicion' for the purposes of carrying out a stop and search. It states that the existence of reasonable grounds depends on the circumstances in each case. It requires the presence of an objective basis for the suspicion based on objective facts and can never be founded on the basis of personal factors alone 'without reliable supporting intelligence or information or some specific behaviour by the person concerned …' Reasonable suspicion might be based on the nature of the property, the time or place or the behaviour of the person. It cannot be based on the person's background or membership of a particular group, eg being black or young or wearing certain clothes.

11.19 In 1997, however, the Code was amended and now states that where there is reliable information or intelligence that members of a group or gang habitually carry weapons or controlled drugs and wear a distinctive item of clothing, the members may be identified by means of that distinctive item of clothing or other means of identification such as jewellery, insignias or tattoos. This amendment was added in response to concerns that certain gangs were regularly carrying and using knives. Its wording, however, is sufficiently wide to encompass other groups, such as Rastafarians who are also identifiable by their clothing and who are known to carry cannabis. The frequent use of stop and search powers in the past against Rastafarians has been the cause of tension between some black communities and the police.

11.20 The note for guidance which accompanies the code recognizes the potential for the power of stop and search to be a cause of resentment if overused or misused. It states:

> It is important to ensure that powers of stop and search are used responsibly and sparingly and only where reasonable grounds for suspicion genuinely exist. Over use of the powers is as likely to be harmful to police effort in the long term as misuse. Both can lead to mistrust of the police among sections of the community. It is also particularly important to ensure that any person searched must be treated courteously and considerately if police action is not to be resented.

The use of stop and search powers in practice

11.21 The use of stop and search powers has been a controversial aspect of police powers for many years, particularly their use in inner city areas against members of minority ethnic groups. The alleged overuse of stop and search powers was an important factor in the Brixton riots of the 1980s. In particular, there was criticism over the use of intensive police operations against drug offences and burglary which involved large numbers of stops during short periods of saturation policing. Since the 1980s, the police have become far more conscious of the political sensitivity of stop and search operations and have tended to consult with local community leaders before carrying out similar operations. Nevertheless, concerns are still regularly voiced that the power is disproportionately used against members of the black communities.

11.22 The research evidence broadly supports this claim. The Policy Studies Institute study cited above found that age, gender and ethnicity were the most important variables in terms of the likelihood of being stopped and searched. Young males of Afro-Caribbean origin were most likely to be stopped. The research found a big difference in the rate at which black and white young men were stopped. Afro-Caribbean males who had been stopped in the last 12 months were stopped four times on average compared with 2.5 for white males.

11.23 Generally the research found that those who were stopped had a reasonably favourable view of the behaviour of the police in relation to the stops, but those who were stopped most frequently had the poorest overall view of the police. More recent research carried out in the late 1990s has found that the greatest objection to the use of the powers by those stopped was not so much the fact of being stopped and searched but rude or aggressive treatment by the police during the process (Fitzgerald, 1999). In response to this finding, the revised code now includes a statement that the powers must be used 'fairly, responsibly, with respect for people being searched and without unlawful discrimination'.

11.24 One means of determining whether or not stop and search powers are being misused or overused is to assess the relationship between the use of the powers and the detection of crime. The Policy Studies Institute study found that of the 1.5 million stops carried out about 8 per cent (100,000) resulted in an arrest. This suggests that a high proportion of stops and searches are unnecessary, but also that the total numbers of offences discovered by the use of the power is relatively large. Whether or not the cost in terms of damage to community relations is worth the benefit in terms of detection of crime is ultimately a political judgment.

Police powers in the police station

11.25 The evidence about the use of PACE on the street suggests that the power to stop and search is widely used and that the checks and formalities set out in the Act are often not applied. One reason for this is that despite the highly public nature of the street interaction, it is usually a relatively low-impact exercise of power which is over quickly. The incentive to challenge the police or to seek legal advice about the legality or the stop and search after the event is not strong.

11.26 By contrast, the exercise of police powers in the police station usually has a longer and more serious impact on people's lives. Arrest and detention is an experience which most people would regard as exceptional and serious, and one in which knowledge of your rights or legal advice becomes important. For this reason, there is greater scrutiny of, and challenge to, police powers in the station and the provisions of PACE regarding this aspect of the statutory regulations have generally had more effect on police practice.

Arrest and detention

11.27 Before 2005, the police had the power to arrest anyone whom they reasonably suspect to be committing, to have committed or to be about to commit an arrestable offence. Arrestable offences are, broadly speaking, the more serious offences. Under the provisions of the Serious Organised Crime and Police Act 2005 the power to arrest was significantly widened from arrestable offences to indictable offences, a category that includes less serious offences such as shoplifting. Once arrested, the premises of an arrested person can be searched for evidence relating to the offence.

11.28 An arrested person can be detained if there are reasonable grounds for believing it is necessary (not convenient or desirable) to preserve evidence relating to an offence which the suspect is held in connection with or to obtain evidence through questioning. Once they have obtained sufficient evidence to charge the person, the police must either charge them or release them.

11.29 Many attendances at police stations are theoretically voluntary, in that the person has not been arrested. In common with the stop and search provisions, the rules on detention do not apply when a person comes to the station voluntarily. The status of such people is something of a grey area under PACE. Code C specifies that even if attending 'to help police with their enquiries' a person must be informed that he or she is not arrested and may leave or have legal advice. The extent to which these guidelines are observed is not known. In practice, it is likely that many people who attend the station voluntarily will not be aware that they are free to leave unless they are formally arrested.

11.30 One of the most significant changes made by PACE to the regime in the police station was the creation of a new post of custody officer. Each station in which suspects are detained must have a custody officer on duty who must be an officer of the rank of sergeant. Their role is to supervise the detention process and to keep a detailed custody record which sets out such information as the time of arrival, periods of interviews and requests for legal assistance.

11.31 Suspects must be brought before the custody officer once they arrive at the station in order for the officer to decide if there is sufficient evidence to charge them. If so, they must then be charged and released unconditionally, bailed to return to the station or appear before the magistrates' court on a given date, or detained in custody to be brought before magistrates. If there is not enough evidence for the person to be charged, he or she must be released unless the custody officer believes that further detention is necessary to preserve evidence or to secure evidence by questioning. The custody officer is under a continuing duty to order the immediate release of suspects if there are no longer grounds for detaining them.

11.32 In addition to the scrutiny of the custody officer, there must be a review of whether detention is still necessary by an officer who is not the custody officer within six hours after the suspect being brought to the station and then every nine hours. Until recently the normal maximum period of detention was 24 hours between arriving at the station and charging unless the offence was a serious arrestable offence (as set out in PACE). In that case the suspect could be detained for up to 36 hours if authorized by a senior officer who believes it necessary and considers that the investigation is being carried out expeditiously. However, in the Criminal Justice Act 2003 the requirement that the offence be a serious arrestable offence was removed so that the extension of time can be authorized in relation to all arrestable offences. If the police wish to detain a person beyond this time they can apply for a warrant of further detention from the magistrates' court for further periods of 36 hours up to a total period of 96 hours.

11.33 Once the suspect has been charged, the custody officer must release the suspect unless:

(a) the person has refused to give his or her name and address;

(b) the custody officer reasonably doubts that the name and address given are genuine;

(c) there are reasonable grounds for believing detention is necessary to protect the suspect or to protect others or prevent damage to property;

(d) there are reasonable grounds for believing that the suspect will fail to attend court or interfere with the administration of justice.

The Criminal Justice and Public Order Act 1994, s 27 allows for conditions to be attached to police bail.

11.34 Overall, therefore, the PACE provisions relating to detention provide for a relatively strict regime in which the emphasis is placed on the requirement for there to be valid grounds for detention and a system for the regular monitoring and checking of the need for detention. In practice, however, the evidence suggests that the reviews by the custody officer and the independent reviewing officer often amount to little more than a rubber stamp. It appears to be rare for a custody officer to order the release of a suspect against the wishes of the officer in charge of the investigation.

11.35 In general, the absence of a strong independent check on detention is mitigated by the fact that the average length of detention tends to be relatively short. Only about 1 per cent of detentions are extended beyond the normal 24-hour maximum, with the average being approximately four hours. However, for very serious offences such as rape and murder this rises to 22 hours. Similarly, long periods of detention are also common for those held under the prevention of terrorism provisions. For this small minority of cases the gap between the letter of the detention provisions and the spirit in which they are implemented can be a cause for concern. Equally worrying are the Government's attempts to extend the detention time limits in terrorism cases. In its Counter-Terrorism Bill, the Government proposed extending the pre-charge detention time limit in exceptional cases from 28 to 42 days. However, this clause was dropped in October 2008 after the House of Lords rejected it by 191 votes. Opponents of the Bill argued that it would breach Article 5(2), (3) and(4) ECHR requirements that arrestees are informed promptly of the reasons for their arrest and the charges against them; that detainees be brought promptly before a judge; and that detainees are entitled speedily to have the lawfulness of their detention ascertained by a court.

Rights of suspects during detention

11.36 In addition to providing limits on the circumstances and length of time for which a person can be detained, PACE also sets out the rights which arrested persons can exercise during the detention. These include important basic standards in the conditions of their detention such as being allowed eight hours' rest in every 24 and the provision of regular meals and adequate lighting and heating.

11.37 One of the most important rights given to suspects in detention is to have someone informed of their whereabouts and to consult a solicitor in private. These provisions are an essential guarantee against being held incommunicado. In order for the right to consult a solicitor to be meaningful in practice, particularly to those who have never been detained before, suspects need to know about it and be able to afford it. The duty solicitor scheme, which was set up at the same time as PACE, provides a list of local solicitors who are on duty 24 hours a day to provide free legal advice. The duty solicitor will attend at the station or give advice over the telephone. In order to ensure that suspects are aware of the scheme, PACE requires that they must be told of the right and that it is free.

11.38 In practice, however, despite these guarantees, only about 40 per cent of those detained ask for legal advice. No doubt some of the remaining 60 per cent are people making well-informed choices who genuinely consider that they do not need a solicitor. However, research suggests that the police sometimes also discourage people from exercising the right in various ways, for example by reading out the right to legal advice very quickly or stressing that contacting a solicitor will delay their release. Under PACE the suspect has the right to see a solicitor 'as soon as is practicable', which gives considerable scope for delay.

11.39 In addition to the potential for informal 'ploys' by the police to discourage the involvement of lawyers, there is also a power to delay access to a solicitor if an officer of the rank of superintendent or above has reasonable grounds for believing it is necessary because the exercise of right might lead to:

- interference with evidence, or
- harm to persons, or
- alerting others suspected of committing an offence, or
- hindering recovery of property.

11.40 Before 2005, this power to delay access to a solicitor was limited to more serious offences but has been extended in the Serious Organised Crime and Police Act 2005 to all indictable offences. In practice this power has, to date, been rarely exercised, except in cases of terrorism. In almost all cases, if a suspect wants a solicitor and is prepared to ask for one and possibly to wait, one will be provided. An unjustified refusal of access to a solicitor is one of the few breaches of the PACE provisions which is taken very seriously by the courts and is likely to lead to evidence such as a confession being excluded by the trial judge.

11.41 This provides a major disincentive for the police to interfere explicitly with the right. Although the low take-up rate for a solicitor may indicate that some suspects may still not be fully aware of the right or may be being deterred from exercising it, the current level of legal advice in the station is far better than in the pre-PACE era.

11.42 Obtaining a solicitor, however, does not automatically guarantee the receipt of competent legal advice. Until recently it was common for legal representatives to be clerks rather than qualified solicitors – either trainees or ex-police officers employed by solicitors' firms for this purpose. As a result of the range of advisers, the quality of the advice was inevitably highly variable.

11.43 In response to increasing concern about poor standards of advice, in the 1990s the Law Society introduced compulsory training for advisers at the station. Recent research on the quality of legal representation suggests that as a result of this change there has been a significant improvement in standards. This development is particularly important in the light of changes to the right of silence (see below). In *Murray v United Kingdom* (1996) the European Court of Human Rights held that there was a breach of Article 6 when a terrorist suspect was denied access to a solicitor when questioned. Under the provisions in effect in Northern Ireland (equivalent to those later introduced in England and Wales) a suspect's failure to answer questions could lead to an inference of guilt being drawn against the defendant at trial. In these circumstances, the court held that access to legal advice was a requirement of a fair trial. In order to comply with this decision in Strasbourg, the Youth Justice and Criminal Evidence Act 1999 amended PACE, s 34 by prohibiting an adverse inference to be drawn from silence at the station when the suspect has not had an opportunity to consult a solicitor.

Questioning

11.44 Since the main purpose of detention is to interview the suspect, the PACE provisions relating to questioning are a key aspect of the Act. Before PACE there were few rules governing the way in which questioning should be conducted and it was common for suspects to claim in court that they had been mistreated during interviews or that an alleged confession was fabricated. PACE addressed this problem by the introduction of tape-recorded interviews. During an interview, two tapes are used. One is sealed until the court hearing, while the other is used to make a summary for the defendant who may also request access to the whole tape.

11.45 The introduction of tape-recording was successful in so far as it resulted in a significant reduction of allegations of police 'verballing' during interviews. However, defence lawyers noted that after the new regime was introduced there was an increase in the number of alleged confessions made in the car on the way to the police station. In general, the use of a tape recorder has provided a check on some of the abuses that could take place or at the very least provided evidence of unacceptable behaviour. In *Paris, Abdullahi and Miller* in 1993 (the 'Cardiff Three'), for example, the Court of Appeal quashed a murder conviction after hearing the tape of an interview in which the defendants denied their involvement over 300 times before confessing. In its judgment, the court expressed its shock at the hostile and intimidating approach which was adopted by the police. Amazingly, the interview had been attended throughout by a solicitor.

The right of silence

11.46   Until 1994, an arrested person was under no legal obligation to answer police questions and solicitors routinely advised their clients simply to reply 'no comment' in police interviews. After four official inquiries and many years of debate on the subject, the Criminal Justice and Public Order Act was passed in 1994 removing the absolute right of silence. On arrest, the police must now administer the following caution:

> You do not have to say anything. But it may harm your defence if you do not mention, when questioned something which you later rely on in court. Anything you do say may be given in evidence.

11.47   If, during an interview, suspects do not answer police questions they run the risk that an 'adverse inference' as to their guilt will be drawn at their trial if they rely in their defence on facts which they could reasonably have been expected to mention to the police. This change has increased the need for competent legal advice during police interviews since the decision as to whether or not to answer questions is now a more difficult one with potentially serious consequences. Legal advisers need to be much more proactive than in the past, for example by ensuring that the police have made adequate disclosure of the case against the suspect so that he or she can know exactly what is being alleged.

11.48   The debate over the removal of the right of silence was an intense one and opinions over the changes were sharply divided. The main arguments put forward in favour of its removal were that a disproportionate number of professional criminals used the right to take advantage of the system and construct 'ambush' defences which they would spring on the prosecution in court. It was also argued that the right not to answer questions was left over from a time when defendants had very few rights and needed protection. The enactment of PACE and the provision of free legal advice were sufficient to protect weak or innocent defendants. The right now merely served to prevent the police and the courts from getting at the truth.

11.49   In contrast, supporters of the right of silence argued that the assumption that the innocent have nothing to hide was flawed. There may be many reasons why inno- cent suspects would wish not to answer questions: they may feel the need to protect others from recrimination; they may be fearful for their own safety or may want to protect their privacy where, for example, the truth would expose an aspect of their personal life unconnected with any criminal activity. They may also wish to remain silent because they do not understand fully the nature of case against them and therefore cannot give a full and clear response to the allegations. Research also suggests that there are categories of vulnerable suspects who are likely to make false confessions (Gudjonsson, 1992). If suspects in these circumstances are forced to answer questions there is a greater risk of a miscarriage of justice, particularly where an adverse inference being drawn by the court results in a conviction in relation to an otherwise weak prosecution case. Lastly, supporters of the right of silence argue that the burden of proof requires that the state brings the case and proves it beyond reasonable doubt. The defendant should not be under an obligation to co-operate in the process in any way.

11.50 In 1992, the Royal Commission on Criminal Justice conducted a survey of research on the use of the right of silence and concluded that 5–15 per cent of suspects remain completely or partially silent when questioned by the police. Therefore the great majority of suspects make some sort of statement, whether to admit or deny the offence. Moreover, the Commission found that those who remain silent are no less likely to be charged or convicted than those who do not. So the relevance of the removal of the right in 1994 related to a small proportion of suspects who were silent and either not prosecuted or acquitted and who might have been prosecuted or convicted if an adverse inference had been allowed to be drawn.

11.51 At the time the provisions were introduced it was not clear how the courts would apply them in practice. A key question was how the courts would interpret the requirement that the suspect should 'reasonably' have been expected to mention a fact to the police (PACE, s 34). From the judgments of the Court of Appeal in the cases which have been decided since 1994, it is clear that the judges are generally supportive of the provisions and reluctant to hold that an adverse inference should not have been drawn. In *Friend* (1997) the Court of Appeal went so far as to hold that an adverse inference could be drawn against a 14-year-old suspect with a men-tal age of 9 who failed to answer police questions. However, in *Maguire* (2008) the Court of Appeal did warn that prosecutors should be cautious about too readily seeking to invite formalized representations under s 34.

11.52 The incorporation of the European Convention on Human Rights into domestic law has made relatively little difference to the approach of the courts in this area. In a number of cases the Court in Strasbourg has reviewed this issue and has held that the right to a fair trial under Article 6 does not require an absolute right of silence. However, in certain circumstances it has held that there has been a breach of a right to a fair trial in the UK where an adverse inference was drawn from silence.

11.53 In *Condron v United Kingdom (No 2)* (2000) the ECtHR held that there was a breach of Article 6 because an adverse inference was allowed to be drawn by the jury without a proper direction having been given by the judge. The facts of the case were that the defendants were drug users who were charged with supplying class A drugs. At the police station their solicitor advised them not to answer police questions because she considered that they were suffering from withdrawal symptoms and therefore not in a fit state to reply. The police surgeon was called, and held that they were fit for interview. They remained silent in interview and the trial judge allowed the jury to draw an adverse inference at trial.

11.54 On appeal, the Court of Appeal held that the judge should have given a clearer warning to the jury that they should not convict unless there was no other reasonable explanation for the defendants' silence other than that they had no answer to the charge, or none that would stand up to cross-examination. However, the Court also held that the inadequate direction by the judge did not render the conviction 'unsafe' and so dismissed the appeal. The defendants took the case to Strasbourg where the ECtHR held that there had been a breach of Article 6 and criticized the Court of Appeal for concluding that a conviction could be 'safe' in such circumstances (see chapter 14).

11.55 The issue of the effect of legal advice to remain silent when questioned by the police was revisited by the Court of Appeal in *Howell* (2003). The Court held that reliance on legal advice not to answer questions will not, of itself, constitute reasonable grounds for silence. It stated that what is reasonable will depend on the particular circumstances of the case. Examples of relevant factors given by the Court were the ill-health of the suspect or a genuine inability to recall events without sight of documents. The Court concluded that there must be 'soundly-based objective reasons' for silence.

11.56 To summarize, the empirical evidence on the right of silence suggests that quantitatively the right was less important than is suggested by the degree of controversy provoked by its abolition. Most suspects answer questions and most plead guilty. But qualitatively, whether there is a right to remain silent in the police station or in court is important in three respects. First, it is an indication of the extent to which the system prioritizes the need to reduce the risk of wrongful convictions. Second, it is evidence of whether the criminal justice process is underpinned by a due process model, emphasizing the rights of suspects, or a crime control model, emphasizing the collective need to tackle crime by maximizing convictions.

11.57 Lastly, it is an example of whether the criminal justice process is more adversarial or inquisitorial in nature. Many continental European systems regard the idea of a defendant's right of silence as anathema. Suspects in legal systems such as those in France or Germany have traditionally been seen as the central focus of the investigation process and, as such, as being under a duty to co-operate in the inquisitorial system. Instead of a right of silence, they are regarded as having a 'right to speak' in order to assist in the discovery of the truth. The abolition of the right of silence in England and Wales, in line with other recent criminal justice legislation, represents a clear move towards a more inquisitorial, crime control model of justice. Supporters of this change argue that it promotes better truth-finding, while its detractors say that it reduces fairness and increases the risk of wrongful convictions.

Photographs, fingerprints, and samples

11.58 Since the purpose of detention is to acquire evidence, it is common for the police to take photographs, fingerprints, and samples from the arrested person. These can now be checked against data held on a national DNA database. Under the provisions of PACE, samples are divided between those which are intimate and non-intimate. Non-intimate samples (hair, saliva, nail scrapings, and mouth swabs) can be taken without consent. Intimate samples (blood, semen, urine) can only be taken with consent and normally by a doctor. However, failure to give consent can lead to an adverse inference being drawn at court in the same way as a refusal to answer police questions.

11.59 The retention of samples raises important human rights questions. In *Marper* (2008) the European Court of Human Rights held that the retention of DNA samples from suspects who had not been charged or had been acquitted breached Article 8 ECHR. The judges noted that the UK was the only state in the Council of Europe to give the police a blanket and indiscriminate right to retain samples without limit of time, regardless of the gravity of the alleged offence. Legislation is expected to provide a more proportionate power to retain certain samples.

11.60 The routine search of suspects on arrest is not permitted. They can be searched only if they may have on them items which could be used to cause injury, damage, the interference with evidence or assistance in an escape. Intimate searches (which are defined as all body orifices other than the mouth) can only be carried out if authorized by a senior officer who reasonably believes that the person has concealed class A drugs or material which he might use to cause physical injury to himself or others. Searches for drugs must be carried out by a doctor at a hospital, but a search for dangerous material can be carried out by an officer in an emergency. In practice, intimate searches are very rare.

The implications of the Human Rights Act 1998

11.61 In the light of the obvious impact on the personal freedoms which PACE authorizes, it is inevitable that the field of police powers has the potential to give rise to a range of different claims under the HRA. In order to decide whether or not it is possible to challenge the exercise of a police power in a particular case as a breach of the European Convention on Human Rights, it is necessary to ask a series of questions. Which Convention right might have been breached by the action? Does the action in fact breach that right? Is the right absolute (such as against inhuman or degrading treatment) or qualified (such as the right to privacy)? If it is qualified, does the breach fall within one of the qualifications? For example, is it in accordance with the law and necessary in a democratic society? Is the breach proportionate, ie is it the minimum necessary restriction which can be imposed in order to achieve the legitimate goal? Lastly, is the right exercised in a discriminatory manner in breach of Article 14?

Stop and search

11.62 In relation to stop and search powers, the answer to the first question is that, in principle, the prevention of movement of a person by a police officer might give rise to claim under Article 5 of the European Convention on Human Rights – the right to liberty and security of person. However, it is unlikely that a stop and search constitutes a breach of Article 5 because most stops and searches are brief and carried out with the intention only of finding stolen or prohibited articles rather than detaining the person.

11.63 There is not yet any case law from the European Court of Human Rights on the question of stop and search under PACE, so the courts in the UK have no guidance on this matter should it come before them, but it appears that a person must be detained for a significant period of time in order to claim that they had been deprived of their liberty under Article 5.

11.64 In practice, the most likely successful claim in relation to stop and search powers would be that they are being used in a discriminatory way against certain sections of the community. However, if it is not possible to argue that stops and searches under PACE amount to a deprivation of liberty, then it is not arguable that the disproportionate application to certain groups constitutes a breach of Article 14. This is because Article 14 is not a free-standing right to freedom from discrimination but only applies to the exercise of the rights in the Convention. If these are not engaged, it does not come into play.

11.65 If in the future the UK signs protocol 12 to the Convention which provides for a free-standing right not to be discriminated against, then it might be possible, for example, for a young, black man who had been repeatedly stopped and searched to succeed in such a claim if he could show that the objective standards of the code of conduct were not being adhered to and that the exercise of the power against him was not proportionate to the threat posed by street crime.

Detention

11.66 In contrast to stop and search, the provisions in the police station provide much more scope for a successful claim under the Human Rights Act 1998. The detention of a suspect for questioning will almost certainly amount to a deprivation of liberty under Article 5. The questions which arise in relation to police detention are therefore:

- whether the deprivation is in accordance with a procedure prescribed by law;

- whether it falls within one of the allowed exceptions; and

- whether the procedural safeguards which are set out in Article 5(2)–(5) have been complied with.

11.67 To be prescribed by law a provision must comply with PACE or the equivalent domestic legislation as well as with the general underlying principles of the Convention, eg that a power must not be exercised in bad faith.

11.68 Under Article 5(1)(c), detention in breach of Article 5 is permissible if there is 'reasonable suspicion' that the suspect has committed an offence and the purpose of the detention is to bring her/him before a court. The European Court of Human Rights has held that reasonable suspicion requires the presence of objective facts (*Fox, Campbell and Hartley v United Kingdom* (1990)). PACE requirements would therefore appear to comply with this since the reasonable suspicion required by PACE before a person can be arrested and detained must be based on objective circumstances.

11.69 Similarly, the time limits, if observed, would appear to conform to the interpretation of the Convention to date. In *Brogan v United Kingdom* (1988), the European Court of Human Rights in Strasbourg held that detention for six days breached Article 5. The Court now seems to have established that four days is the maximum acceptable detention before bringing the suspect to court, so that it is unlikely that there could be any claim of breach in respect of PACE unless a claimant could persuade the UK courts that the Strasbourg jurisprudence is a 'floor not a ceiling' and that the UK courts should impose stricter time limits.

11.70 However, in *Murray v United Kingdom* (1996) the European Court of Human Rights held that refusing access to a solicitor for 48 hours was a breach of the right to a fair trial. In the rare cases when suspects are denied access to a solicitor under PACE, it is likely that the police would need to show that there were clear grounds which justified this action, if they are to avoid a successful claim under the HRA, particularly in the light of the removal of the right of silence, which the European Court of Human Rights recognized as increasing the importance of legal advice.

Summary

11.71 In assessing the fairness and effectiveness of police powers, it is necessary to consider both the legal rules which govern the powers and the culture and attitude of the police in exercising them. This is because the legal powers allow for a wide measure of discretion in the way they are exercised. In practice, it is hard to see how any other system could work. Police interaction with the public requires the constant exercise of judgment and the right approach in any one situation will be dependent on the particular facts and context. The police could not take action in relation to every instance of illegal behaviour without a massive increase in resources. Nor would such a level of criminalization be an acceptable or desirable development.

11.72 Striking the right balance in the exercise of police powers is not easy. If the police are liberal, avoiding where possible intervention which interferes with the rights of private individuals, then they are criticized for failing to protect society from criminals, and vice versa. PACE and the HRA provide the legal framework for the exercise of the powers, but the practice of policing ultimately depends on the political culture both of the police and society as a whole. In general, the current trend is towards strengthening police powers. Despite the Human Rights Act, there is a general willingness to allow the police greater discretion in the exercise of their power. This approach is further evidence of the shift away from a justice system which prioritizes the rights of suspects and defendants in favour of one where victims and crime control are put first.

FURTHER READING

M Zander *The Police and Criminal Evidence Act* 1984 (2008, 6th edn, London).

M Zander 'The Joint Review of PACE: A Deplorable Report' (2003) New Law Journal, 14 February.

Fitzgerald et al (2001) *Policing for London* (http://www.kcl.ac.uk/depsta/law/research/icpr/publications/findings.pdf).

Starmer, Strange and Whitaker *Criminal Justice, Police Powers and Human Rights* (2001, London: Blackstone Press).

G Gudjonsson *The Psychology of Interrogations, Confessions and Testimony* (1992, Chichester: J Wiley).

USEFUL WEBSITES

Home Office website police section
http://www.homeoffice.gov.uk/police/

SELF-TEST QUESTIONS

1 'The provisions of PACE give the police an unacceptably wide measure of discretion which allows them to infringe the rights of suspects with impunity.' Discuss.

2 Are the current rules governing the length of time a person can be detained at a police station adequate?

3 'Now that the right to silence has been abolished, the suspect in the police station is left with little protection.' Discuss.

4 Why has the regulation of police powers in the station been more effective than those exercised on the street?

5 List six questions which will need to be addressed in order to determine whether or not police action may be successfully challenged under the Human Rights Act 1998.

6 What impact has the HRA 1998 had on the exercise of police powers? Does the HRA 1998 undermine efforts to detect, prevent and prosecute crime?

12

The prosecution process

SUMMARY

This chapter describes the role and functions of the Crown Prosecution Service (CPS). It reviews the criticisms which have been made of the CPS: in particular, that it fails to secure convictions and is too ready to discontinue cases, that it is not willing enough to disclose evidence to the defence, and that it is guilty of discriminatory practices in relation to victims, defendants and the personnel who work for it. It argues that these concerns are partially justified but concludes that the performance of the CPS has generally improved in recent years.

12.1 The high level of discretion which the police must exercise in relation to their powers to stop and search, arrest, detain and investigate crime does not stop at the point of charging. Once a person has been charged it is not automatic that he or she will be prosecuted and there has never been a legal obligation to bring an offender to court. The decision to prosecute rather than to issue a caution or to drop the case involves another important exercise of discretion in the criminal justice process.

The creation of an independent prosecution service

12.2 Before 1986, the decision to prosecute, or not, was taken by the police. Each of the 43 police forces was free to implement its own policies as to the kind of cases which would be prosecuted. Inevitably, this localized prosecution process led to a degree of inconsistency around the country. An equally serious objection to this system was that the police, having spent time and resources investigating a crime and identifying an offender, could not be expected to be sufficiently independent to decide whether it was in the interests of justice for a prosecution to proceed.

12.3 In 1981, the Philips Royal Commission on Criminal Procedure, which was set up to review police powers, was also asked to examine the prosecution process in the light of these concerns. It concluded that a new independent body was needed which would take over the case once a charge had been brought. The Government accepted the proposals, and the Crown Prosecution Service was formed in 1986. Private prosecutions can still be brought by individuals and other bodies such as the Serious Fraud Office, Customs and Excise, the Inland Revenue and local authorities, but the great majority of prosecutions are now handled by the CPS.

12.4 The head of the CPS is the Director of Public Prosecutions, who is responsible to the Attorney-General. The latter is directly responsible for the decision to prosecute in certain cases such as terrorism offences or offences under the Official Secrets Act 1989. The Attorney-General is a political appointee who combines a number of different roles. As well as deciding whether or not it is in the public interest for certain sensitive and serious cases to be prosecuted, she or he is also the legal adviser to the Government. The potential conflict of interest, real or apparent, which can arise when the Attorney-General must decide whether or not a case should be prosecuted which may expose the Government to criticism is a source of recurring concern. The draft Constitutional Renewal Bill 2008 proposed the removal of the Attorney-General's role in individual prosecutions, as opposed to general prosecution policy. However, in its response to the Justice Committee's report on the Bill, the Government stated that it considered that legislation was not necessary. Instead, a protocol will be agreed between the Attorney-General and the directors of the prosecution authorities, detailing their respective roles.

12.5 The role of the CPS at the time it was set up was to take over the case once a person has been charged and to decide whether or not to proceed or drop the case. Increasingly, however, it is involved in the charging process itself. The Criminal Justice Act 2003 set up a new charging regime in which the CPS is directly involved in determining what charges, if any, are to be brought, the aim being to reduce the danger of inappropriate charges being laid. Once a case proceeds after charge, the CPS prepares it for trial, and either presents it in court or instructs a self-employed barrister to do so.

12.6 Before 1999, prosecutors employed by the CPS could not act as advocates in the Crown Court. Since then, employed lawyers have had rights of audience in the higher courts provided they have the necessary advocacy qualification. This means, in practice, that they are barristers or they are solicitors who have gained the higher rights of audience qualification. The CPS currently has over 400 solicitors with higher rights of audience. It has argued that this allows for the more efficient and cost-effective handling of cases.

12.7 Critics of the move, however, argue that it undermines the quality of justice by reducing the independence of the advocate. The fear is that, as salaried employees,

CPS prosecutors presenting a case are less likely than self-employed barristers or solicitor advocates instructed by the CPS to feel able to make decisions which might damage the prosecution case but which are in the interests of justice. For example, the decision by prosecuting counsel to disclose evidence to the defence which supports its case or undermines that of the prosecution is one which may be necessary in the interests of justice, but which may lead to the collapse of the prosecution case. This result may have more impact on the career prospects of an employee of the Crown Prosecution Service than a self-employed barrister or solicitor advocate.

The prosecution criteria

12.8   The decision to prosecute is based on two tests. First, there must be a 'realistic prospect of success', and second it must be 'in the public interest' for a prosecution to proceed.

12.9   A Code for Prosecutors gives the CPS detailed guidance on the circumstances relating to the offence and the offender which should be taken into account in deciding whether or not to proceed. It sets out a non-exhaustive list of the factors which can count for or against prosecution. Public interest factors in favour of prosecution include the seriousness of the offence; the use of violence; the likelihood of a significant sentence; and the fact that the offence is committed by a person serving the public. In contrast, circumstances which might render it inappropriate for the prosecution to go ahead include the fact that the offence may be trivial or the harm caused minimal; or that the offender is old or very ill.

12.10   Like the PACE codes of practice, the code for prosecutors is periodically revised to take account of changing attitudes and circumstances. For example, in 2001 the code was updated to place more emphasis on the position of the victim. It also includes as a factor in favour of prosecution that the offence was motivated by any form of discrimination. This reflects the increasing political pressure to tackle racist crimes in the light of the MacPherson report into the Stephen Lawrence murder.

The record of the CPS

12.11   Throughout its existence, the CPS has faced a range of different criticisms. In the early years the main source of concern was the allegation of incompetence and inefficiency, largely due to understaffing. The starting salaries offered to prosecutors had been set too low to attract sufficient numbers of experienced and well-qualified lawyers. As a result, it developed a reputation for mediocrity which in turn deterred good candidates from applying. This problem was slowly tackled during the 1990s through an increase of funding and by 1993 the CPS was at last fully staffed. At the end of March 2008 the CPS employed 8,351 staff, including 2,913 prosecutors, 945 of whom were eligible to appear in the Crown Court and above.

12.12 However, other criticisms have also been voiced. A recurring concern has been that the CPS discontinues or downgrades cases in an inappropriately large number of instances. In particular, it has been alleged that serious assaults have been downgraded to the summary offence of common assault so that the cases could be tried in the magistrates' courts at less cost.

12.13 In addition, the CPS has been accused of being overly bureaucratic and top-heavy. In response to these concerns, in 1997 the new Labour Government decided that it should be restructured into 42 areas, so closely mirroring the 43 police forces. The aim of the change was to decentralize control within the organization and give greater discretion to regional Chief Crown Prosecutors.

12.14 This greater emphasis on regional decision-making may make sense in terms of the internal efficiency of the institution, but it is difficult to reconcile with the original premise for establishing an independent prosecuting authority, which was to ensure nationally consistent practices and policies and to break the localized differences in decision-making.

12.15 In the light of the depth of the criticisms of the CPS, the Government also appointed a former Court of Appeal judge, Sir Iain Glidewell, to conduct an inquiry into the organization. In 1999, his report concluded that: 'In various respects there has not been the improvement in the effectiveness and efficiency of the prosecution process which was expected to result from the setting up of the CPS in 1986.' In 2002, a further report from the independent CPS inspectorate identified a number of serious weaknesses in the system (HMCPSI, May 2002). In July 2009 the DPP published a plan 'to take the prosecution service to a new level of effectiveness, responsiveness and transparency'. In particular he highlighted the need for out-of-court disposals to be properly regulated, consistently applied, and publicly transparent.

Discontinuance

12.16 One of the issues which both reports considered was the claim that too many prosecutions were being dropped. The Glidewell report found that the CPS discontinued, on average, 12 per cent of cases. It found no firm evidence of inappropriate downgrading of charges, although it concluded that it suspected that this practice did occur.

12.17 Assessing whether or not a 12 per cent discontinuance rate is too high, or indeed, too low is not easy. The answer depends on the reason why cases are being dropped. If it is because they have been badly prepared and so are not ready for court, then clearly the system is failing. Some evidence to support the argument of inadequate preparation was found by Sir Iain in the high rate of directed acquittals.

12.18 His report criticized the fact that over half of all acquittals are directed by the judge after she or he has concluded that there is not sufficient evidence for the case to continue. A high proportion of directed acquittals indicates that the prosecution is proceeding with cases which are not strong enough to put before a jury. However, even in such cases the failing may not be the fault of the CPS but rather, as the CPS has sometimes claimed, the police who carried out the investigation.

12.19 In addition, many discontinuances occur because witnesses for the prosecution fail to attend court or do not give the same version of events once they do take the witness stand. It is difficult to see how the CPS could prevent this happening or avoid dropping cases once it does. It should also be remembered that directed acquittals make up a very small proportion of all cases which are prosecuted and that the success rate of cases which do reach a verdict is high.

12.20 The dilemma which the CPS faces is that if it discontinues a high proportion of cases this suggests that it is failing in its duty to bring offenders to court. However, if it rarely discontinues, it can be accused of simply rubber-stamping the decisions of the police and failing to provide a rigorous and independent scrutiny process. Without detailed research on the reasons why cases are dropped or proceeded with it is difficult to determine what the 'right' level of discontinuance should be. Nevertheless, the CPS inspectorate report in 2002 concluded that the approach of the CPS: 'too often tended to be one of only considering any weaknesses, rather than also playing a more proactive role in ... trying to build or develop a case'.

12.21 Some of the criticism of discontinuance has focused on the approach of the CPS to cases which involve the prosecution of suspects in positions of authority. In particular, there has been concern about the way the CPS applies the evidential test in cases involving corporate manslaughter and police malpractice. The decision not to prosecute a number of police officers involved in cases of deaths in custody in 1999 led to a critical inquiry by Judge Gerald Butler. He concluded that in these cases the CPS had taken an unnecessarily pessimistic view of the chances of securing a conviction.

12.22 A year later in *R v DPP, ex p Jones* (2000), the High Court came to a similar conclusion in relation to the decision not to prosecute in a case of corporate manslaughter. The family of a worker killed while unloading a ship at a dock brought a successful action for judicial review of the decision of the CPS not to prosecute his employer.

The Court held that the CPS had behaved 'irrationally' and not considered the law properly in deciding that there was not a realistic prospect of success. It directed the DPP to reconsider the decision.

12.23 One explanation for the high rate of discontinuance in cases involving powerful or authoritative defendants is that the traditional approach to the evidential test has been to ask whether a properly directed jury or bench of magistrates would be *likely* to convict, not whether they *ought* to convict. The danger with this approach is that it may simply reproduce the inherent biases of the trial system. In relation to the prosecution of people from groups who enjoy higher credibility than most defendants, magistrates and juries may be unlikely to convict because of a bias in favour of their evidence.

12.24 In such a case, the public-interest test might favour prosecution, particularly where the offence is one committed by a person serving the public. However, since the evidential threshold must be passed before the public interest is considered, the prosecution would not go ahead. If it is desirable on the grounds of public policy that public figures or powerful bodies who are suspected of committing offences are prosecuted, then consideration should be given to the CPS routinely adopting a lower evidential threshold in relation for these cases. However, whether such a practice would survive a challenge under the Human Rights Act 1998 is open to question since it might be held to be a discriminatory practice under Article 14.

12.25 The most recent change designed to reduce the discontinuance rate is for the CPS to advise the police on the initial charge in all cases so as to reduce the chances of over- or undercharging. As a result of the Glidewell report, criminal justice units which are jointly staffed by the CPS and police were set up in most police service areas. The Criminal Justice Act 2003 built upon this development to give the CPS a central role in the formulation of the charge at an early stage. This change is one example of the Government's response to the problem of the 'justice gap' – the difference between the numbers of crimes recorded and the numbers of crimes where the offender is brought to justice. Narrowing this gap is a key feature of the current official approach to reform of the prosecution process (CPS, 2002).

Disclosure

12.26 Another growing area of concern has been the approach of the CPS to the disclosure of evidence to the defence, in particular material such as witness statements or forensic evidence gathered by the police which the prosecution does not intend to use at trial and which might help the defence case. This issue is particularly important in the light of the greater investigative resources which the police almost always have compared to the defence. This means that the police may well gather evidence, such as witness statements, which supports the defence case but which the defence is not aware of.

12.27 In the early 1990s, the courts expanded the duty of the prosecution to disclose unused evidence to the defence in the cases of *Ward* (1993), *Davis* (1993), *Keane* (1994) and *Brown* (1994). However, these decisions attracted strong official criticism. In 1993, the report of the Royal Commission on Criminal Justice concluded that the arrangements for prosecution disclosure of unused matter had become unworkable and open to abuse by the defence. In response to these concerns, the Criminal Procedure and Investigations Act (CPIA) was passed in 1996, reducing the duty of the prosecution to disclose all the evidence it has in its possession.

12.28 The CPIA 1996 established a new three-stage process. It requires the CPS to make 'primary disclosure' of the material in its possession which, in the opinion of the prosecutor, 'might undermine the prosecution case'. Once this disclosure has been made, the defence is obliged to disclose its own case to the prosecution in general terms. If the defence fails to disclose its case, two things may happen. First, in Crown Court cases the jury may be invited to draw such adverse inferences 'as appear proper' in deciding whether the accused is guilty. Second, in both Crown Court and magistrates' courts cases the prosecution need not provide any secondary disclosure. This secondary disclosure requires the prosecution to disclose matter in its possession which: 'might reasonably be expected to assist the accused's defences as disclosed in the defence statement'.

12.29 The aim of the new statutory disclosure regime was to reduce the burden on the prosecution of having to reveal large amounts of material to the defence. The creation of a new obligation on the defence to disclose its case was intended to reduce the incidents of so-called 'ambush defences' in which the defence is produced in court at the last moment, too late for the prosecution effectively to check or challenge it.

12.30 In addition, the linking of prosecution and defence disclosure represents another example of the tendency to move towards inquisitorial approaches in the criminal justice system where both sides are required to set out their cases in advance. However, the danger which the CPIA rules pose is that by penalizing the defence for failing to disclose its defence through non-disclosure by the prosecution, innocent defendants may be convicted because they have not had access to vital material which would support their case.

12.31 The former Director of Public Prosecutions, David Calvert-Smith, expressed anxiety about the weaknesses of the disclosure regime and emphasized the need for prosecutors to exercise their discretion carefully in order to ensure that the defence has sight of relevant material. Lord Justice Auld in his review of the criminal courts concluded that the regime for disclosing unused material was not working properly and did not command the confidence of criminal practitioners (Auld, Chapter 10, para 163). The Criminal Justice Act 2003 included a number of provisions relating to disclosure of unused material. Most were designed to ensure fuller disclosure by the defence. The changes did little to address the concerns of defence solicitors that they are being denied access to important material which supports their case. However, this problem may arise not because prosecutors have failed to disclose evidence to the defence, but rather because it has not been passed on by the police to the CPS in the first place. The loss or suppression of relevant material at an early stage in the investigation is particularly difficult to identify and remedy.

Discrimination

12.32 The most recent problem to hit the CPS has been the allegation of racist practices both in relation to the decision to prosecute and in terms of staff employment, promotion and treatment. In 2000, a senior prosecutor brought a successful action against the CPS in the employment tribunal for race and sex discrimination. In 2001, an independent report commissioned by the CPS found that the service was suffering from 'institutional racism'– the term used by the MacPherson report in relation to the police to describe the situation where the procedures and practices of the institution result in racist outcomes, irrespective of the attitudes of the individuals who work for it (Denman, 2000).

12.33 These findings were reinforced by the CPS Inspectorate report in 2002 which concluded that: 'In a significant proportion of racist incident cases, the charges selected and pursued by the CPS do not reflect the seriousness of the offending or give the courts adequate sentencing powers.' Although the former DPP, David Calvert-Smith, publicly stated his determination to address this problem both in terms of staff treatment and prosecuting decisions, the findings of the two reports represented another blow to the confidence and reputation of the organization.

Summary

12.34 The CPS was set up to ensure independence in the prosecution process. Thus far, it has failed to provide the level of competence, efficiency and fairness which had been hoped for. Some progress has, however, been made, but there is some way to go before it fulfils the goals for which it was created. In 2002, the Attorney-General, Lord Goldsmith, identified three stages in the development of the CPS. The first, from 1986–1999, was characterized by: 'a long period of inadequate work, loss of public confidence and lack of self-worth'. From 1999, he claimed that the organization had improved as a result of restructuring and better resources. Finally, he argued that the CPS was about to move into a third phase in which it would become a 'fighter for justice' taking a more central role in all stages of the criminal justice process, from bringing charges to influencing sentencing. Whether or not the CPS can fulfil this new function and command public confidence in doing so depends largely on the extent to which the continuing problems in the areas of discontinuance, disclosure and discrimination discussed in this chapter can be successfully addressed.

FURTHER READING

The Glidewell Report *Review of the Crown Prosecution Service, Summary of Main Recommendations* (1998) (http://www.archive.official-documents.co.uk/document/cm39/3972/3972.htm).

Crown Prosecution Service Annual Report 2008–9 (http://www.cps.gov.uk/publications/reports/2008/).

Crown Prosecution Service Inspectorate Annual Report 2008–9 (http://www.official-documents.gov.uk/document/hc0809/hc08/0872/0872.pdf).

Lord Justice Auld *A Review of the Criminal Courts of England and Wales* (September 2001) (http://www.criminal-courts-review.org.uk/).

Michael Zander *Cases and Materials on the English Legal System* (2007, London: Butterworths), pp 241–273.

Crown Prosecution Service Inspectorate *Thematic Review of Attrition in the Prosecution Process* (the Justice Gap) (2002).

The Government's Response to the Justice Committee Report on the Draft Constitutional Renewal Bill (provisions relating to the Attorney General) (2009) (http://www.justice.gov.uk/publications/docs/CM-7689.pdf).

Crown Prosecution Service *The Public Prosecution Service – Setting the Standard* (2009) (http://www.cps.gov.uk/news/articles/the_public_prosecution_service_setting_the_standard/).

USEFUL WEBSITES

Crown Prosecution Service website home page
http://www.cps.gov.uk/

Crown Prosecution Service Inspectorate website home page
http://www.hmcpsi.gov.uk/

SELF-TEST QUESTIONS

1   Why was the CPS established?

2   What are the two tests which the CPS must apply in determining whether or not to proceed with a prosecution?

3   What is meant by the claim that the CPS suffers from 'institutional racism'?

4   'My vision is of a world class prosecuting service, that reduces crime, protects the public, by dealing effectively with criminal behaviour, by protecting and respecting the rights of victims and witnesses, and by inspiring the confidence of the communities that we serve.' Kier Starmer DPP (2009). How far is the CPS from realizing this vision?

13

The trial process

SUMMARY

This chapter describes the process whereby cases are allocated to the magistrates' court or the Crown Court for trial and outlines the trial process in the two courts for both adult defendants and young people. It highlights the tendency to adopt more inquisitorial approaches at trial such as the relaxation of strict rules of evidence. It emphasizes the central and growing role of guilty pleas and the possible explanations for the differences in the rates of guilty pleas in the Crown Court and magistrates' courts. It concludes by reviewing the sentencing process and the tension between executive and judicial control of this aspect of the criminal justice process.

13.1 By the time a criminal case reaches court for trial, it is very near the top of the justice pyramid. In order to have reached that stage a series of discretionary decisions must have been made. The crime must have been reported, the police must have decided to record the offence and investigate it and, having identified a suspect, to arrest and then charge him or her. Finally, the CPS must have exercised its discretion to proceed with the case. Of the estimated 15 million crimes committed each year, a total of approximately 1.4 million cases make it through this process. The great majority of these, about 1.3 million, are dealt with in the magistrates' courts, with the remaining 100,000 going on to the Crown Court.

Deciding on venue

13.2 All criminal cases start life in the magistrates' court. Whether a case stays to be tried in the magistrates' court or is sent up to the Crown Court depends on a number of factors. The first is the seriousness of the offence. Crimes such as homicide, rape and robbery are classified as 'indictable only' and may only be tried on indictment in the Crown Court. At the other end of the scale, 'summary only' offences (eg minor motoring offences and low value criminal damage) are the least serious and may only be tried in the magistrates' court. In between these two are a range of 'either way' offences (eg theft) which, as the name suggests, may be tried in either the Crown Court or the magistrates' court.

13.3 When the CPS introduces an either way case in the magistrates' court they will tell the magistrates whether or not they think the offence is suitable for summary trial or should go up to the Crown Court. It is then for the magistrates to decide whether or not they are willing to hear it. As their range of penalties is restricted, currently a maximum fine of £5,000 and/or 12 months' imprisonment, they will only agree to try a case if they consider that an appropriate penalty in case of a conviction is within their powers.

13.4 If the magistrates decide that the case is too serious and must go to the Crown Court, the defendant has no option but to be tried by a jury. However, if they decide to keep the matter in the magistrates' court the defendant has the right *not* to consent to summary trial, but to demand trial by jury in the Crown Court. This is what is meant by the defendant's right to trial by jury. It is a right which only arises in the case of either way offences which the magistrates have agreed to try.

Jury trial

13.5 For many years now, the existence of a defendant's right to elect trial has been the topic of considerable public debate. Critics of the system argue that it allows professional criminals to put off the day of the trial and to clog up the more costly higher courts with less serious cases in the hope that the case will be dropped or the jury will acquit. They also argue that no other country gives the defendant the right to choose which court to be tried in and that the decision should be made by the courts on the basis of the seriousness of the offence.

13.6 Supporters of the right claim that jury trial is a cornerstone of the democratic system and that trial by one's peers is a right which goes back to the Magna Carta of 1215. They point to the many 'either way' cases in which defendants have elected trial in the Crown Court and been acquitted by juries reaching so-called 'perverse' verdicts which reflect the jury's view that the case should never have been brought or that the law is oppressive. In recent years, in cases where the evidence of guilt is clear, juries have acquitted protesters charged with criminal damage of genetically modified crops and people charged with possession of cannabis who were suffering from painful illnesses and took the drug to ease their symptoms.

13.7 When the Labour Government came to power in 1997 it was persuaded that the decision as to where the case should be heard should be left to the magistrates and that cost savings of up to £100 m per year could be made if less serious cases were tried summarily. However, resistance to the move was strong. Two Bills introduced to remove the right were defeated in the House of Lords.

13.8 In 2003, the Government again sought to curb the right to jury trial. Under the provisions of the Criminal Justice Act, it allowed for future measures to be introduced that would remove serious and complex fraud trials from the jury system so that they could be heard by a judge alone. The provisions attracted considerable opposition as the 'thin edge of the wedge' in the ongoing process of eroding the jury system, and plans to introduce the changes were shelved. The provisions of the 2003 Act which allow a case to be heard by a judge alone in the case of jury tampering are, however, in force. Applying this provision, on 18 June 2009, the Court of Appeal allowed the first-ever Crown Court trial to be held without a jury (*R v T, B, C, H* 2009).

13.9 Despite the failure to date of these legislative initiatives, other reforms have had an indirect impact on the jury system. Most importantly, the increase in the custodial sentencing powers of magistrates from 6 to 12 months in the Criminal Justice Act 2003 was intended to encourage magistrates to try more cases themselves and reduce the number of jury trials by about 6,000 per year.

Proceedings in the magistrates' courts

13.10 In approximately 90 per cent of cases in the magistrates' court the defendant pleads guilty and the role of the magistrates is limited to deciding on sentence (outlined below). A contested trial is therefore a relatively rare event in the magistrates' court. Most trials will last from one hour to a day, with an average time of one to one and a half hours. The prosecution may outline what it aims to prove in a short opening, or more likely will call its witnesses straight away.

13.11 The prosecution advocate, who will be either a member of the CPS or an agent employed by the CPS on a daily basis (a solicitor or barrister), will draw out evidence from the witness in what is known as 'examination in chief'. The defence advocate (again either a barrister or solicitor) or the defendant him- or herself, may then challenge any of the evidence, or try to discredit the credibility of the witness in what is known as 'cross-examination'. The prosecutor then has the right to conduct a 're-examination' to clear up any points arising from cross-examination. When the advocates have finished their questioning, the magistrates may wish to clarify some points and may ask their own questions.

13.12 Once the prosecution has called all its witnesses, which in the daily practice of the magistrates' courts are likely to be police officers, it will close its case. The defence may, at this stage, ask the court to discharge the defendant on the basis that there is no case to answer. The court then has to ask itself whether a reasonable tribunal, properly directed, *could* (not would) convict on the basis of what it had heard so far. The court may ask itself the same question without a defence application, but in practice such an intervention is rare.

13.13 On the assumption that the court finds that there is a case to answer, or if no submission of 'no case to answer' is made, it is the turn of the defence. The defence is under no obligation to call any evidence at all. It is for the prosecution to prove its case beyond reasonable doubt, and the defendant need not give nor call any evidence, which would be liable to testing by cross-examination. In practice most defendants do wish to give their side of the story from the witness box, and the process of examination in chief, cross-examination, re-examination and questions from the bench is repeated.

13.14 When the defence witnesses have been called the defence may sum up its case through an address to the bench. Lay magistrates may, and often do, call for any comments on the law from their legally qualified clerk, and indeed the advocates may also make some legal points even at this stage. In the great majority of cases tried summarily, however, it is the facts which are in issue and there is very little law involved. The magistrates will then retire to discuss the matter and return to court with their verdict.

13.15 If it is 'not guilty' the case ends there, possibly with a further debate on costs. If it is guilty, then the process moves towards sentence. A simple matter may be dealt with at once, but often the sentencing decision is postponed to an adjourned date for a variety of reasons. Perhaps the bench will be considering a community sentence or imprisonment, in which case in the great majority of cases they will need a report from the probation service about the defendant.

Proceedings in the Crown Court

13.16 The work of the Crown Court resembles more closely than the magistrates' courts the popular image of a criminal court and full trials are regular occurrences. Nevertheless, much of the court's time is taken up with other matters such as bail applications, appeals from the magistrates' courts, guilty pleas, and pre-trial reviews. These shorter hearings are often listed for the mornings, leaving the rest of the day free for a trial. In comparison with the magistrates' courts, the proceedings are relatively formal and ritualized.

13.17 The judge is referred to as 'My Lord' if a High Court judge or 'Your Honour' if a circuit judge or recorder. Judge and counsel wear gowns and wigs. Supporters of these trappings argue that they instil respect for the proceedings and reinforce continuity. Critics say that they are archaic, intimidating, and alienating. In 1992, the then Lord Chancellor, Lord Mackay, and the then Lord Chief Justice, Lord Taylor, both came out in favour of the removal of wigs, arguing that they detract from, rather than strengthen, the dignity of the court. Since then more senior judges have expressed their support for the removal of wigs.

13.18 Interestingly, a major survey of the Crown Court carried out by the Royal Commission on Criminal Justice in 1992 found that 88 per cent of jurors thought that judges should retain their wigs. Pressure for reform of court dress has most recently come from solicitor advocates who are not allowed to wear wigs and claim that this undermines their authority and suggests to the jury that they are second-class lawyers. In 2008 the Lord Chief Justice, Lord Phillips, announced that solicitor-advocates would be entitled to wear wigs in criminal cases.

13.19 The trial procedure in the Crown Court differs in some respects from the magistrates' courts. Before being asked whether he or she pleads guilty or not guilty, the defendant is 'arraigned' before the Court to answer the indictment, which, in practice, means being asked to confirm his or her name and address. If the defendant pleads not guilty a jury is sworn in. The jury of 12 women and men are there to decide all questions of fact, leaving the judge to decide on the law and, if necessary, the sentence. At a summary trial, these tasks are performed by the magistrates alone with the assistance of the clerk. The presentation of the prosecution and defence cases proceeds broadly in the same way as in the magistrates' courts.

13.20 In serious cases each side may have two counsel, a senior (usually a Queen's Counsel) and a junior. In contrast with summary trials where defendants often appear without a lawyer, it is rare for a defendant to be unrepresented in the Crown Court and legal aid is much more commonly available than for summary hearings because of the greater seriousness of the offences. Once the defence counsel has finished his or her closing speech, the judge explains the law to the jury and summarizes the evidence for them.

13.21 This aspect of the trial is controversial as it gives the judge a role in the facts of the case. The judge is in a position to stress some aspects of the evidence and play down others, thus influencing the jury's view of the case. Even the best judges can find it hard to produce a totally balanced, fair and accurate summing-up, particularly in a long or hard case. They do not always succeed and appeals are sometimes based on the grounds that the summing-up was partial or biased. In the US, judges do not sum up on the facts, and some commentators have suggested that England and Wales should adopt this system.

13.22 After the summing-up the jury will retire to consider its verdict, which must initially be unanimous. If no decision is reached after some hours of deliberations, the judge will recall the jury and inform them that she or he can accept a majority verdict if they cannot reach a unanimous decision. The judge will send them back to try to do so. If full agreement is still not reached, an 11:1 or 10:2 majority will be accepted. Anything less, and the result is described as a 'hung jury' and the jury will be discharged. The CPS will then decide whether to proceed to retry the case before a new jury.

13.23 If the defendant is convicted the judge will often adjourn to consider the sentence and for social enquiry reports to be prepared if necessary. At the sentencing hearing the defence will usually present a plea in mitigation to the judge which sets out the reasons why she or he should pass a lenient sentence.

The trial process for young defendants

13.24 The description above applies to the trial of adults. For young people, ie under 17 years old, the process is rather different. For most cases, even relatively serious offences, the young person will be tried summarily in the magistrates' court sitting as the Youth Court. These hearings are conducted in private and the identity of the defendant cannot be made public without the permission of the court.

13.25 The process is intended to be less intimidating than in an adult court and only magistrates who have received special training can sit in the Youth Court. In practice, the extent to which the needs of the child or young person are accommodated differs from court to court. This is partly because there is an unresolved tension within the court system as to whether the youth justice process should prioritize the welfare of the young person or the protection of society from crime and the punishment of offenders.

13.26 Only in much more serious cases are young people tried in the Crown Court. Before 1999, such cases were very similar in procedure to an adult trial. However, in 1999 two boys convicted of killing a 2-year-old child went to the European Court of Human Rights arguing that their right to a fair trial had been breached because they were tried when aged 10 and 11 in a full adult court. The Court upheld their claim, finding that the proceedings were inappropriate for defendants of their age, having at times been frightening and beyond their levels of understanding (*V and T v United Kingdom* (1999)).

13.27 As a result of the ruling, the Lord Chief Justice, Lord Woolf, issued a Practice Direction regarding the conduct of Crown Court trials for those under 17. The changes which it instituted included the requirement that young children should usually not sit in the dock but in the main well of the court with their family and lawyers. It also encouraged the removal of wigs and the use of shorter periods sitting in court which accommodated the concentration levels of young defendants.

13.28 In 2002, the new procedure was applied in the trial arising from the murder of South London schoolboy Damilola Taylor. The accused, who were in their mid-teens, did not sit in the dock (which was instead given to journalists!) and wigs were not worn. The changes were widely considered to have been successfully implemented and it will be interesting to see whether the arguments for removal of wigs and unnecessary formalities in adult trials will be boosted by the reforms of trials of young people.

Evidence

13.29 Just as the procedure of a criminal trial broadly follows that of a civil hearing, the rules regarding the admissibility of evidence are in outline the same, although with some important differences. Being a common law system, the rules of evidence are, compared to a civil law jurisdiction, relatively strict and formal. The basic rule is that evidence must be relevant to the issues in dispute for it to be allowed in evidence. However, not all relevant evidence will be allowed in. Where the judge or magistrates believe that the prejudice which it would induce outweighs its probative value it is usually excluded.

13.30 Under the common law, certain types of evidence, such as a defendant's previous convictions, were felt to be so prejudicial that a rule prevented these being admitted. Relevant evidence, such as hearsay evidence, may also be excluded if it is not possible to test it in court. A simple example of hearsay evidence is when someone comes to court to explain what another person has told her or him as evidence of the truth of that statement. Because the person with the knowledge of the statement is not there in court it is not possible to cross-examine them effectively about it.

13.31 However, these rules are complicated by the fact that many exceptions to them have grown up under the common law. For example, defendants' previous convictions can be admitted if they 'lose their shield' by attacking the credibility of the prosecution witnesses. This means that if, as often happens, a defendant argues that the police are lying when they say that he made a confession in the police car, or that they found drugs on him, the police are then entitled to cast doubt on his credibility by showing that he has previously been found guilty of a crime by a court. Similarly, there are many exceptions to the hearsay rule; for example, if someone dies their written evidence can usually be read out in court.

13.32 Over the years, these rules and exceptions have built up into a complex law of evidence which lawyers, magistrates and judges must be familiar with. However, the trend in recent years has been towards the relaxation of these rules and the tendency to allow in a much wider range of evidence. This change is an example of the more general move towards the inquisitorial approach to the trial process.

13.33 Just as the area of pre-trial disclosure has developed a 'cards on the table' approach which is more typical of a civil law system, so at trial there is an increasing willingness to allow in all relevant evidence and for the court to give it whatever weight seems appropriate. The Criminal Justice Act 2003 included provisions which extended the circumstances in which previous convictions or misconduct on the part of defendants or witnesses should be allowed to be raised in court. This change is evidence of how far attitudes towards this issue have shifted in recent years. In 1989, Professor Michael Zander, commenting on the suggestion of the police that there should be limited disclosure of previous convictions, was able to say that ' ... there is not the slightest prospect of the proposal being implemented. At no time since 1972 has there been any significant level of support for the idea – even the police have apparently felt that it was not worth promoting' (1989, pp 195–196). The 2003 Act also extended the circumstances in which hearsay evidence could be introduced.

13.34 One argument against this more open approach to evidence is that some rules are required to ensure that the system functions fairly by maintaining some 'equality of arms' between the prosecution and defence and by preventing breaches of defendants' human rights. The relaxation of the rules of evidence poses a particular problem in terms of human rights for the system in England and Wales because of the reliance on lay adjudicators, magistrates and juries, in contrast to the civil law jurisdictions which make much more use of professional judges. The stricter rules of evidence in England and Wales are partly based on the assumption that lay participants are less able than professional judges to attach the appropriate weight to, say, a defendant's previous convictions and are more likely to be unduly prejudiced by the knowledge of previous bad conduct. It is quite possible that this argument could form the basis of a challenge to the new law under the Human Rights Act 1998 as a breach of Article 6 on the grounds that defendants tried by a lay magistrate or juror will not receive a fair trial if their previous convictions are routinely put before the court.

13.35 One response to these criticisms is to say that even though the exclusionary rules are being increasingly whittled away, there has always been, and remains, a wide discretion on the part of the judge to exclude evidence which has been illegally or unfairly obtained. For example, under PACE, s 78, the judge can exclude evidence which would have an 'adverse effect on the fairness of the proceedings'. Under the common law, judges have always also had the power to prevent evidence being admitted if to do so would be an 'abuse of process' because, for example, it was obtained illegally.

13.36 In practice, this discretionary process has always worked best in the Crown Court where the judge could decide, in the absence of the jury, whether or not to exclude certain evidence. If the decision is to exclude, the jury then goes on to hear the case without any knowledge of the excluded evidence. In contrast, if magistrates decide that evidence should be excluded, they must then perform the superhuman task of putting out of their mind the knowledge of the evidence which they have already heard, in deciding on guilt.

Guilty pleas, sentence discounts, and charge bargaining

13.37 The principle that a defendant is innocent until proven guilty is often said to be the bedrock of the criminal justice system. Like many other time-honoured principles, it often applies more in theory than practice. The description of the trial process set out above only occurs in a minority of cases because over 70 per cent of defendants plead guilty (58 per cent in the Crown Court and 88 per cent in the magistrates' courts) so removing the necessity of proving guilt.

13.38 On the face of it, the fact that so many defendants plead guilty is not only inconsistent with the main principle underpinning the criminal justice system but also appears to run counter to the defendant's interests. Why plead guilty when you have a chance of being acquitted? The answer is found in the practice of plea bargaining, which takes two forms. In the first, the defendant agrees to plead guilty in return for a reduced sentence. In the second, he or she agrees to plead guilty to a less serious charge, for example a defendant charged with a malicious wounding, which is denied, may well be persuaded to plead guilty to the much lesser charge of assault occasioning actual bodily harm. Or alternatively, if a defendant is charged with four or five offences, the prosecution may agree to drop one or two of them if the defendant pleads guilty to the others.

13.39 Until recently the courts did not officially recognize that plea bargaining existed and judges were not willing to enter into any deals in relation to sentence. However, it was common for defence counsel to speak to the judge privately to be given some indication of the likely sentence in the event of a guilty plea. The Royal Commission on Criminal Justice Crown Court survey in 1992 found that 88 per cent of barristers and 67 per cent of judges believed that there should be a 'realistic discussion of plea' between counsel and judge. The Director of Public Prosecutions agreed and argued that: 'It can be done without putting pressure on defendants – that is something you must never do.' However, critics of the change feared that such a move would add to the pressure on defendants to plead guilty.

13.40 Although the more open and formal plea-bargaining process recommended by the Royal Commission has not been implemented, in practice it is now openly acknowledged that defendants who plead guilty are entitled to a discount of between one-third to one-quarter of their sentence depending on how early the guilty plea is entered. As a result of a recommendation by the Royal Commission, this was given legislative effect in the Criminal Justice and Public Order Act 1994, s 48, which states that when determining what sentence to pass in relation to an offender who has pleaded guilty the court shall take into account (a) the stage in the proceedings for the offence at which the offender indicated his or her intention to plead guilty, and (b) the circumstances in which this indication was given. Lord Justice Auld in his report supported the increasingly open and formal plea-bargaining arrangements by recommending the introduction of a graduated scheme of sentence discounts with higher discounts for earlier pleas and a system of advanced indication of sentence for a defendant considering a guilty plea. This proposal is partially implemented in the Criminal Justice Act 2003 which states that the court must take into account the stage in the proceedings at which the offender indicated his or her intention to plead guilty and the circumstances in which this indication was given.

13.41 In most cases, where the defence and prosecution have agreed to accept a guilty plea to a lesser charge, the judge accepts this decision. However, the court is not obliged to do so and can order the prosecution to proceed on the original charge. One high-profile example of such a case arose in the trial of the 'Yorkshire Ripper', Peter Sutcliffe, who was charged with the murders of a number of women in 1981. He agreed to plead guilty to manslaughter on the grounds of diminished responsibility and the prosecution accepted that offer. However, the judge concluded that there was sufficient evidence for him to be tried for murder and required that the trial should proceed on that basis. The jury duly convicted him of murder, although he was transferred from the prison system to a secure hospital after his trial because of his mental disorder.

13.42 The obvious advantage for the prosecution of plea bargaining is that a conviction is secured without the risks and costs of a trial. The objection to this practice is that innocent defendants may be pressurized into pleading guilty while guilty defendants will receive a punishment which does not match the seriousness of the crime they committed. Plea bargaining has become an everyday feature of the system without which delays and cost would soar, but it is a practice which does not sit comfortably with the presumption of innocence and one which inevitably incurs a cost in terms of the risk of miscarriages of justice. Although plea bargaining is likely to continue, there are calls to formalize the process and in 2008 the Attorney-General published a consultation on the *Introduction of a Plea Negotiation for Fraud Cases in England and Wales.*

Differences in guilty plea rates

13.43 One of the most notable features of the guilty plea rate is that it is significantly higher in the magistrates' courts where trials are relatively rare occurrences. One explanation for this discrepancy is that when a defendant intends to plead guilty in relation to an either way offence he or she is much more likely to elect for the case to be dealt with by the magistrates, whose sentencing powers are more limited than those of a judge in the Crown Court.

13.44 Another explanation may be the roll of the Bind Over. This order allows the court to bind a defendant over to be of good behaviour and/or to keep the peace, for a specified time, with the penalty that he or she must forfeit a sum of money in the event of misbehaviour within the time limit. In order to Bind Over the court must be convinced that the defendant must have demonstrated by past behaviour which was in some way blameworthy that there is a danger of a future breach of the peace.

13.45 In practice, an agreement to avoid a trial by offering a Bind Over is usually made between the CPS and defence advocates and then rubber-stamped by magistrates, with little or no regard to the criteria. An endorsement of the advocates' decision to Bind Over, which results in no criminal conviction to the defendant and no necessity to prove the case by the prosecution, can often be plea bargaining under another name.

13.46 A final reason why defendants who wish to plead 'not guilty' to an either way offence elect trial before a jury is because there is a higher conviction rate in the magistrates' courts than the Crown Court. One explanation for the higher conviction rate is that magistrates become 'case hardened', in that they hear similar defences and allegations (for example of police lies and pressure) many times and tend to adopt a more sceptical attitude towards defendants' accounts of events.

13.47 Moreover, magistrates, although usually lay people, are regular players in the criminal justice system and have a vested interest in ensuring its smooth running which may mean that they instinctively tend to support the police and prosecution who appear before their court on a daily basis. Whatever the explanation for the discrepancy in the conviction rates between the two courts, its effect is that an acquittal is a relatively rare event in the magistrates' courts.

Sentencing

13.48 From what has been said about guilty pleas and the rate of conviction, it should come as no surprise that one of the principal activities of magistrates is sentencing. With the majority of cases being uncontested, magistrates are sometimes called upon to sentence many times in a day's sitting. Sentencing may be for a day's list of those charged with having no TV licence, or vehicle tax, where lists can be packed with 80 or 90 cases in a morning, and the same in an afternoon, or a few sentences to be passed in both uncontested and contested cases. The range of penalties, from discharges to custody, is the same as in the Crown Court, but fines are restricted to £5,000 and imprisonment to 12 months. In practice, the most common sentence is the fine, but large numbers of people are sent to prison each year by magistrates, albeit for relatively short lengths of time.

13.49   Research has shown that there are major variations in sentencing practice through-out the country. In response to this problem, the Criminal Justice Act 2003 included a provision for a new Sentencing Guidelines Council (SGC) to improve consistency for offences across the board. The SGC began work in 2004 and has already pro-duced a number of important guidelines.

13.50   The process of sentencing in the Crown Court is essentially the same as the magis-trates' courts, but with fewer restrictions on the sentencers' powers. The discretion of the judges in sentencing is limited only by the statutory maxima set down for many offences and by sentencing guidelines which are periodically set out by the Court of Appeal to ensure consistency in sentencing practices between different courts in relation to similar cases.

13.51   The freedom to tailor a sentence to each particular case, in contrast to jurisdictions such as the US which have much stricter mandatory sentencing tariffs, is, however, currently under threat. The 'two strikes and you're out' legislation introduced in the Crime (Sentences) Act 1997 which imposed mandatory life sentences in the case of certain repeat offenders was one example of the growing determination on the part of politicians to curb judicial discretion and impose more rigid (and punitive) responses to certain crimes.

13.52   The judges have strongly resisted this trend, arguing publicly against the erosion of their discretion. They have had some success in fighting their corner. The effective-ness of the 1997 legislation was reduced by the House of Lords under the Human Rights Act 1998 as a breach of the right to a fair trial. The court 'read in' to the statute a discretion on the part of the judges not to pass a life sentence where the interests of justice so required (*Offen* (2001)).

13.53   Similarly, the right of the Home Secretary to set the tariff in the case of life sentences has been gradually dismantled by the European Court of Human Rights and the domestic courts and the power has been transferred to the judges (*Anderson* (2002)). Nevertheless, the Government is planning to introduce further restrictions on their discretion and the battle for control of sentencing between judges and politicians is far from over.

13.54 Sentencing in the youth justice system has been reformed by the Criminal Justice and Immigration Act 2008 which introduced a new generic community sentence for children and young people called the 'youth rehabilitation order'. The Act also requires the sentencing court to have regard to the 'principal aim of the youth justice system' which is 'to prevent offending (or re-offending) by persons aged under 18'.

Summary

13.55 Although the criminal trial is the final outcome for only a small fraction of criminal cases, this does not mean that only the most serious cases reach that point. Much of the work of the courts is relatively mundane and routine. The bulk of magistrates' courts cases are minor offences in which the defendant pleads guilty and receives a fine in proceedings lasting less than an hour.

13.56 Nevertheless, the sheer quantity of cases heard in the lower courts means that a significant number involve issues in which the reputation, livelihood or liberty of the defendant is at stake. In those cases, the quality of summary justice received does not always match the seriousness of the issue. By contrast, proceedings in the Crown Court represent the upper end of the market in terms of time, resources and quality of personnel. The continuing erosion of the range of cases which can be heard in the Crown Court and the transfer of more serious cases to be disposed of summarily undoubtedly saves money, but it also raises pressing questions about the standards of justice found in the magistrates' courts.

FURTHER READING

Criminal Justice Act 2003 (http://www.hmso.gov.uk/acts/acts2003/20030044.htm).

Lord Justice Auld *A Review of the Criminal Courts of England and Wales* (2001) (http://www.criminal-courts-review.org.uk/).

Michael Zander *A Matter of Justice* (1987, London: Tauris), pp 192–203.

Michael Zander *The State of Justice* (2000, London: Sweet and Maxwell), ch 4.

Andrew Ashworth and Mike Redmayne *The Criminal Process* (2005, Oxford: Oxford University Press).

Attorney General's Office *Introduction of a Plea Negotiation Framework for Fraud Cases in England and Wales* (2008) (http://www.attorneygeneral.gov.uk).

USEFUL WEBSITES

Publications, links and news on the criminal justice system
http://www.homeoffice.gov.uk

Judgments, history, and statistics on the criminal justice system
http://www.cjsonline.org/home.html

Guide to the criminal justice system of England and Wales
http://www.cjsonline.gov.uk/the_cjs/

Judicial statistics 2007
http://www.official-documents.gov.uk/document/cm74/7467/7467.asp

Sentencing Guidelines Council
http://www.sentencing-guidelines.gov.uk/

SELF-TEST QUESTIONS

1   Describe the process by which a case is allocated to the magistrates' court or the Crown Court.

2   What is meant by a 'hung jury'?

3   Give three possible reasons for the higher rate of guilty pleas in the magistrates' court than Crown Court.

4   List one advantage and one disadvantage of reducing the restrictions on the admission of evidence in court.

Criminal appeals and the post-appeal process

SUMMARY

This chapter describes the appeal process from the magistrates' court and the Crown Court and the hurdles which convicted defendants face in getting to the Court of Appeal. It analyses the confusion over the interpretation of the term 'unsafe' in the Criminal Appeal Act 1995 (CAA 1995) and traces the historical reluctance of the Court of Appeal to quash convictions where there is concern about their safety. It argues that further reform of the CAA 1995 to encourage a more liberal approach by the judges is likely to have less effect than a change of attitude on the part of the judges of the Court of Appeal. It explains the background to the establishment of the Criminal Cases Review Commission and assesses its record to date. It also analyses the appeal process to the House of Lords, Attorney-General's references, and prosecution appeals. It concludes that tension caused by the competing goals of ensuring finality to proceedings, due process, and factually accurate verdicts will continue to run through the appeal and post-appeal process.

14.1 At the top of the criminal justice pyramid sits the appeal and post-appeal process. Only a tiny fraction of cases ever reach the Court of Appeal and only a handful go on to be reviewed by the final review body, the Criminal Cases Review Commission (CCRC). However, although these are small in number they often involve serious or high-profile cases. The outcome of the appellate and review process therefore can be very significant for the lives of the individuals concerned and for public confidence in the system. Where convictions for offences such as murder and rape are overturned on appeal or later identified as a miscarriage of justice and referred back to the

Court by the CCRC, public confidence in the system of investigation, prosecution and trial can be undermined for many years.

14.2 Over the years, a number of high-profile cases have generated a great deal of controversy. In the 1980s and early 1990s in particular, a series of terrorism cases including the Guildford Four, the Birmingham Six and the Maguire Seven were overturned after long campaigns questioning the safety of the convictions. A common feature of these cases was the emergence of new evidence about police malpractice, such as the fabrication of confessions or the mistreatment of suspects in custody.

14.3 Most of the cases had also been initially reviewed by the Court of Appeal and their convictions upheld, and the apparent failure of the Court to identify these cases as unsafe gave rise to widespread criticism of the appeal and post-appeal process and led to subsequent reform.

The structure of the appeal process

14.4 Although a small number of high-profile cases attract a significant amount of media coverage, most appeals go unreported. The majority of cases are from the magistrates' court and appeal lies to the Crown Court where they are heard by two magistrates and a judge. About 13,000 appeals are heard each year from the lower courts and there is an absolute right of appeal against fact and law from the judgment of the magistrates. Appeals on questions of law alone lie to the Divisional Court of the High Court by way of case stated.

14.5 In contrast, appeals from the Crown Court lie to the Court of Appeal (Criminal Division) and, interestingly, there is no automatic right of appeal in relation to these more serious cases. Permission must be granted by the Court of Appeal. In practice, a single High Court judge decides whether or not to grant leave on reading the application on paper without an oral hearing. If leave is refused there is an automatic right to renew the application to the full court.

Hurdles to the Court of Appeal

14.6 The Court of Appeal is a small body. Although all Court of Appeal judges are eligible to sit in the Criminal Division, most spend their time hearing civil appeals. There are usually four panels of judges hearing criminal appeals at any one time, almost always sitting in the Royal Courts of Justice in London. All the appeals against sentence and conviction from approximately 100 Crown Courts must be heard by this relatively small group of judges. To help the appeal judges to manage the Court's workload their numbers are supplemented by High Court and Circuit judges who sit with the Lords Justices.

14.7 About 8,000 applicants a year apply for permission to appeal, of which approximately 2,000 are successful. Most of these are appeals against sentence. Only about 2,000 defendants appeal against conviction each year, of which approximately 600 are given permission to appeal and heard by a full court of three judges. Of these, about one-third are successful.

14.8 The chances of a person convicted in the Crown Court having their conviction overturned is therefore very small indeed. On the face of it, the low appeal rate is difficult to explain. Why would anyone choose not to appeal? What has a convicted defendant got to lose? The answer is that just as the legal system provides the accused with incentives to plead guilty, so the convicted person faces a number of disincentives to appeal.

14.9 The first is that legal aid is only available for the preparation of the application for permission to appeal if counsel advises in favour of an appeal. If she or he does not consider that there are grounds for appeal, or if permission is not granted by the single judge, legal aid ends. Many convicted persons draft their own application and grounds of appeal, but the quality of these is often poor and very few are ever successful.

14.10 Another major disincentive is the so-called 'time loss' rules. These are set out in a practice direction which states that time spent in custody on appeal should not count against sentence in the case of frivolous or vexatious appeals. Many convicted defendants believe, quite mistakenly, that they face a real risk of serving a longer sentence if their appeal is unsuccessful. In practice, it is very rare for the court to order 'time loss' and any order will be for a maximum of 28 days.

14.11 One of the reasons why defendants are deterred by the time loss rules is that they are wrongly advised by their lawyers that there is a real danger that the Court will apply them. Overall the quality of advice and information provided to convicted defendants, particularly for those in prison, was found by the Royal Commission on Criminal Justice to be highly variable. Reviewing the evidence about the difficulties faced by potential appellants, the Commission concluded that the inconsistent standards and availability of legal advice and assistance were 'serious matters'. It proposed that the Law Society and Bar Council should clarify their guides to practitioners so that convicted persons would be ensured up-to-date and accurate advice about their prospects for appeal. We do not know whether or not these recommendations have led to improvements since 1993.

14.12 Finally, many defendants do not appeal because they know that the chances of success are small as a result of the restrictive approach which the court has taken to its powers to review convictions.

The approach of the Court of Appeal to its powers

14.13 Before 1907, when the first Criminal Appeal Act set up the Court of Criminal Appeal, there was, incredibly, no system for appealing against a conviction by a jury. Even though, in the nineteenth century and earlier, many defendants were sentenced to hard labour or death after a very cursory trial.

14.14 The Criminal Appeal Act 1907 gave the new court wide powers to overturn a conviction but, in practice, the judges interpreted these narrowly and were very reluctant to overturn a verdict, preferring to emphasize the importance of the sovereignty of the jury:

> Where there is evidence on which a jury can act and there has been a proper direction to the jury this court cannot substitute itself for the jury and re-try the case. That is not our function. If we took any other attitude it would strike at the very root of trial by jury. (*McGrath* 1949)

14.15 As a result of concerns about this approach in the following decades, a new Criminal Appeal Act was passed in 1966 which gave the Court the power to quash a conviction where there was an error of law, a procedural irregularity or where the conviction was 'unsafe or unsatisfactory'.

14.16 In 1969, in *Cooper* the Court appeared to have changed its attitude as a result of the new provisions. The Lord Chief Justice, Lord Widgery, stated that:

> Now our powers are somewhat different, and we are indeed charged to allow an appeal against conviction if we think that the verdict of the jury should be set aside on the ground that under all the circumstances of the case it is unsafe and unsatisfactory. That means that in cases of this kind the Court must in the end ask itself a subjective question, whether we are content to let the matter stand as it is, or whether there is not some lurking doubt in our minds which makes us wonder whether an injustice has been done.

14.17 In practice, however, the *Cooper* (1969) approach was rarely applied. The organization JUSTICE was only able to discover six reported cases between 1969 and 1989 where the Court had quashed a conviction on the basis of a 'lurking doubt' about the safety of the conviction.

14.18 By the time the Royal Commission on Criminal Justice was asked to review the criminal justice system in 1991, there was widespread concern that the Court was failing to identify and correct miscarriages of justice. However, there was no agreement about what changes were needed. The majority of the Commission felt that the statutory grounds of appeal should be reduced to one simple umbrella term; that the Court should quash a conviction if it 'is or may be unsafe'. A minority of the Commission considered, however, that this formula would mean that the Court would be less likely to quash a conviction when something had gone wrong in the pre-trial or trial process, such as a breach of PACE rules by the police.

14.19 The Commission was split over the question of what the Court should do in such a case when a procedural irregularity was serious but did not raise a possibility that the conviction was unsafe, in the sense that the defendant may be factually innocent, perhaps because of the presence of other overwhelming evidence. The minority felt serious failures in the procedure undermined the integrity of the criminal justice system so that the conviction should be quashed:

> The moral foundation of the criminal justice system requires that if the prosecution has employed foul means the defendant must go free even if he is plainly guilty. Where the integrity of the process is fatally flawed, the conviction should be quashed as an expression of the system's repugnance at the methods used by those acting for the prosecution.

14.20 In contrast, the majority of the Commission argued against allowing a conviction to be overturned when there was strong evidence that the defendant had committed the offence:

> In the view of the majority, even if they believed that quashing the convictions of criminals was an appropriate way of punishing police malpractice, it would be naïve to suppose that this would have any practical effect on police behaviour. In any case it cannot in their view be morally right that a person who has been convicted on abundant other evidence and may be a danger to the public should walk free because of what may be a criminal offence by someone else.

14.21 This disagreement goes to the heart of the appeal system. Is it there to ensure only that the innocent are not convicted, or does it also serve the function of setting standards and regulating the system?

14.22 In the event, the Government accepted a modified version of the majority recommendation. In the Criminal Appeal Act 1995, it gave the Court the power to quash the conviction on the simple ground that it is 'unsafe'. Almost immediately, in a series of cases, the Court confirmed the fears of those who argued that the Court would interpret the new provisions as a restriction on their power. In *Chalkley* (1998) the Court stated:

> ... in our view, whatever may have been the use by the Court of the former tests of 'unsatisfactoriness' and 'material irregularity,' they are not available to it now save as aids to determining the safety of the conviction ... The court has no power under the substituted

s 2(1) to allow an appeal if it does not think that the conviction is unsafe but is dissatisfied in some way with what went on at the trial.

14.23 However, since the passing of the Human Rights Act 1998, this narrow interpretation has given rise to the question of whether the Criminal Appeal Act 1995 is compatible with the right to a fair trial under Article 6 of the European Convention on Human Rights.

The effect of the Human Rights Act 1998 on the approach of the Court of Appeal

14.24 A considerable amount of conflicting case law has emerged on the question of whether a conviction which is secured after an unfair trial can be upheld as safe. Defence lawyers have argued that in such circumstances a conviction must be quashed, otherwise the Court would be failing to 'read and give effect to' the Criminal Appeal Act 1995 in a way which is compatible with the convention as it is obliged to do under HRA 1998, s 3.

14.25 In *Condron (No 2)* (2000) the European Court of Human Rights held that the conviction was not unsafe when the defendants had been convicted after an adverse inference had been drawn from their silence in the police station. The two defendants had claimed that they had been suffering from the effects of heroin withdrawal at the time and their solicitor advised them not to answer questions in the light of their condition. The Court in Strasbourg criticized the Court of Appeal's approach to the Criminal Appeal Act 1995, arguing that:

> The question of whether or not any rights of the defence guaranteed to an accused under Article 6 of the Convention were secured in any given case cannot be assimilated to a finding that his conviction was safe in the absence of any inquiry into the issue of fairness ...

14.26 The Court of Appeal in *Davis Rowe and Johnson* (2001) held that the two concepts of safety and fairness should be kept apart: 'we reject therefore that a finding of a breach of Article 6(1) by the ECHR leads inexorably to the quashing of the conviction'. Since *Condron*, the UK courts have produced a number of contradictory decisions about whether a conviction which results from an unfair trial will always be unsafe. Some have suggested that this must be the case:

> A breach of a defendant's constitutional right to a fair trial would inevitably result in the conviction being quashed. (*Mohammed (Allie) v The State* (1999))

> ... in our judgment, for a conviction to be safe, it must be lawful; and if it results from a trial which should never have taken place, it can hardly be regarded as safe. (*Mullen* (1999))

> if a defendant has been denied a fair trial it would almost be inevitable that the conviction would be regarded as unsafe. (Lord Woolf in *Togher* (2001))

14.27 In *Cranwell* (2001), the Court of Appeal appeared to retreat from the view that an unfair conviction would 'inevitably' (*Allie Mohammed* (1999)) or 'almost inevitably' (*Togher* (2001)) be unsafe and reverted to the line of reasoning in *Davis, Rowe and Johnson* that the strength of the evidence of guilt will be a factor in determining the safety of the conviction:

> Although in very many cases a trial which is unfair will result in a conviction which is unsafe, this is not necessarily the case. There may be cases, for example, in which, though there has been unfairness, the evidence of the guilt of the defendant is so strong that there can be no doubt that the verdict is safe.

14.28 More recently, Lord Steyn has stated that: 'It is well established that the guarantee of a fair trial under Article 6 is absolute: a conviction obtained in breach of it cannot stand' (*R v A (No 2)* (2001), para 38 referring to *Forbes* (2001)). However, he went on to say that: 'The only balancing permitted is in respect of what the concept of a fair trial entails: here account may be taken of the familiar triangulation of interests of the accused, the victim and society' (para 38).

14.29 But despite the authoritative ruling of the House of Lords that a conviction cannot stand in breach of Article 6, the Court of Appeal still appears to be following the approach it adopted in Cranwell. In *Alami and Botmeh* (2002) Rose LJ held:

> even if there were an assertable breach of Article 6, we would not regard that breach as, in itself, calling for any remedy other than a declaration of violation, unless, by virtue of the breach, the jury's verdicts were unsafe.

And in *Skuse* (2002) Rix LJ stated that '... had we held that there has been a breach of Article 6(1), we consider that we would not have been bound to hold that the conviction is unsafe'.

14.30 Thus the definition of what constitutes a fair trial remains within the discretion of the Court and it is clear that it is to be understood as a concept which refers to the trial as a whole, so that individual elements of unfairness do not necessarily render it in breach of Article 6 and so unsafe.

14.31 In the light of this confusion over the definition of an unsafe conviction, Lord Justice Auld has proposed that there should be a statutory amendment to the Criminal Appeal Act 1995 which clarifies how the term should be interpreted. He did not, however, say which approach was to be preferred. If the decision of the ECtHR in *Condron (No 2)* is followed, then the only amendment which would be compatible with the convention is one which recognizes the power to quash a conviction when the defendant may be factually guilty but has been convicted unfairly.

14.32　Such a statutory amendment would usefully establish the principle that unfair convictions are unsafe and help to stem the flow of contradictory decisions from the Court of Appeal. It would not, however, establish what types of error, irregularity or abuse of process constitute unfairness sufficient to amount to a breach of Article 6.

14.33　This problem is less likely to be solved by statutory amendment than by a change in attitude on the part of the Court of Appeal. The history of the Court's approach to its powers has been one of external pressure on the system to take a more liberal approach and to quash convictions more readily. This has been met by internal resistance on the part of the judges who are reluctant to interfere with the verdict of the jury and to open the floodgates to many more appeals.

14.34　The response to this problem has been to change the statutory wording of the Criminal Appeal Acts. But past experience suggests that this has had little effect on the Court's approach. The tension between the competing goals of the appeal process which underpins the Court's approach to its powers is not a problem which can be legislated away.

Appeals to the House of Lords

14.35　Appeals from the Court of Appeal lie to the Supreme Court (formerly the Appellate Committee of the House of Lords), which is the highest court of appeal for England and Wales (see chapter 2). It hears cases from the Divisional Court of the Queens Bench Division, the Court of Appeal and the High Court of Justice in Northern Ireland, but it does not have jurisdiction to hear criminal appeals from the High Court of Justiciary in Scotland. The Supreme Court decides appeals on questions of law of general public importance and all cases which are heard must be granted permission to appeal either by the Court of Appeal or by the Supreme Court itself. The criminal jurisdiction was only a relatively small aspect of the work of the, House of Lords which heard fewer than 20 criminal appeals each year.

The post-appeal process

14.36　Because of the seriousness of the effects of miscarriages of justice, the rejection of an appeal by the Court of Appeal was historically subject to a final, very limited power of review by the Home Secretary. Historically, this was exercised through the royal prerogative of mercy exercised on behalf of the monarch. This role was extended under the Criminal Appeal Act 1968 (originally given in the Criminal Appeal Act 1907, s 19) to a power to refer cases back to the Court of Appeal.

The role of the Home Secretary

14.37 The power of the Home Secretary to refer back cases to the Court of Appeal was a broad one. Under CAA 1968, s 17 he could refer back a case at any time: 'if he thinks fit'. In practice this power was exercised very sparingly. An average of six cases a year were referred back to the Court in the period between 1981 and 1992. This handful of cases was sifted from a total of around 700–800 petitions received by the Home Office each year.

14.38 Over a period of many years a number of criticisms emerged of the restrictive way in which successive Home Secretaries had interpreted their statutory powers. It was argued that they had consistently refused to refer back cases unless strong fresh evidence had emerged. Nor did they undertake a proactive role in seeking out that evidence where concerns about a case had been raised. Instead they relied upon lawyers and supporters of the convicted person, often working without funding, to produce fresh evidence.

14.39 When the Home Secretary did consider that investigation was needed because the first police investigation was flawed, he invariably instructed a police force to carry out that work, giving rise to the criticism that the police were being asked to investigate themselves. This approach was partly the result of the fact that the Home Office had very little funding or staff to carry out this task. There was also concern that the Home Office tended to operate in a secretive manner and was reluctant to disclose material to the convicted person or explain the reasoning behind its decisions. Finally, there was a view that it was constitutionally inappropriate for a member of the executive to be carrying out an essentially judicial task.

The Criminal Cases Review Commission

14.40 In the light of these criticisms, the proposal of the Royal Commission on Criminal Justice for the establishment of a new independent review body to replace the Home Office was probably the most predictable and least controversial of all its recommendations since there was almost universal support for the change. The RCCJ proposed that the new body would be better resourced and independent from the executive, and these proposals are broadly reflected in the provisions of the Criminal Appeal Act 1995 which established the Criminal Cases Review Commission.

14.41 The purpose of the Commission is to investigate and refer cases back to the Court. It has no powers to interfere with the verdict itself and a referral is treated by the Court of Appeal as a normal appeal under CAA 1995, s 9. The Commission must be made up of a minimum of 11 members, one of whom is the Chairman. Its members are appointed by the Queen on the recommendation of the Prime Minister. The Act specifies that the members will include both lawyers and lay persons.

14.42 In order for the Commission to refer back a case to the Court of Appeal, it must present an argument or evidence not raised at trial or on appeal other than in 'exceptional circumstances'. It must also consider that there is a 'real possibility' that the conviction would not be upheld by the Court if the reference were made. Thus, the approach of the CCRC is closely tied to that of the Court of Appeal. If the Court is unwilling to quash convictions in certain types of cases the CCRC is unable to refer those cases back, however strongly it considers the case for an appeal to be.

14.43 Despite this limitation, in general, the CCRC has been regarded as making a significant improvement to the post-appeal process. It had referred back many more cases than the Home Office and over half the cases it has referred back to the Court have been successful. In terms of its operation, a review by the Home Affairs Select Committee praised its 'professionalism, independence and openness'. Its main problem to date has been a large backlog of cases waiting to be dealt with, suggesting that it is a victim of its own success. In the first decade of its existence the CCRC received 10,288 applications, only 9,618 of which it had managed to deal with (a total of 376 applications resulted in referrals to the Court of Appeal and in 241 of those cases convictions were quashed). This backlog has led to criticisms that the CCRC is not prioritizing its case load correctly and is wasting its resources on investigating and referring back very old cases to the Court of Appeal where the defendant had died in prison or been executed many years earlier, such as *Mattan* (1998), *Bentley* (2001) and *Hanratty* (2002). However, in his evidence to the Home Affairs Select Committee the former Chairman, Sir Frederick Crawford, defended this approach. He argued that these were cases which it inherited from the Home Office when it was established and which they were under a duty to investigate in order to close the files one way or the other. He confirmed that once these cases had been dealt with, priority would be given to those who were currently in custody.

Prosecution appeals

14.44 Thus far this chapter has concerned appeals by the defence rather than the prosecution. Traditionally, the same principle which underpins the double jeopardy rule preventing a second prosecution of a defendant for the same offence has prevented the prosecution from appealing against an acquittal. However, although the prosecution does not have a general right to appeal against a conviction or sentence, there are a number of exceptions to this rule which have developed in recent years.

14.45 The first of these exceptions relates to acquittals in the magistrates' courts where the prosecution may appeal against a decision of the magistrates on a point of law or jurisdiction by way of case stated to the Divisional Court of the Queen's Bench Division (Magistrates' Courts Act 1980, s 111(1)). If the High Court upholds the appeal it can remit the case back to the magistrates' court to be redecided. No equivalent provision exists for prosecution appeals from the Crown Court. Under the Criminal Justice Act 1972, s 36, the Attorney-General has a power to refer an acquittal to the Court of Appeal on a point of law. However, the Court's decision does not affect the outcome in the particular case. The intention of the provision is to allow for errors of law to be put right so as to ensure accuracy and clarity in the law for future cases. The Court of Appeal, after it has given its view, can refer the case to the House of Lords for its opinion.

14.46 The one instance in which an appeal by the prosecution can affect the verdict arises where the prosecution alleges that an acquittal is 'tainted' under the Criminal Procedure and Investigations Act 1996, ss 54–57. This provision was passed as a result of a recommendation by the Royal Commission on Criminal Justice and gives the High Court the power to quash a conviction if satisfied that the acquittal would not have occurred had it not been for the interference with or intimidation of the jury. In practice, the provision does not appear to be used.

14.47 The power of the prosecution to appeal against a sentence is also a relatively new one. Under the Criminal Justice Act 1988, s 36, the Attorney-General has the power to refer an 'unduly lenient' sentence to the Court of Appeal which may increase the sentence as it sees fit. In contrast to the tainted acquittal provisions, this power is relatively frequently used. Between 2003 and 2006, the Crown appealed against 35 sentences, over half of which were increased by the Court of Appeal.

14.48 The most controversial development in the area of prosecution appeals has been the emergence of a debate about whether to give the prosecution a right of appeal when fresh evidence emerges after an acquittal which casts doubt on the verdict. The MacPherson report into the death of Stephen Lawrence recommended that 'consideration should be given to the Court of Appeal being given the power to permit prosecution after acquittal where fresh and viable evidence is presented' (MacPherson, 1999). A Law Commission report on the subject in 2001 proposed that the prosecution should be given the right to appeal against an acquittal by the jury where there is apparently reliable and compelling new evidence of guilt. This recommendation was limited to the offence of murder (Law Commission,

March 2001). In his review of the criminal courts, Sir Robin Auld adopted and extended the recommendations of the Law Commission report but argued that the prosecution right of appeal should not be limited to murder but extended to other grave crimes. These proposals were accepted by the Government and included in the Criminal Justice Act 2003.

14.49 In addition to this new right of appeal in certain cases involving fresh evidence, the Criminal Justice Act also incorporated a right for the prosecution to appeal against a ruling by the trial judge before and during trial which leads to the termination of the case. This provision was also put forward by Sir Robin Auld who proposed that the prosecution should be able to appeal against rulings such as the decision to stay a prosecution on the grounds of abuse of process or to direct the jury to acquit because there is no case to answer. The Attorney-General, Lord Goldsmith, has said that it is 'wholly wrong' that if a judge decides to bring a case to an end in such circumstances he should do so without the possibility of being challenged. In view of the significant proportion of cases in the Crown Court which result in acquittal after a judge's direction, this power represents an important change in the trial and appellate process and is likely to be exercised relatively frequently.

Summary

14.50 The recent extension of prosecution appeal rights is one further example of the shift towards a more victim-centred and prosecution-orientated criminal justice system in which the term miscarriages of justice is applied equally to a wrongful acquittal as a wrongful conviction. In practice, however, it is unlikely that the Court of Appeal will regularly overturn acquittals, any more than it has been willing to overturn convictions. This historical reluctance of the Court of Appeal to interfere with a jury verdict is perhaps the only example of consistency in its approach since it was set up in 1907. The pervasive feature of the appeal process is the lack of a coherent rationale for reviewing decisions of the trial courts. The explanation for this is found in the presence of the competing, and often irreconcilable, goals within the criminal justice system identified in chapter 10. The appellate process is an area in which the tension between these goals is particularly evident. The need to ensure finality in decision-making and to promote the efficient and cheap disposal of cases must always be balanced against the requirements of a fair system in which the risk of miscarriages of justice is minimized. The long history of contradictory decisions of the Court of Appeal concerning the circumstances in which an appeal will be heard and the definition of an 'unsafe' conviction is evidence of the unresolved, and perhaps unresolvable, nature of the tension between these underlying goals.

FURTHER READING

David Schiff and Richard Nobles 'Due Process and Dirty Harry Dilemmas: Criminal Appeals and the Human Rights Act' (2001) 64(6) Modern Law Review 911.

Lord Justice Auld *A Review of the Criminal Courts of England and Wales* (2001) ch 12. (http://www.criminal-courts-review.org.uk/chpt12.pdf).

Kate Malleson and Stephanie Roberts 'Streamlining and Clarifying the Appellate Process' (2002) Criminal Law Review 272.

David Schiff and Richard Nobles 'The Criminal Cases Review Commission: Reporting Success' (2001) 64(2) Modern Law Review 280.

Criminal Cases Review Commission Annual Reports available from the Criminal Cases Review Commission (http://www.ccrc.gov.uk).

Home Affairs Select Committee Report on the Work of the Criminal Cases Review Commission (http://www.publications.parliament.uk/pa/cm199899/cmselect/cmhaff/106/10602.htm).

MacPherson *The Stephen Lawrence Inquiry, Report of an Inquiry by Sir William MacPherson* (Cmnd 4262, 1999, London: HMSO).

Law Commission *Double Jeopardy and Prosecution Appeals* (Report No 267, March 2001).

USEFUL WEBSITES

The Criminal Cases Review Commission
http://www.ccrc.gov.uk/

Ministry of Justice judicial statistics section (appellate courts)
http://www.justice.gov.uk/publications/docs/judicial-court-stats-chapter1.pdf

SELF-TEST QUESTIONS

1 'The approach of the Court of Appeal to its powers is driven by the judges' reluctance to interfere with a jury verdict. Unless this changes, no amount of statutory reform will change the system.' Discuss.

2 List three reasons why defendants convicted in the Crown Court do not appeal to the Court of Appeal.

3 What is meant by the 'Lurking doubt' test set out in the Cooper case in 1969? What effect has the test had on the approach of the Court of Appeal to its powers?

4 Summarize why s 2 of the Criminal Appeal Act 1995 might be incompatible with Article 6 of the European Convention of Human Rights.

5 Does the Criminal Cases Review Commission represent an improvement over the Home Office as a final reviewing body for miscarriages of justice?

15

The provision of legal services

SUMMARY

This chapter outlines the extensive and ongoing changes in the way legal services are provided in England and Wales. It summarizes a range of provisions intended to open up the legal services market through the removal of restrictive practices which limit competition. In particular, it discusses the current focus on the regulatory system and the likely reforms which are to be introduced in this area. It places these changes in the context of the expansion in size of the legal services market and the increasing specialization and diversification of legal work and highlights the criticisms which the legal profession is facing over the lack of diversity in its composition. It concludes that the tension running through the legal system between quality of justice and efficiency in this area is expressed as a desire for cheaper legal services provided in a more flexible and competitive market versus the need to protect vulnerable citizens from unscrupulous or poor-quality advisers. At the same time a fundamental imperative is to ensure access to justice and to maintain lawyers' constitutional independence.

Providers of legal services

15.1 Most discussions of the provision of legal services in England and Wales begin and end with a description of the role and function of solicitors and barristers. Traditionally legal services have been regarded as the preserve of the legal profession; the body of lawyers whose members hold a qualification which allows them to undertake legal work which cannot be carried out by unqualified people and which imposes upon them regulatory and ethical requirements. These lawyers account for a significant proportion of those who provide legal services, but it is important to remember that although the work of solicitors and barristers is the most formal and visible part of the system, an array of legal services are supplied by other providers, some more and some less regulated by government. In England and Wales there are surprisingly few official restrictions on who can provide legal services for profit or otherwise. The only functions which are restricted to those with particular qualifications are advocacy in the courts (but not tribunals), litigation (the commencement of action in the courts), probate (the administration of an estate in the courts), conveyancing (buying and selling property), and immigration advice. The provision of general legal advice, eg on commercial law, welfare law and employment law; will writing; representation in tribunals; the administration of estates (other than formal probate) and many other areas, does not need to be carried out by a lawyer and very often is not. Legal executives, clerks, employment advisers, general and specialist advisers and volunteers at law centres and advice centres, trades union representatives, and many others provide legal services for profit or for free. The total number of these providers and the value or quantity of services they offer is not known, but it is likely that most legal advice and assistance is supplied by providers who are neither barristers nor solicitors.

The legal profession

15.2 Although qualified lawyers may represent a minority of those offering legal services, they are undoubtedly the most powerful players in the legal services market and the economic impact of their work is very great. As a result, much of the debate and proposals for reform in this area have focused on the organization and regulation of barristers and solicitors.

15.3 One area which has attracted considerable attention over the years is the division of the legal profession into two separate branches. The distinction between the two branches of the legal profession has traditionally been that barristers work as self-employed individuals in buildings called chambers and must be members of one of the four Inns of Court (Lincoln's Inn, Gray's Inn, Middle Temple, and Inner Temple). In contrast, solicitors usually work in partnerships. This form of division is now relatively unusual around the world. In most countries the legal profession is made up of one body and all lawyers undertake a common training before going on to specialize in different areas such as advocacy or commercial work. In contrast, England and Wales have maintained the traditional division between solicitors and barristers. This arrangement is often described by supporters of a divided profession as if it has been in existence since time immemorial. In fact, it was only in the

Victorian period that solicitors emerged as a distinct branch of the profession. Moreover, in practice there has always been a significant overlap in the working arrangements of the two branches. Many solicitors spend a great deal of their time working as advocates in the magistrates' courts and county courts, and many barristers have 'paper practices' in which they primarily give specialist advice to solicitors rather than appearing in court. In addition, a significant proportion of solicitors and barristers work as employed lawyers in government or as in-house counsel for companies.

15.4 Despite these overlaps, many solicitors and barristers remain strongly committed to a divided profession, arguing that it ensures the highest quality of case preparation and advocacy. The main argument against the divided profession is that its effect is to hinder competition and protect the vested interests of lawyers by protecting their markets and keeping new providers out. During the 1960s, a number of proposals were put forward for ending the division and creating a fused profession. In the event, these did not materialize, and it was accepted that the legal profession would continue in its present divided form. Until the 1980s, the rules which governed the training, professional conduct, and division of responsibilities of the two branches remained relatively strict. During that decade, however, the attacks on restrictive practices by the Conservative Government began to have an impact on the legal profession. A programme of reform was put in motion which has been continued with equal enthusiasm by the Labour Government since it came to power in 1997.

Advocacy

15.5 The main focus of the reforms in the 1980s and 1990s was the arrangements for the provision of advocacy services. Since the nineteenth century, barristers have enjoyed an exclusive right to present cases in the higher courts (rights of audience). The starting point for the changes was the introduction in 1985 of a Private Member's Bill supported by the Conservative Government which removed the monopoly on conveyancing work (buying and selling property) enjoyed by solicitors.

15.6 This measure allowed licensed conveyancers to compete in a market which made up a significant proportion of many solicitors' work. Although in practice the reform has been less effective than was intended and the great majority of conveyancing work is still carried out by solicitors, it was a key factor in changing the approach of solicitors towards the division between the two branches of the profession. The threat to the conveyancing monopoly led solicitors to turn their attention to the advocacy monopoly which barristers still enjoyed and to campaign for its removal. In 1989, the then Lord Chancellor, Lord Mackay, introduced a major programme of reform to open up rights of audience in the higher courts.

15.7 The Courts and Legal Services Act 1990 retained existing common law rights of audience in the courts but put in place a system by which applications could be made by bodies such as the Law Society, the Crown Prosecution Service or the Institute of Legal Executives for permission to institute new training arrangements which would qualify their members for additional rights of audience. The additional training requirements were, however, costly and time-consuming and few solicitors obtained the new advocacy qualification.

15.8 Further changes were therefore made in the Access to Justice Act 1999. The Access to Justice Act 1999 stated that all barristers and solicitors would obtain full rights of audience on qualification. It then authorized the professional bodies to determine what further training or qualification is required before being entitled to practise in the higher courts and required that this must be approved by the Lord Chancellor.

15.9 Since 1999, rules proposed by the Law Society have been introduced which have liberalized the process by which solicitors can gain rights of audience in the higher courts. In particular, the requirement that applicants should have recently completed a number of hours' advocacy in the lower courts can now be substituted for litigation experience. This new 'development' route to qualification is particularly important for solicitors working in large commercial firms who are unlikely to have any recent experience of advocacy in the county court or magistrates' courts. Initially, the number of solicitors applying to be solicitor-advocates was relatively small. However, by 2009 approximately 4,000 solicitors had obtained higher rights of audience, including 12 who had been made QCs, and it is likely that this figure will rise. Solicitors who work in firms which do a high proportion of international work, in particular, have found that their clients from countries, such as the US, which do not have a divided profession, find it difficult to understand why the senior and well-paid solicitors they instruct in the UK cannot represent them in court. As a result, it is now routine in some city firms for solicitors working in their litigation departments to obtain higher rights of audience.

Assessment of the advocacy reforms

15.10 The Government's objectives in introducing the Courts and Legal Services Act 1990 was stated as being: 'to see that the market for legal services operates freely and efficiently and gives clients the widest possible choice from those who had the necessary expertise'. Predictably, the Law Society gave its strong support to the reforms, while, equally predictably, the Bar's response to the proposals to remove its advocacy monopoly in the higher courts was defensive. It argued that: 'Justice cannot be measured in terms of competition and consumerism: justice is not a consumer durable; it is the hallmark of a civilised and democratic society.'

15.11 Setting aside the inevitable vested interests which drive the different positions adopted by the two branches of the profession, a number of arguments can be advanced both for and against opening up the rights of advocacy. One argument in support of the status quo is that it is needed in order to ensure that junior barristers have enough work to build up a practice. Despite the large sums which some senior barristers earn, the early years of life at the Bar are almost always difficult ones, with the great majority of junior barristers struggling to earn enough to pay the rent in chambers and cover their bills. This situation has become more difficult with the introduction of student loans, with graduates entering the profession already in debt. Opening up advocacy is likely to increase the pressure on junior members who are now competing with solicitors. If they cannot survive the first few years, the future of the Bar may be in danger.

15.12 Whether or not this matters depends on whether or not the Bar is considered necessary. The main argument in favour of the preservation of a self-employed body of advocates and specialists is that it promotes independence. Because barristers are not employed by one institution, they can appear one day for the prosecution and the next for the defence (or for a claimant or insurance company in the civil courts). They are not directly beholden to the demands of either side and have an arm's length relationship with the client.

15.13 This is important because advocates are often required to make decisions which comply with the requirements of justice but which may conflict with the interests of the parties they represent. For example, they may be under a duty to disclose material to the other side which would help its case or advise that a case should be dropped even if this is unpalatable to the client. Employed lawyers, whether working in private practice or public employment such as the Crown Prosecution Service or a government department, are likely to be more directly affected by their employers' interests in reaching these decisions.

15.14 An additional argument in favour of the Bar is that it provides a valuable pool of specialists. The quality of barristers' advocacy will be higher on average than that of solicitor-advocates because that is their main occupation, whereas solicitors must divide their time between the demands of an office and appearing in court. The use of a referral system in which solicitors instruct barristers with expertise in particular areas has the advantage of giving lay clients the benefit of the knowledge and experience which the solicitor has gained of the abilities of members of the Bar.

15.15 Against this, it can be argued that the threat to the Bar has been overstated. It is an organization which is quite capable of adapting to changed conditions. The competition from solicitors will force the Bar to seek out areas of work at which it can compete effectively, to moderate its fees and to provide a better quality service. The requirement for a specialist Bar will always be present and there will be plenty of work for a leaner, more competitive body of advocates.

15.16 In addition, even if the Bar does suffer as a result of the changes, it may be that this cost is more than compensated for by the greater choice which clients will have as to who will represent them in court. If people know and trust their solicitors and consider them capable on the basis of past experience it cannot be justified that they should have to employ additional lawyers who do not know the case to present it in court. The cost and inefficiency of this 'double-manning' do not justify propping up the Bar.

15.17 In relation to the question of independence, it can be argued that solicitors are equally capable of fulfilling their obligation to the courts as independent professionals who are officers of the court and bound by the rules of conduct of the Law Society. Moreover, there is a case for saying that the independence of the Bar has been exaggerated. For example, the so-called 'cab-rank' rule whereby barristers will take any case which is offered them in their areas of expertise is often breached in practice. It is difficult to know how often barristers find spurious reasons to turn down work which they should take under the cab-rank rule. Solicitors acting for unpopular defendants such as those charged with terrorism offences have, in the past, reported that they have had to approach many different barristers before they have found one willing to take on the brief. Barristers may be self-employed but the economic and cultural pressures they are under may be just as threatening to their independence as the employed status of solicitors. Equally worrying is the trend away from accepting legally aided work. As the rates of legal aid pay have fallen, the Bar Council has changed its rules so that barristers in some areas such as family work are no longer in breach of the cab-rank rule if they refuse to take certain legally aided work.

Direct access to the Bar

15.18 Despite the strong resistance of the Bar to any erosion of the divided profession, there have been some important reforms to the rules which govern the working practices of the Bar. In particular, the rule which prevented barristers from taking instructions directly from the public has been gradually weakened.

15.19 In the past, anyone who needed representation in court had to go first to a solicitor, who then instructed a barrister if necessary. In the 1980s, in the face of criticism of this restriction, the Bar Council relaxed the rule by allowing that certain professional clients, such as accountants, could instruct a barrister directly. During the 1990s, the number of organizations who were granted direct access to the Bar grew. Nevertheless, pressure to remove the restriction altogether increased. In 2001, the Office of Fair Trading strongly criticized the prohibition on clients having direct access to a barrister as a barrier to competition. In response to the OFT report on competition in the professions (discussed below), the Bar Council agreed to allow more general direct access by January 2003. However, its initial plans for widening access were restricted to a more 'cautious' relaxation of the rule in areas of family and criminal work.

Queen's Counsel

15.20 Another aspect of the legal profession which has been the subject of considerable criticism and change is the system for designating certain barristers as senior advocates known as Queen's Counsel (QCs). Approximately 10 per cent of the Bar is made up of QCs and, until recently, these were appointed by the Lord Chancellor on an annual basis. The competition for the rank of QC (also known as Silk) was always very strong and only a minority of those who applied each year were appointed. As well as being an important mark of status, taking Silk allowed barristers to charge considerably more for their services.

15.21 During the 1980s and 1990s, an intense debate about the value of the QC system developed. Supporters of the system argued that it was a merit-based process which allowed solicitors and litigants who used the services of the Bar to identify the most able and distinguished advocates. In contrast, critics claimed that the system did not provide a genuine kite mark of quality because appointments were not based on objective and rigorous criteria, but the subjective views of a small number of senior judges consulted by the Lord Chancellor on the quality of the applicants.

15.22 In addition, the narrow background of those appointed became a subject of increasing attention. The proportion of women taking Silk remained the same between 1993 and 2003 at approximately 8 per cent despite the significant increase in women entering the legal profession during that period. Likewise, the proportion of QCs from minority ethnic backgrounds was significantly less than their proportion of the profession as a whole. Similarly, despite the fact that solicitor advocates became eligible for Silk in 1995, the highest number appointed in any one year was 12, in 2001. In addition, those appointed QCs tended to be clustered in certain chambers, particularly commercial sets which included a high proportion of judges.

15.23 The exclusion of large sections of the legal profession from the QC system, combined with growing concern about whether it was appropriate for the government to be involved in the appointment process of a professional body at all, led to the decision in 2003 to suspend the system while consultations on reform were undertaken. In 2005, a new appointments system was established consisting of an Independent Selection Panel, chaired by a lay member and including both lay and legal representatives. Under the new arrangements the Panel's recommendations are passed to the Lord Chancellor who puts them to the Queen. The Lord Chancellor has no power to veto names or to add names of his own. The process is intended to produce a fairer and more merit-based selection system. Applicants must provide a self-assessment as to how they meet a number of competences, including integrity, understanding, using the law, working with clients, and persuading. Applicants also provide the names of referees who have recently encountered them at work such as judges or arbitrators, fellow practitioners, and professional clients.

15.24 In July 2006, the first round of QCs appointed under the new system were announced. These included significant increases in the number of women and minority lawyers appointed, with 33 women – 49 per cent of the 68 who applied and 24 minority lawyers – 42 per cent of the 24 such applicants being selected. The second round of appointments in January 2008 saw the appointment of 20 women – 39 percent of the 51 who applied and 4 ethnic minority lawyers – 18 per cent of the 22 who applied.

15.25 While it is too early to draw firm conclusions about the workings of the new QC selection process, what is clear is that the underlying motives for these reforms are not unique to the area of Queen's Counsel, but are part of a much wider process of reform of the regulation of the provision of legal services as a whole.

Regulation of the legal services market

15.26 A recurring concern driving forward recent and current changes is the desire to ensure that the market for the provision of legal services is sufficiently competitive. An important development in this debate was the publication of a report on the professions in March 2001 by the Office of Fair Trading criticizing a range of restrictive practices.

15.27 The report prompted responses from the Government and lawyers. In general the profession was both defensive and critical of the report, though certain changes were implemented in response to the report. For example, the Bar Council agreed to allow barristers to advertise their comparative charges, while the Law Society changed its rules to allow solicitors employed by non-solicitors to provide services to third parties. The Government, on the other hand, was generally sympathetic to the report and in 2002 the Lord Chancellor's Department published a consultation paper, *In the Public Interest?*, asking for views about such matters as the regulation of conveyancing services, probate, and appointing Queen's Counsel. The paper provided evidence of the shift in Government thinking away from a professional orientated towards a market-orientated approach to legal services, stating that:

> ... the Government's position is that the market should be opened up to competition unless there are strong reasons why that should not be the case, such as evidence that real consumer detriment might result from such a change.

15.28 A particular feature of the more recent approach to the question of regulation has been to expand the scope of the debate to include the full array of regulatory mechanisms in the legal services market place. In the past, almost all the attention has focused on the professional bodies of the legal profession – the Bar Council for barristers and the Law Society for solicitors. But there is now much more awareness of the role played by the other bodies which regulate the work of other legal services providers, such as the Institute of Legal Executives and the Council for Licensed Conveyancers. To date, all these regulators have been allowed to continue to determine their practice rules and to operate their complaints and disciplinary machinery within the broad statutory framework set down by the Government. However, increasing concern over this self-regulatory system has led to greater government scrutiny of the existing regulatory system. The latest, and most extensive, is the review undertaken for the Department for Constitutional Affairs by Sir David Clementi. The main recommendations of the Clementi review was that a new Legal Services Board (LSB) should be set up to oversee the regulatory activities of those bodies whose members offered legal services. The Legal Services Act 2007 implemented this recommendation and established the LSB, which acts as single, independent regulator. The intention is to ensure greater consistency and fairness in the provision of these services in line with the Act's aim of placing the interests of the consumer at the centre of the regulatory system.

15.29 One way in which Clementi envisaged that this change of focus could be achieved was by dividing the regulatory and representative functions of the professional bodies. This proposal has been accepted by the Law Society and the Bar Council, which have both decided to create independent regulatory bodies – the Solicitors' Regulation Authority and the Bar Standards Board.

15.30 In addition to proposing an overarching Legal Services Board, the Clementi report recommended changes in the following areas, many of which have been implemented in the Legal Services Act 2007.

The complaints system

15.31 One of the key factors in the decision to establish a review of the regulatory system was the long-standing weakness of the existing complaints system. Most of the concern focused on the system for solicitors, who have direct contact with clients and therefore are far more likely to be the subject of complaints. Despite efforts by the Law Society to improve the complaints system, including setting up the Office of Supervision of Solicitors, it continued to be the subject of criticism for its failure to deal effectively with complaints and to make significant progress in reducing the serious backlog of cases. As a result of these concerns, the Legal Services Ombudsman argued the case for the creation of a single dispute resolution mechanism for handling all complaints relating to the provision of legal services. David Clementi accepted this argument and proposed the establishment of a new independent Office for Legal Complaints to fulfil this function. The Legal Services Act 2007 provides for there to be an Office for Legal Complaints and the body is expected to be fully operational by the end of 2010.

Multi-Disciplinary Partnerships and Legal Disciplinary Partnerships

15.32 As the legal services market has expanded and diversified, the attention of the profession and the government has been drawn to the question of whether solicitors and barristers can practise in Multi-Disciplinary Partnerships (MDPs) with other professionals. In practice, many lawyers from both branches do already work with other professionals but simply avoid working within a partnership structure. In 1991, solicitors and barristers were given the statutory right to form partnerships with non-lawyers and each other and the legal professions were given the authority to regulate that process. Both the Law Society and the Bar Council maintained their restrictions on such practices, but the pressure for change has grown. In 2001, the Office of Fair Trading report 'Competition in the Professions' recommended removal of the restrictions in both branches of the profession. The Lord Chancellor's Department consultation paper in response to the report stated that it was 'keen to remove practices that were not in the public interest'.

15.33 The enthusiasm for MDPs which developed in the 1990s was tempered, however, by public concern over the dangers of unregulated free markets in the world of accounting and finance. The revelation of fraud scandals in large companies such as Enron and the prosecutions of solicitors involved in money laundering served to inject a note of caution in the deregulation of MDPs. The argument against them is that requirements such as the need to protect client confidentiality, to which solicitors and barristers are subject, do not affect the non-lawyer members of the partnership. The effect may be to undermine the ability of lawyers to uphold their professional obligations.

15.34 The Clementi review considered this issue in detail. It concluded that restrictions should be lifted to allow a form of MDP, called Legal Disciplinary Partnerships, to be set up which would allow a range of legal service providers to practise together as 'managers', provided the non-lawyers in the partnership remained in a minority. Such partnerships could, however, be funded by investment from non-lawyers. Although the proposals include safeguards for such arrangements, such as the fact that the non-lawyer owners would have no right of access to clients' files, consider-able concern has been expressed about the danger that such practices might suffer from a conflict of interest between their legal professional duties and the demands of their owners. Despite these concerns, this aspect of the Clementi proposals too has been included in the Legal Services Act 2007. The Act will allow legal services firms to have up to 25 per cent non-lawyer partners and will allow different kinds of lawyers to form firms together.

Expansion, diversification, and specialization

15.35 The future of the divided profession and changes to the regulatory regime are only two aspects of the current developments in the legal profession. Equally important have been the effects of the very significant increase in the size of the profession in recent years. In the 1950s, there were around 2,000 barristers and 17,000 solicitors. These figures have risen to approximately 12,000 and 108,000 respectively. Over 80 per cent of barristers now practise in chambers which are made up of over 20 members.

15.36 At the same time as numbers have grown, the degree of diversification in the work-ing arrangements of different lawyers has increased. This is particularly marked in relation to solicitors. The majority of solicitors still work in small firms or as sole practitioners, but the number and size of big firms has increased dramatically.

15.37 There are now five city firms with over 1,000 fee earners. The turnover of the largest of these, Clifford Chance, was in excess of £1bn in 2005. The presence of these 'super firms' is a relatively recent phenomenon. In 1952, the largest city firm was Slaughter & May, with 16 partners and a total annual turnover of £274,000. At the time, practice rules still limited the number of partners which any firm could have to 20.

15.38 These historical figures show that 50 years ago the difference between the largest and smallest practices in terms of partner numbers and turnover was relatively small. Today, the gap between them is staggering. The large city practices make up less than 2 per cent of firms but they employ 30 per cent of solicitors and generate over half of solicitors' turnover. The needs, priorities, and interests of a partner in a large city firm specializing in international commerce and a sole practitioner in a small general practice are now so different that it is becoming hard to talk about them as members of the same profession. This division is compounded by the increasing numbers of solicitors who are not sole practitioners or partners in a firm but are employed by other companies. These employed solicitors now make up over 20 per cent of the total. The role of the Law Society in reflecting the interests and regulating the activities of such diverse groups of lawyers is now very difficult indeed.

15.39 One example of the increasing division between large commercial practices and other solicitors which emerged recently was the decision by a consortium of city firms to set up an independent vocational training course to be taken by the graduates offered training contracts by those firms. This was provoked by their concerns that the standard Legal Practice Course did not specifically address the particular skills and knowledge which their trainees would require. In response to the proposal, the Master of the Rolls, who has an historical responsibility for the solicitors' branch of the profession, spoke out about the dangers of such a divisive move in the training of the profession.

15.40 While many in the profession supported his intervention, there is also a growing recognition that the one-size-fits-all training course is increasingly inappropriate for young lawyers who are likely never again to encounter the majority of the subject-matter of the vocational course. The Law Society sought to address this problem several years ago by restructuring the Legal Practice Course into a skills-based rather than knowledge-based course in order to provide a more relevant training for all lawyers.

15.41 The problem still remains, however, that solicitors work in increasingly specialized areas and are often wholly unqualified in practice to undertake work outside that narrow field. Thirty years ago it was common for solicitors to carry out a relatively large range of work perfectly competently. As each area of law has become more extensive and complex, this has become less and less possible. Small firms of generalist practitioners are now rare. Other professions, such as medicine, have dealt with this problem through the introduction of compulsory specialist training.

Doctors wishing to work in areas such as anaesthetics, surgery or obstetrics must undertake further training and pass exams before they can practise those skills. It may be that solicitors will need to move in that direction.

15.42 Among barristers the equivalent division in working arrangements which has emerged is between employed members of the Bar and those working in a traditional self-employed capacity in chambers. Increasingly barristers are being employed in the public sector, in-house in large international firms of lawyers and accountants and in private and public companies. Their needs and interests are often very different from their self-employed counterparts. Being unable to have direct access to clients, for example, has in the past been a major difficulty for employed barristers while the restrictions on conducting litigation may be a significant limitation.

Composition of the profession

15.43 As the profession has grown its significance in society has increased. Most people today will use the services of a solicitor at some point in their lives. As a result, its composition has become more important. In particular, there is now a debate about whether access to the profession is based on merit alone or whether there is direct or indirect discrimination in recruitment, training or working practices. When the legal profession was a relatively small and elite group it was drawn disproportionately from those with wealthy and privileged backgrounds and was almost exclusively made up of men. The expansion in higher education which began 40 years ago and has accelerated in the last decade and the change in social attitudes towards women and minority groups has opened up the possibility of a legal career to graduates from a much wider range of backgrounds.

15.44 Among solicitors there are now slightly more women than men at the point of qualification and, likewise, the proportion of those qualifying from a minority ethnic background is now greater than that of the general population. The problem of imbalance is found higher up the ranks, among partners, where women and minorities are significantly under-represented. There are currently two schools of thought about this problem. The first, the 'trickle-up' school, believes that the imbalance is a product of historical bias and will naturally change as the younger lawyers move up the ranks. The second holds that structural and cultural barriers still exist for those who do not come from traditional legal backgrounds and that only some form of positive action will produce equality.

15.45 Support for this view is found in the fact that women solicitors are on average paid less than their male counterparts at the equivalent level of experience and are less likely to be made partner. Similarly, the proportion of women barristers among the senior rank of Queen's Counsel (see above) is still less than 10 per cent. Moreover, the evidence suggests that discrimination is not limited to the upper ranks of the legal profession, where the number of men is much greater, but is equally prevalent among recent entrants to the profession. In 2002, a report by the Equal Opportunities Commission found that female law graduates were paid an average of £18,500 three years after graduation compared with £21,500 paid to their male counterparts. The report concluded that that the legal profession had one of the worst records in terms of pay disparity among the professions. Similar disadvantages are suffered by young solicitors and barristers from minority ethnic groups, who are under-represented in successful commercial firms and chambers.

15.46 Another important structural factor in the composition of the legal profession is economic. At the Bar, the problem of recruiting graduates from less well-off backgrounds is made more acute by the fact that the training year (pupillage) was traditionally unpaid. For those who do not come from wealthy backgrounds the economic realities of building a practice at the Bar may be a deterrent to some capable graduates.

15.47 The Lord Chancellor and other senior judges have recently been publicly urging the Bar to ensure that it has sufficient funding for pupils in order to attract the brightest young lawyers from a diverse range of backgrounds, and the Bar has responded by trying to ensure that all pupils are paid a minimum salary. As of 1 January 2003, all pupils have been entitled to an annual award of not less than £10,000 and to receive reasonable travel expenses. However, proposals from the Bar Council in 2002 for barristers to contribute annually to a central fund which would support paid pupillages had to be abandoned after opposition from commercial sets of chambers. The argument in favour of this proposal is that the requirement that pupils be paid will deter less wealthy chambers from offering places. Since these chambers are often the most diverse in terms of ethnicity and gender, the effect of this may be to reduce still further access opportunities for graduates from non-traditional backgrounds. The danger of economic and social elitism at the Bar is particularly worrying in view of the fact that the upper ranks of the judiciary are still almost exclusively drawn from the Bar. If the next generation of barristers is drawn predominantly from the more wealthy graduates, the chance of greater diversification in the background of the judiciary is remote.

15.48 Economic and social elitism are the most pressing concerns in terms of entry to careers in the legal profession. In 2007 a Bar Council working party led by Lord Neuberger carried out a major review of the barriers of entry to the Bar. It found that, although the Bar had a relatively good record in relation to race and gender balance, financial considerations and social background and hence familiarity with the professions remained significant barriers to entry. Lord Neuberger made 57 detailed recommendations aimed at tackling problems of social mobility at all stages, from school through to pupillage and tenancy. In 2009 Alan Milburn MP chaired a study on access to high status jobs and he too highlighted significant barriers to access to the legal profession. His report suggested that the legal profession was becoming more, rather than less, exclusive and that entrants to the profession were increasingly likely to come from affluent families. Problems of social mobility are complex and deep-rooted and any action to reverse this trend must by systemic, involving schools, careers advisers, and universities as well as the legal profession itself.

The future

15.49   Despite the heated debates and various statutory reforms which have taken place in relation to rights of advocacy in recent years, there is little evidence to suggest that the formal division between barristers or solicitors is likely to end nor that the future of the Bar is in jeopardy. Indeed, current figures show that the Bar is continuing to expand in size and that barristers' incomes are still growing. Nevertheless, the working practices of both branches have clearly undergone very significant change and this seems likely to continue.

15.50   The reforms to advocacy should be seen as part of a wider process of change which is having a real impact on the way that lawyers work. Some of these changes are driven by a Government agenda, but equally important are the effects of the fast changing market conditions in which solicitors and barristers must operate. Lawyers in private practice are business people and they have to adapt to economic realities. The general trend towards global business and large international practices has had a significant impact on the interests of commercial firms.

15.51   These ongoing changes may ultimately prove to have as significant an effect on the legal profession as a formal merger of the two branches would have done. The driving force behind the changes of the last 15 years or so has been to open up the legal services market and strip away many of the remaining restrictive practices in both branches of the profession. The goal of increasing consumer choice, reducing excessive costs and improving quality through the promotion of a more open market in legal services is uncontroversial. However, the assumption on which the reforms ultimately rest, that the legal profession is no different from any other business, is not. Lawyers in private practice are business people, but they are also required to fulfil obligations other than to their profit margins. Their duty to the court, to their clients, and to the codes of conduct of their governing bodies are the distinguishing features of legal professionalism. Unlike other businesses, lawyers are also expected to fulfil a constitutional role by providing an independent body of professionals who will play their part in upholding the rule of law.

15.52 These competing obligations are not, of course, always adequately fulfilled and lawyers regularly fail to live up to the high ethical standards set for them. Nevertheless, many lawyers defend unpopular clients, take cases challenging the legality of government action, undertake unpaid work for deserving causes and consider their underlying rationale as being to promote the interests of justice. These lawyers join the legal profession because its culture and values are not limited to those of the free market. The relationship between the pressure on lawyers to run a successful business and to uphold their ethical and professional standards of conduct has always been, and always will be, a source of tension. Whether or not the current range of reforms intended to increase competition in the legal profession will benefit the public as consumers more than they will damage them as citizens is the most difficult question currently facing the legal profession and the Government in this area of the legal system.

15.53 Whether or not the process of relaxing the restrictive practices of the profession improves the quality of service to the consumer, it will undoubtedly liberalize the career options of lawyers. The number of different providers of legal services is likely to grow and if movement between solicitors and barristers is increasingly easy and flexible, young lawyers will be able to develop their careers in response to their particular needs and interests at any one time and will not be forced to make a lifetime's choice on entering the profession.

15.54 It is possible, for example, that in the future many young lawyers will choose to begin their careers as solicitors where they can command a reliable salary (and pay off student debts) and that later those with an aptitude and ability in advocacy who would prefer a more independent career will move to the Bar, no doubt taking with them the connections forged while in practice as a solicitor. Likewise, barristers who later in their career wish for the security of a salary and a pension may take their advocacy skills and specialist expertise with them to employment in the public or private sector. The cost of this flexibility is that the 'job for life' which many lawyers once took for granted no longer exists. Members of the legal profession are now subject to the vagaries of the market in the same way as all other business people.

15.55 Whatever the particular working patterns which emerge among lawyers and other providers of legal services in the coming years, it is likely that the current market orientated reform process will continue. Those regulations and practices which have been identified as restrictive and anti-competitive will come under increasing pressure. Unless their supporters can make a strong case to show that they are justified in the public interest, they are unlikely to survive.

FURTHER READING

The Future of Legal Service: Putting the Consumer First (October 2005, Department for Constitutional Affairs) (http://www.dca.gov.uk/legalsys/folwp.pdf).

David Clementi *Report of the Review of the Regulatory Framework for Legal Services in England and Wales* (December 2004) (http://www.legal-services-review.org.uk/content/report/index.htm).

In the Public Interest? (July 2002) Lord Chancellor's Department Consultation Paper following the publication of the Office of Fair Trading Report on competition in the professions.

Competition in the Professions (March 2001, Office of Fair Trading) (available on the Office of Fair Trading website below).

Constitutional Reform: The Future of Queen's Counsel (March 2003, Department for Constitutional Affairs) (http://www.dca.gov.uk/consult/qcfuture/index.htm).

David Bean 'A Bar to Competition or a Competitive Bar?' (2002) 152 New Law Journal 657.

The Bar's Consultation Paper in response to the Office of Fair Trading report on competition in the professions (2002) (http://www.barcouncil.org.uk/consultations/consultationpapers/).

The Law Society's response to the Office of Fair Trading report on competition in the professions (2002)

Annual report of the Legal Services Ombudsman 2008–9 (http://www.olso.org/publications/AnnualReports/AR2009.asp).

Statistics on the composition of the Bar http://www.barcouncil.org.uk/about/statistics/.

Bar Council, *Entry to the Bar Working Party Final Report* (2007) (http://cms.barcouncil.rroom.net/assets/documents/FinalReportNeuberger.pdf).

Cabinet Office, *Unleashing Aspiration: The Final Report of the Panel on Fair Access to the Professions* (2009) (http://www.cabinetoffice.gov.uk/media/227102/fair-access.pdf).

USEFUL WEBSITES

New QC selection process
http://www.qcapplications.org.uk/

Bar council website home page
http://www.barcouncil.org.uk

Law Society website home page
http://www.lawsoc.org

Office of Fair Trading website. Includes 2001 report on competition in the professions and 2002 report on progress
http://www.oft.gov.uk

Legal Services Board home page
http://www.legalservicesboard.org.uk/index.htm

SELF-TEST QUESTIONS

1 'Opposition to the extension of rights of audience by the Bar is driven solely by crude vested interests. By opening up advocacy in the higher courts the quality of the service offered to litigants will improve and the costs will come down.' Discuss.

2 What is meant by an independent Bar? Why is the idea of an independent Bar considered important?

3 Are the proposals for reform of the regulation of the provision of legal services put forward by Sir David Clementi likely to achieve their goals?

4 What evidence is there to challenge the 'trickle-up' approach to improving diversity in the legal profession?

5 'Lack of social mobility is the single biggest hurdle to entry into the legal profession.' Discuss.

16

The structure and functions of the judiciary

SUMMARY

This chapter describes the different judicial ranks and discusses the tension which exists between the requirements of judicial independence and accountability. It highlights the growing debate over the increasing role of judges in politically sensitive decision-making through the development of judicial review and the Human Rights Act 1998 and contrasts this with their more traditional functions of applying the law, fact-finding and sentencing. It outlines their new role in case-management and the growing importance of judicial training and extra-judicial work. It concludes that the role of the judges has become more diverse and demanding and that this change has led to a greater degree of professionalization in the judiciary.

The judicial ranks

16.1 In common with the court structure, the judiciary in England and Wales is organized hierarchically. Its ranks do not, however, tally neatly with the tiers of courts and most of the judges can and do sit in more than one court while many members of the judiciary hear trials and appeals in both civil and criminal cases.

Lord Chancellor

16.2 Until 2005, the Lord Chancellor sat at the top of the judicial hierarchy. He was head of the judiciary, speaker of the House of Lords, and a member of Cabinet. He also carried the primary responsibility for appointing the judges (see chapter 17).

However, these overlapping constitutional roles became increasingly controversial as they breach the principle that there should be a separation of powers between the judiciary, the legislature, and the executive. In 1998, a Commons motion signed by 50 Labour MPs called for the Lord Chancellor to be replaced by an elected Minister of Justice directly accountable to the House of Commons. In 2003, pressure also grew from Europe for reform of the role of the Lord Chancellor when the Council of Europe parliamentary assembly debated a resolution calling on the UK to end the practice of the Lord Chancellor sitting as a judge.

16.3 As a result of these and other similar criticisms, the Government decided in 2003 to implement a root and branch reform on the role of the Lord Chancellor. Under the provisions of the Constitutional Reform Act 2005 (CRA), the Lord Chief Justice has replaced the Lord Chancellor as head of the judiciary and responsibility for judicial appointments has been given to a new independent judicial appointments commission. The legislation as originally drafted removed the office of Lord Chancellor completely and his political post was reformulated into that of the Secretary of State for Constitutional Affairs. However, as a result of strong opposition in the House of Lords to this change, the cabinet minister in charge of the Ministry of Justice retains the title of Lord Chancellor, though he has lost all his judicial functions and is no longer the speaker of the House of Lords.

16.4 There is no doubt that the reformed role of Lord Chancellor will not carry with it the prestige it once enjoyed and it is now much closer to a normal cabinet post. Opponents of the change argued that this special office was a vital means of maintaining judicial independence and that its 'demotion' will weaken the protection given to judges. Supporters of reform argued that the Lord Chancellor's multiple roles were anachronistic and inappropriate in a modern democracy. They claimed that the judges themselves are perfectly able to guard their independence provided a political culture of respect for the rule of law is maintained. To this end, the CRA includes a provision requiring the Lord Chancellor to protect and promote judicial independence.

Lord Chief Justice

16.5 As a result of the CRA the Lord Chief Justice is now the formal head of the judiciary as well as the most senior sitting judge. He is also President of the Courts of England and Wales and head of the Criminal Division of the Court of Appeal. The CRA states that as President of the Courts of England and Wales, the Lord Chief Justice is responsible for representing the view of the judiciary of England and Wales to the Lord Chancellor and ministers; maintaining the welfare, training, and guidance of the judges; and making arrangement for the deployment of judges and case allocation. Before 2005, the Lord Chief Justice was also head of the Queen's Bench Division (QBD) of the High Court. Under the provisions of the CRA a separate post of President of the QBD has been created.

Master of the Rolls

16.6 The most senior civil judge is the Master of the Rolls, who is head of the Court of Appeal (Civil Division) and hears the most serious civil appeals. The title is derived from his role in the supervision of the solicitors' branch of the profession which requires him to keep the roll of those qualified as solicitors.

President of the Family Division

16.7 The head of the Family Division of the High Court is the President who hears the most difficult cases involving children or ethical matters such as contested medical treatment cases. Under the CRA the President is now also entitled the Head of Family Justice. The President also sits in the Court of Appeal.

Chancellor of the High Court

16.8 Under the provisions of the CRA, the post of Vice Chancellor was renamed Chancellor of the High Court. He is head of the Chancery Division of the High Court and hears the most difficult Chancery cases (eg those involving trusts and company matters). The Chancellor of the High Court also sits in the Court of Appeal.

Law Lords and Supreme Court Justices

16.9 Members of the Appellate Committee of the House of Lords were known as Law Lords. They were almost always appointed from among the judges in the Court of Appeal. They heard both civil and criminal appeals involving questions of law of general public importance. They also sat as members of the Judicial Committee of the Privy Council. The Law Lords were full members of the House of Lords (the upper chamber of Parliament) and so could play a role in the legislative process. Although most of the Law Lords chose not to participate in voting or debates on the passage of legislation, their presence in the legislature was been the subject of growing criticism as a breach of the separation of powers. Under the provisions of the CRA the Law Lords will become Supreme Court Justices in the new independent Supreme Court when it opens in October 2009. Their powers and functions will, however, remain essentially the same (see chapter 2).

Lords Justices of Appeal

16.10 Judges in the Court of Appeal are usually appointed from the High Court. They hear both civil and criminal appeals. They may sit predominantly in one or the other Division of the Court (Civil or Criminal). The Civil Division sits in panels of twos or threes while the Criminal Division sits in threes made up of one Lord or Lady Justice sitting with two High Court judges or a High Court judge and a Circuit judge.

High Court judges

16.11 Judges in the High Court are usually appointed from among part-time Recorders or Deputy High Court judges. Occasionally they are appointed from the Circuit bench. On appointment they are allocated to one of the three Divisions of the High Court: the Queen's Bench Division, the Family Division or Chancery Division. High Court judges regularly travel around the country 'on circuit' hearing the most important civil and criminal cases, although the Lord Chancellor has indicated that this practice is to be replaced by shorter visits to hear particular cases where the need arises.

16.12 Some High Court judges are Presiding Judges. These oversee one of the six geographical circuits into which the country is divided for the purposes of the administration of the courts. Presiding judges are responsible for deciding which judges will hear which cases and for the general management of the circuit. They work together with the Resident judges (see below) and the Court Service, which is the administrative agency which runs the courts.

Circuit judges

16.13 Circuit judges are usually appointed from among Recorders or District Judges. They sit in the Crown Court hearing middle-ranking and more serious cases and in the county court hearing civil cases. Resident Judges are senior circuit judges who have management responsibilities for a circuit dealing with administrative matters and the deployment of judicial resources.

District judges

16.14 District judges are appointed from among Deputy District judges. Most are former solicitors. They handle the bulk of less serious judicial work in the county court and hear a wide range of different cases such as family work, breach of contract, and negligence claims.

District Judges (Magistrates' Courts)

16.15 These are professional magistrates (formerly called Stipendiary Magistrates) who are trained lawyers (unlike the majority of magistrates, who are lay people). They sit in the magistrates' courts generally hearing the more serious criminal cases dealt with there. They also hear some civil work such as family cases.

Recorders

16.16 These are part-time judges. They are practising lawyers (barristers or solicitors) who sit as judges for approximately 20 days per year. They can hear both criminal and civil cases sitting in the Crown Court and county court, but often specialize in one area or the other.

Deputy High Court judges

16.17 These are also senior practising lawyers who sit as part-time High Court judges. They do not have security of tenure and are currently appointed when the workload of the court requires more temporary judges. Some will go on to be appointed to the full-time High Court bench.

Masters

16.18 Pre-trial interlocutory work in the High Court in London is handled by masters in the Queen's Bench and Chancery Divisions. District judges undertake the equivalent work outside London in District Registries which are located in county courts.

Part-time (fee-paid) judges

16.19 The extensive use which is made of judges who are paid to sit from time to time while continuing their legal practice is an unusual feature of the judiciary in England and Wales. Such part-time judges, who make up two-thirds of the judiciary, are not found in civil law systems nor even in most other comparable common law systems such as Australia, New Zealand, or Canada. In 2001, 24 per cent of Crown Court and county court work was carried out by part-time judges. These posts raise particularly acute problems of independence since they do not enjoy the same security of tenure as full-time judges and the Lord Chancellor can simply decide not to renew their contracts.

16.20 However, the Human Rights Act 1998 has brought a change in this area. In Scotland the Courts held in *Starrs* in 1999 that the use of part-time judges (Sheriffs) was a breach of Article 6 of the European Convention on Human Rights which guarantees the right to be heard by an impartial and independent tribunal. Part-time Sheriffs could no longer be used after the decision. In England and Wales the arrangements for employing part-time judges were changed in order to avoid a similar adverse decision. Assistant Recorders, who previously had limited security, were made into Recorders. They are now appointed for fixed five-year periods and must be guaranteed a certain number of days in court each year.

16.21   Concern remains, however, over the position of deputy High Court judges, who do not enjoy the same guarantees. Since the cases they hear are more likely to involve challenges to official action, public expenditure or other politically sensitive cases, it is the use of part-timers at the higher end of the court system which should attract more attention than it does. The former Lord Chief Justice, Lord Woolf, expressed concern about the increasing use of deputies. He argued that some of the less demanding High Court work should instead be given to Circuit judges (Woolf, 2001).

Independence

16.22   The debate over the role of part-time judges is evidence of the centrality of the concept of judicial independence in England and Wales which requires that judges should not be subject to any improper pressure from politicians or interest groups, or even other judges, which might prevent them from deciding a case with impartiality.

16.23   The most obvious practical expression of this concept is seen in their tenure and salary arrangements. If judges are in danger of being sacked or having their pay cut if they reach decisions which are unfavourable to the Government, judicial impartiality is bound to suffer. Full-time judges are therefore appointed until the age of 70 and can only be removed in the most exceptional circumstances. Judges in the High Court and above can only be dismissed by the Queen after both Houses of Parliament have voted for removal. This has never happened. Senior judges therefore enjoy a great deal of job security and, in practice, only serious criminal conduct would justify removal.

16.24   Judges below the High Court are formally less secure. They can be removed by the Lord Chancellor on the grounds of 'incapacity and misbehaviour'. In practice, these powers appear to be similarly restricted to conduct which amounts to criminal behaviour, having only been used once in recent times, against a circuit judge caught smuggling whiskey and cigarettes. In cases involving other serious misconduct, the threat of action has usually been enough to induce a resignation.

16.25   In addition to job security, the salaries of the judges are protected and, by statute, cannot be reduced. The government periodically reviews judicial salaries and seeks the advice of an independent review body, called the Senior Salaries Review Body, on the levels of salaries (though it does not always follow that advice). In practice, salary levels are high in comparison with average incomes, but lower than a successful solicitor or barrister might expect to earn. Lawyers are often willing to take a pay cut on being appointed to the bench in return for a secure post, high status, interesting work and a very generous pension. The formal protection of the judges' salaries from reduction by the executive or legislature does not, however, immunize the judiciary from the day-to-day political reality of the politics of pay rises. In 2003, the then Lord Chancellor, Lord Irvine, was the subject of extensive media criticism when it was revealed that he had been given a 22 per cent pay rise on the advice of the Senior Salaries Review Body. In response to this criticism he decided to forgo the rise in favour of a much smaller increase in line with inflation.

Accountability

16.26   The other side of the coin of judicial independence is judicial accountability. The development of mechanisms of accountability has been strictly limited by the competing requirements of judicial independence which has traditionally been taken to require that judges must occupy 'a place apart' in the social and political world (Friedland, 1995). Nevertheless, the judiciary has argued that it is a highly accountable body in that its decisions are reached in public, reasons are given for those decisions and these can be overturned on appeal. While the appeal process may provide an effective internal accountability process, the effect of the prioritization of judicial independence has been to exclude most forms of external accountability by which decision-makers in other spheres of public service explain their actions and answer for the consequences of their decisions.

16.27   Judges have almost complete immunity from action in the courts, either civil or criminal, in the conduct of their work (Olowofoyeku, 1993). In addition, there was, until recently, limited scope for the scrutiny of the judiciary by Parliament. It was not until the early 1990s that the Lord Chancellor's Department became subject to review by the parliamentary select committees and acquired for the first time a minister in the Commons to account for its activities. In 2003, a parliamentary select committee was established specifically dedicated to review of the Department, rather than it coming under the auspices of the Home Affairs Select Committee. The Justice Committee now scrutinizes the work of the Ministry of Justice.

16.28   In addition to the limited review by Parliament, the judges have traditionally attracted very little media scrutiny. In the past, the press did not generally report on the personal beliefs and values of the judges and, with the exception of sentencing decisions, did not subject the judiciary to the same degree of scrutiny as other public institutions. This approach is, however, changing. In recent years the public and the media have been more willing to scrutinize and criticize the judges, so much so that some senior judges have expressed the view that these criticisms are severe enough to have a 'chilling effect' on judicial independence. One particular area which has attracted growing attention has been the lack of diversity in the composition of the judges (see chapter 17). This has led to the commonly heard accusation that judges are 'out of touch'. Recent research into public attitudes and the justice system has found that 66 per cent of a representative sample of the public agreed or strongly agreed with the statement that most judges were out of touch with ordinary people's lives. There was no difference in the response rate on the basis of age, education, employment or previous experience of the courts (Genn, 1999). However, the research did find that the proportion of respondents who expressed negative views of the judiciary was lower among those respondents who had actually appeared before a judge, which suggests that there is a credibility gap between the real and perceived attributes of the judges. This would appear to be confirmed by recent findings from a large-scale survey of people who had undertaken jury service. The research found that 'the vast majority of respondents were extremely impressed with the way judges performed'. The researchers noted that there was 'particular praise for their perceived professionalism, the consideration they showed, particularly to juries, their ability to clarify and summarize information and their impartiality' (Matthews, Hancock, and Briggs, 2004).

16.29   As a result of these sorts of findings, judges have slowly begun to realize that public confidence must be won and cannot simply be assumed. The judiciary has begun to make efforts to seek to improve its public image to counter this criticism and to engage more actively in public debate about matters of justice. In January 2003, for example, the then Lord Chief Justice reacted to public criticism of his sentencing which suggested that burglars should not automatically receive a custodial sentence by issuing a press notice via the Lord Chancellor's Department (Press Notice 10/03). In 2005, this process of improving the ability of the judiciary to engage with the public and to strengthen public confidence in the judges was taken a step further with the creation of a judicial communications office and an official judiciary website.

Constitutional position of the judiciary

16.30   As will be clear from the reforms to the judiciary described in the sections above, the constitutional role of the judiciary in England and Wales is undergoing significant and long-term change. The Former Lord Chief Justice, Lord Phillips, on his appointment in 2005, noted that: 'We are on the brink of a new era in the role of the judiciary in England and Wales – I am proud to be the first Lord Chief

Justice who will become the head of that judiciary.' A key aspect of this change is the development of the judiciary into a more distinct third branch of government, structurally removed from that of the executive and legislature. An important indicator of the more separate constitutional role that is being developed by the judiciary is the revitalization of the Judges' Council, a body made up of representatives of the different ranks of the judiciary. Until recently, the Council was a relatively moribund body, but it is expected in the future to play a vital role in representing the interests of the judges at a collective level both to the senior judiciary and to the other branches of Government.

16.31 These institutional changes need to be understood as a reflection of a more substantive change in the role played by the judiciary in the constitution. Until relatively recently the function of judges was widely seen as being limited to the settlement of disputes and the application of the law. Even the most senior judges were rarely perceived as occupying a place in the constitution as a branch of government in the same way as, for example, the US Supreme Court. This view of the judges' role explains why judicial independence has been so heavily prioritized over accountability.

16.32 Increasingly, however, the role of the judges as part of the checks and balances of democratic government is acknowledged by judges, politicians, and academics. The provisions of the CRA dismantling the multiple roles of the Lord Chancellor and creating a separate Supreme Court is key to this process of change. The changes introduced in the Act are based on a belief that there needs to be greater separation of powers between the judiciary and the other branches of government. One reason for this change in approach has been the growth of judicial review, the process by which the judges scrutinize the legality, procedural fairness, and reasonableness of the decisions of government and officials.

Judicial review

16.33 Over the last 40 years judges have used ancient prerogative orders which give them certain limited powers to ensure that the Government exercised its powers legally, to develop a new wide-ranging function of scrutinizing official decision-making. The role is a controversial one since it brings the judges much further into the policy-making process.

16.34 However, until recently, the test which the judges applied for overturning an official decision was a stringent one. Unless the decision was illegal because it went beyond the decision-maker's powers or had been arrived at through an unfair or irregular procedure, it could only be quashed if it was 'so unreasonable that no reasonable decision-maker could reach it'. Applying this standard the judges could maintain that they were not involved in assessing the merits of policy-making decisions, but rather only ensuring a basic standard of rational and fair decision-making.

16.35 However, since the passing of the Human Rights Act 1998, this threshold appears to have been lowered and now the judges have said that where decisions involve human rights they will apply a more intense scrutiny of the decision-making and consider whether it was a proportionate response to the problem which it addressed. This approach is likely to bring the judges nearer to the examination of the actual merits of official decisions. Whether this amounts to an unconstitutional usurpation of the function of elected politicians or a legitimate function for a judiciary in a system based on the rule of law is the subject of growing debate.

Fact-finding

16.36 The controversy surrounding the appropriate role of the judiciary in carrying out judicial review, and indeed in setting human rights standards generally under the Human Rights Act 1998, is really only of relevance to the senior judges who sit in the High Court and above and are the final arbiters in complex and sensitive cases. Most judges, in contrast, still spend almost all their time carrying out more traditional adjudication roles.

16.37 In the civil courts in particular, where lay decision-makers play a minor role, judges are responsible for handling day-to-day disputes in cases involving such areas as contracts, negligence actions and divorce. Most of their time is spent in deciding which facts are proved and applying settled law to those facts, reaching a decision and writing a judgment setting out the reasons for that decision.

Sentencing

16.38 An equally important function for all judges who work in the criminal courts is sentencing. Since most defendants plead guilty or are found guilty this is a fundamental function of a criminal judge. The sentencing system in England and Wales, in contrast to that of other jurisdictions such as many US states, involves a wide measure of discretion. Although judges are obliged to follow sentencing guidelines, and may find their sentences overturned on appeal if they do not, each sentencing exercise is intended to reflect the particular circumstances of each case, and there are relatively few mandatory sentences and a relatively wide range of different sentencing options which judges can choose from.

16.39 In determining the appropriate sentence, therefore, the judge is expected to fulfil an important role of reflecting and articulating social values. This is the area in which judges attract the most criticism and the media regularly highlight sentencing decisions which may appear to be too lenient or too severe. The judges, in response, have argued that this coverage is often ill-informed and distorted and fails to reflect the vast number of uncontroversial sentencing decisions passed each year. In 2000, the Lord Chancellor's Department issued to judges a guidance pack on dealing with the media to help them explain their decisions and respond effectively to unjustified criticism.

Case management

16.40 Until recently judges were expected to take a relatively neutral and passive role in the trial and pre-trial process. Most of the judge's involvement came at the later stages, summing up the case to the jury in a criminal trial, deciding and writing the judgment in the civil trial, passing sentence and determining what costs should be paid by whom. Traditionally, the judge was generally expected to leave the detailed management of the trial to the advocates, intervening only when a decision on a rule of law or procedure was required. The Woolf reforms have changed this in the civil justice process and given the judges a new role in actively managing cases (see chapter 9). A similar development is also underway in the criminal process. One result of this change is that judges are expected to spend a much greater proportion of their time reading and preparing for cases.

Training

16.41 Changes such as the new role in case management, the Human Rights Act 1998, and the increase in the range of sentencing options available to judges have all increased the need for judges to receive appropriate training. Traditionally, however, judges did not consider that training was necessary and, indeed, regarded it as a potential threat to their independence. The establishment of the Judicial Studies Board in 1979 was only considered acceptable because it was run by judges, for judges, and the training provided was largely voluntary.

16.42 Since then, however, the range and amount of training has increased in response to the growing complexity and speed of change in so many areas of the law. Judges now generally welcome all the training they can get, which still only amounts to a few days a year on average. In practice, judges are still generally expected to be able to 'pick up' the law in areas which they may have had little experience and to apply a wide range of different skills with little formal support and guidance.

Extra-judicial activities

16.43 In addition to the diverse range of judicial work which judges carry out, many also fulfil a number of different responsibilities not directly related to their case load. Most members of the public who have been in court probably believe that judges work from 10 am to 4 pm with long lunch breaks. In reality, as well as the work of pre-trial reading and preparation, judges increasingly carry a heavy administrative burden. Many senior judges will be involved in decisions about human resources and deciding which cases will be heard by which judges and when. Almost all judges will be involved in the consultation process for the appointment to judicial office. Some will spend time dealing with the media, developing information technology, consulting with court users' groups, receiving and giving judicial training, delivering lecturers and public speeches, writing journal articles, and giving evidence to or heading government inquiries.

16.44 Moreover, traditionally judges in England and Wales had limited support staff such as secretaries or clerks to help them in this work. It is only recently that the judges of the Court of Appeal and the Law Lords have begun to appoint American-style law clerks to help them research their cases. But it is still the case that by international standards the judiciary has relatively few resources and is a highly cost-effective institution.

Summary

16.45 Judges in England and Wales fulfil a very wide range of responsibilities. Many of their day-to-day functions have changed considerably in recent years through such developments as the Woolf reforms and the growing need for more professional and efficient working practices. The relatively amateur approach of former times, which rejected any form of training and expected unquestioning deference from court users and society as a whole, has largely disappeared. Nevertheless, some aspects of the modernization programme which has changed so many areas of public life in recent years have not yet significantly affected the judiciary. The pressure for greater judicial accountability is likely to increase, as is the need for greater diversity in the composition of the judiciary. In addition, the greater separation of powers between the judiciary and other branches of government instituted by the provisions of the CRA is likely to have a significant long-term effect on the structure and role of the judiciary.

FURTHER READING

Lord Woolf *The Needs of a 21st Century Judge*, Address to the Judicial Studies Board, London (22 March 2001) (http://www.jsboard.co.uk/downloads/annual_lecture_2001.pdf).

Martin Friedland *A Place Apart: Judicial Independence and Accountability in Canada* (1995, Canadian: Canadian Judicial Council).

Abimbola Olowofoyeku *Suing Judges* (1993, Oxford: Oxford University Press).

Professor Hazel Genn *Paths to Justice: What People Think and Do about Going to Law* (1999, Oxford: Hart Publishing).

Kate Malleson *The New Judiciary* (1999, Hampshire: Ashgate Press), chs 3, 5, and 6.

Roger Matthews, Lynn Hancock, and Daniel Briggs *Jurors Perceptions, Understanding, Confidence and Satisfaction in the Jury System: A Study in Six Courts* (2004, Home Office No 05/04) (http://www.homeoffice.gov.uk/rds/pdfs2/r227.pdf)

USEFUL WEBSITES

Judicial Studies Board website home page
http://www.jsboard.co.uk/

Judiciary of England and Wales official website
http://www.judiciary.gov.uk/

SELF-TEST QUESTIONS

1   What is meant by the term 'judicial independence'?

2   What effect did the Scottish case of *Starrs* have on the tenure of judges in England and Wales?

3   Outline the effect of the Human Rights Act 1998 on the test for judicial review.

4   List five functions which judges may perform when they are not sitting in court.

5   Can judges be made more accountable without compromising their independence?

17

Judicial appointments

SUMMARY

This chapter reviews the way in which judges are chosen in the light of the increasing constitutional and political significance of the judiciary discussed in chapter 16. It considers the tension between the requirements of judicial independence and accountability in the judicial appointments process and the growing pressure for more openness and greater diversity in the composition of the judiciary. It reviews the radical changes to the judicial appointments process which are set out in the Constitutional Reform Act 2005 and considers whether the new system will meet the challenge of maintaining the legitimacy and high levels of competence of the judiciary, whilst ensuring that all well-qualified lawyers have an equal chance of being appointed to the bench.

17.1 Approximately 900 full-and part-time judges are appointed each year, making it a major administrative process. Unlike the civil law systems found elsewhere in Europe, the judiciary is not a career which a young lawyer can embark upon after graduation, but is a second career taken up usually after many years of successful practice as a solicitor or barrister. Full-time appointment nearly always follows on from a period of part-time sitting, so the first step in a judicial career will be for a middle-aged lawyer to apply to sit as a deputy district judge, recorder or deputy High Court judge.

17.2 The way judges are selected is something of a mystery to most people. In contrast with some countries such as the US, where the selection of a judge is a public and highly scrutinized affair, the appointment of judges in England and Wales has not, to date, been considered a subject of general interest. This situation is changing rapidly, however, as a result of the greater public attention which the work of judges has been attracting. Over the last three decades or so, the growing role of the judges in checking official action through the law of judicial review has brought them into the political arena to an extent which would have been unthinkable before the Second World War.

17.3 More recently, the passing of the Human Rights Act 1998 has given the judiciary a new function in determining the nature and boundaries of human rights in the UK. Whether the judges ultimately take an activist or restrained approach to these new powers, there is little doubt that more sensitive political and ethical questions are coming before the courts to be decided. This judicialization of politics will inevitably mean that the spotlight of public attention and media interest will fall on the judges more intensively than in the past. The individual backgrounds, opinions, and interests of the top judges in particular will receive far greater public scrutiny than ever before.

17.4 The growing importance of the judicial appointments process is reflected in the number of official reports and inquiries carried out on the judicial appointments process in recent years. In 1999, the House of Commons Home Affairs Select Committee took evidence from a wide range of groups and individuals and came up with a number of recommendations for reform. This was followed in 2000 by an inquiry conducted by the retiring commissioner for public appointments, Sir Leonard Peach, which was commissioned by the Lord Chancellor. As a result of the Peach recommendations, a number of changes were instituted which built on reforms carried out by the Ministry of Justice (then Lord Chancellor's Department) since the early 1990s. Most importantly, these included the establishment of a Commission for Judicial Appointments which was given the role of scrutinizing the appointments process for Silk and judicial office and advising the Lord Chancellor on reform. Despite these changes, the pressure for more root and branch reform of the system continued to build up. In 2003, the Government unexpectedly responded to this pressure by announcing the introduction of a complete overhaul of the appointments system in the Constitutional Reform Act 2005 (CRA).

17.5 Under the provisions of the Act, the primary role of the Lord Chancellor in selecting the judges has been replaced by two independent judicial appointments commissions. One commission is responsible for appointing the judges in England and Wales. It consists of 15 members made up of judges, lawyers, a magistrate, a tribunal member and lay people (that is, non-lawyers with experience of appointments in other areas of public and commercial life). The commission, which began work in April 2006, is chaired by a lay person, currently Baroness Usha Prashar, formerly the first civil service commissioner. The second commission is responsible for appointing the justices of the new Supreme Court. It is an *ad hoc* body meeting only when a vacancy arises. Its membership consists of the President and Deputy President of the Supreme Court and one person from each of the judicial appointments commissions covering the separate UK jurisdictions (England and Wales, Scotland, and Northern Ireland). The role of both the Supreme Court Commission and the Judicial Appointments Commission for England and Wales is to recommend an appointment to the Lord Chancellor for each relevant vacancy within its remit. One name is put forward by the Commission which the Lord Chancellor can reject only if he has reason to believe that the person is not fit for office. If the Lord Chancellor believes that better qualified candidates were passed over by the Commission, he can send the name back and ask it to reconsider its decision.

17.6 In order to assess what effect these changes are likely to have, it is necessary to consider why they have been introduced. Three areas can be identified as the main foci of criticism which have led to the reforms: first, the extent to which the appointments system promotes the independence of the judges from political control; second, its lack of openness and democratic accountability; and, third, the lack of diversity in the composition of the judiciary.

Independence

17.7 Under the previous judicial appointments process, the judges of the Court of Appeal and above were chosen by the Queen on the recommendation of the Prime Minister, acting on the advice of the Lord Chancellor. For High Court judges and below, the Prime Minister played no role and the Queen was advised by the Lord Chancellor directly. In practice the monarch rubber-stamped the decision of her ministers.

17.8 Traditionally, therefore, politicians played a central role in selecting the judges. Yet despite the apparently politicized nature of the process, it is conventional to state that judges in England and Wales were chosen on merit alone and that politics played no part in the process. This statement needs some qualification. While it is true that party politics had not played a role in the system for many years, the relevance of political consideration in a wider sense of the word is not so easily dismissed. Indeed, the whole appointments process was intimately tied to the political system through the involvement of the Lord Chancellor, who carried the main responsibility for all judicial appointments.

17.9 By convention, it was understood that the Prime Minister followed the advice of the Lord Chancellor and did not seek to influence the decision in terms of party politics. However, we do not know exactly how the different Prime Ministers and their Lord Chancellors have gone about deciding between different candidates, whether, for example, a shortlist of names is provided by the Lord Chancellor. We do know that when Margaret Thatcher was Prime Minister she did not always accept the first choice of her Lord Chancellor. The dangers of possible political manipulation in the previous system were clear, particularly in the light of the growing political role of the judges.

17.10 While it may be the case that recent Prime Ministers have chosen to have only a limited input into judicial appointments, it is arguable that the convention of non-political involvement at this point in the system was not so clearly defined or firmly established that it could not have been eroded. While 20 or 30 years ago there was little incentive for the Prime Minister to take the time or trouble to intervene over appointments to the senior judiciary, this was less the case in recent years and critics of the system feared that as the potential for judicial decision-making to impact on government policy increased, the temptation to seek to affect the overall political outlook of the bench on the part of future Prime Ministers would have grown. For this reason, the Prime Minister now only plays a formal role in the new judicial appointments process, passing the name of candidates from the Lord Chancellor to the Queen. The Constitutional Reform and Governance Bill which is currently before Parliament goes one step further and will remove the Prime Minister's role in all judicial appointments in England and Wales.

17.11 For the same reason, the provisions of the CRA reduce the role of the Lord Chancellor to that of providing a safeguard against the appointment of unqualified candidates. During the 1990s, increasing concern was expressed about the suitability of leaving almost total control of the process in the hands of one cabinet minister. In 2003, an inquiry set up by the Bar Council and headed by a former Court of Appeal judge, Sir Iain Glidewell, concluded that the Lord Chancellor's powers to appoint judges should be removed. The report argued that the growing role of High Court judges in scrutinizing executive action meant that it was 'politically unacceptable' for senior judges to continue to be appointed by a member of the executive.

Accountability

17.12 Set against these concerns, however, is the equally valid argument that the selection of judges by politicians provides an element of accountability by maintaining the link between the judiciary and elected representatives. Although the Lord Chancellor has, to date, been a member of the House of Lords and therefore not elected, he has, at least, been part of the political system and is answerable to Parliament. During the passage of the Constitutional Reform Bill a number of speakers argued strongly that the Lord Chancellor should retain a greater degree of involvement in the judicial appointments process for this reason. Indeed, the original Bill proposed that in the case of appointments to the Supreme Court, the Supreme Court Commission should recommend two to five names to the Lord Chancellor, leaving her or him to make the final selection. A number of MPs and ministers argued that this proposal ensured that there was some accountability in the selection of the highest, and therefore most powerful, judicial posts. The House of Commons Constitutional Affairs Committee, which carried out a full inquiry into the proposals for constitutional reform, was sympathetic to these arguments and recommended that the provisions of the Bill should allow the Supreme Court Commission, if it so chose, to decide whether to provide the minister with a choice of more than one name (para 50). In the end, the arguments in favour of independence won over those of accountability and the Constitutional Reform Act 2005 provided that only one name would go forward to the Lord Chancellor.

17.13 The removal of any significant input from the Lord Chancellor might be less of a concern if the level of scrutiny by Parliament of judicial appointments was greater, so providing an alternative means of democratic accountability. But, to date, Parliament has taken the view that it is inappropriate to scrutinize individual judicial appointments. This is a very different situation from that which exists in some countries such as the US where judicial appointees appear before legislative committees for questioning at confirmation hearings. These are occasionally highly controversial, but more often simply provide a useful mechanism for legislators and the public to know something about the ideas and approach of those who have been given extensive judicial power.

17.14 One positive recent development in this regard has been the growing willingness of the House of Commons Constitutional Affairs Committee to call senior judges before it to give evidence about different aspects of the legal system and the judicial appointments process generally. To date, the judges have always been willing to attend and have provided full and helpful information and opinions to the committee. In its report on the current constitutional changes, the Committee recommended that this trend be encouraged as a way of maintaining a dialogue between the judiciary and Parliament (para 79).

17.15 Since judicial independence requires that judges be to some extent removed from the pressures of direct democratic accountability, one other channel through which the appointments process can be subject to public scrutiny is the media. To date it has played a limited role, and judicial appointments have received very little coverage, but this is changing. In 1998, for example, the appointment of Lords Millett and Hobhouse to the House of Lords were the first to receive significant media coverage reviewing their backgrounds, legal experience, and reputations. More recently, the promotion of Lady Justice Hale to the House of Lords in 2004 as the first female Law Lord, was widely reported and analysed in the press.

Openness

17.16   These various means of ensuring public accountability in the judicial appointments process can only be effective if the system itself is open to scrutiny. Until relatively recently, the process for appointing judges could be described as operating much like a club, with members recommending their friends and colleagues for advancement. In the 1980s, in response to criticisms of its lack of transparency, the Lord Chancellor's Department introduced a number of changes designed to open up the process. For the first time it published its policies and procedures, job descriptions, and selection criteria. In addition, vacancies for all ranks below the Court of Appeal were advertised, though senior posts remained effectively appointed by invitation only.

17.17   Since 1998, the Lord Chancellor's Department (and its successors the Department for Constitutional Affairs and the Ministry of Justice) has produced an annual report explaining the priorities and goals of the process and setting out figures for applicants and appointments for all the ranks. This exercise is inevitably something of a public relations exercise, but it is also a valuable source of extensive information on the system.

17.18   In comparison to the situation 20 years ago, it is clear that the degree of openness in the system has increased. Nevertheless, criticism remains of the lack of transparency in the consultation process. This is the process whereby the opinions of judges and senior lawyers are sought on the suitability of applicants. The consultation process is the heart of the system and no candidate will be appointed without a significant body of support among the consultees. This process is described by critics as a 'secret sounding system' by which those already on the bench can promote those they know, excluding other equally competent candidates outside the social and work network of a 'golden circle' of judges and barristers.

17.19   Lord Irvine, when Lord Chancellor, objected to the term 'secret soundings' on the grounds that the names of those consulted are made public, and he fiercely defended the system as a highly professional and effective means of obtaining a wide range of different views and opinions of candidates. He argued that judges are well placed to assess the merits of those applying for judicial office and insisted that the consultations process was objective and fair. In a speech to the Minority Lawyers' Conference in 1997, he stated:

> To the sceptic I ask, what do you think happens at one of these consultation meeting? Do you honestly believe that my Permanent Secretary turns up at a senior judge's door asking whether old Copperfield is a good chap or whether young Pickwick is a bit suspect because, rumour has it, he voted for the Green Party at the last election? No, our consultations are not like that.

17.20 However, concern about the potentially subjective and biased nature of the process remains. While unsuccessful candidates can now get feedback explaining in general terms why their application failed, they are still not told what has been said about them by those consulted and there have been claims in the past that inaccurate or biased information has unfairly affected people's chances of appointment. The Department for Constitutional Affairs responded to these concerns by stating that the policy is that one bad comment will not prevent appointment if the others are good and it is expected that the judicial appointment commission will continue this approach. In addition, it is claimed that unsubstantiated allegations of impropriety made against candidates in the consultations process will be disregarded.

17.21 Nevertheless, criticism remains strong and lawyers from non-traditional backgrounds in particular remain sceptical about the fairness of the system. Although the consultation process was generally praised by the Peach report, it recognized that it was poorly regarded. Research commissioned by the LCD in 2000 found that lawyers, particularly from non-traditional backgrounds, were most likely to consider that the system encouraged self-replication (Malleson and Banda, 2000).

17.22 Pressure for change in the system was also increased by growing criticism from the Commission for Judicial Appointments set up to scrutinize the system (not to be confused with the new judicial appointment commission). Although it accepted the need for confidentiality in the system, the Commission's 2002 annual report raised serious concerns about the objectivity and quality of some of the consultations it had observed. In 2004, it went further and argued that the whole consultation process should be scrapped and replaced by a more objective and rigorous process. It appears that the consultation process will continue in some form under the new system of appointments, but how, in practice, the new Judicial Appointments Commission and Supreme Court Appointments Commission will respond to increasing criticism of the process remains to be seen.

17.23 A more radical option for improving openness in the judicial appointments process is that of holding the interview process in public. This option has been rejected on the grounds that it would deter candidates from applying and undermine judicial independence. However, it is a process which is used successfully in some other countries. In South Africa, for example, the Judicial Service Commission interviews all candidates, including those for the Constitutional Court, in public. Although the introduction of this system was highly controversial and the Bar and judiciary at first claimed that good candidates would not put themselves through such an ordeal, the process has proved itself to be successful and generally well regarded both by observers and those who have been interviewed.

17.24 The public interviews in South Africa have also had the unexpected advantage of allowing judges to reveal certain information about themselves in a controlled environment. In 1999, Justice Edwin Cameron, an openly gay member of the South African High Court and a highly respected judge, informed the Commission that he was living with AIDS at his interview for a post on the Constitutional Court. His subsequent appointment undoubtedly reinforced the Judicial Service Commission's reputation for making non-discriminatory appointments on the grounds of merit alone.

Make-up of the judiciary

17.25 Concerns about independence, accountability, and openness in the judicial appointments process are still generally limited to those in the legal world who have a close knowledge or involvement in the system. In contrast, criticisms of the composition of the judiciary are commonly heard in wider public debate about the courts and the justice system. The one fact that almost everyone will claim to know about the judges in England and Wales is that they are elderly, male, white, and educated at elite establishments. This thumb-nail sketch remains very largely accurate, particularly at the top of the judicial hierarchy, where all judges are white, under 10 per cent of judges are women and only one woman, Baroness Hale, has ever been appointed to the Appellate Committee of the House of Lords (now the Supreme Court).

17.26 Clearly the judiciary is lacking in diversity, but it is not necessarily obvious why this matters. Some judges (and academics) have argued that the need for judges to be independent and impartial means that we should not talk about a representative judiciary in the same way as we might the legislature or executive. Judges are not there to represent the interests of any particular group but to ensure that the law is applied fairly and equally to all. In addition, while the judiciary as a whole might be demographically representative of society, the judge in each case cannot. As Lord Taylor, when Lord Chief Justice, argued:

> No judge trying a case can be representative of all sections of the community. To take the gender issue, even with a judiciary of equal numbers male and female the judge in any given case can only be one or the other. (Lord Taylor, 1992)

17.27 One response to these arguments is to say that while the background of the judges should not affect their decision-making, the composition of the judiciary as a whole does affect public confidence in their work and so undermines its legitimacy. For this reason, if no other, greater diversity is needed.

17.28 In 2003, research carried out by Hood, Shute, and Seemungal into perceptions of fair treatment in the courts among members of minority ethnic groups produced some very interesting data about confidence in the judiciary. One of the most positive findings of the study was that very few defendants perceived racial bias in the conduct or attitude of judges or magistrates – only 3 per cent in the Crown Court and 1 per cent in the magistrates' courts. Nor were there any complaints about racist remarks from the bench. Nevertheless, the report concluded there was a clear link between the question of the composition of the magistracy and judiciary and confidence in the courts:

> Among black defendants and lawyers in particular there was a belief that the authority and legitimacy of the courts, and confidence in them, would be strengthened if more personnel from ethnic minorities were seen to be playing a part in the administration of criminal justice. Indeed, in the Crown Court 31% of ethnic minority defendants, and in the magistrates' courts 48%, said they would like more people from ethnic minorities sitting in judgment and among the staff of the courts. Many judges agreed that more could be done to avoid the impression of the courts as 'white dominated institutions'. (Hood, Shute, and Seemungal, 2003)

17.29 The former Lord Chief Justice, Lord Woolf, also recognized the need to enhance public confidence through a more diverse judicial composition: 'The public has the right to demand not only a highly professional judiciary but also a judiciary that is more representative of the population than it is at present' (Lord Woolf, 2001).

17.30 How this change is to be achieved, however, is the subject of a sharp division of views. The official response to the problem of the homogenous composition of the judiciary is the 'trickle-up' hypothesis. This holds that the current make-up is the result of the fact that judges are chosen from among middle-aged lawyers who joined the legal profession 15 to 20 years ago at a time when it included very few women and minority lawyers. It is claimed that as the younger lawyers from more diverse backgrounds move up through the profession and join the recruitment pool the composition will change naturally and automatically:

> The present imbalance between male and female, white and black in the judiciary is obvious ... I have no doubt that the balance will be redressed in the next few years ... Within five years I would expect to see a substantial number of appointments from both these groups. This is not just a pious hope. It will be monitored. (Lord Taylor, 1992)

17.31 This comment by Lord Taylor was made 17 years ago and the evidence suggests that his expectations that a more diverse body of lawyers would 'trickle up' onto the bench have not been fulfilled. There are a number of reasons why this may be so. First, although more women and minority lawyers have entered the legal profession in recent years, they do not move up at the same speed and in the same career patterns as those from traditional backgrounds (see chapter 15). They do not have the connections or patterns of work which allow them to compete equally for judicial office. The tradition of appointing to the senior judiciary almost exclusively from the Bar, and within the Bar from among QCs practising mostly in a small number of elite chambers, discriminates against those outside those groups. Solicitors, in particular, have attacked the consultation process as unfairly advantaging barristers, and in 1999 the Law Society withdrew from the system in protest at its discriminatory effects on solicitors.

17.32 Critics of the system argue for the need for reforms which will open up appointments to candidates from a wider range of backgrounds. One common suggestion, which was supported by the Peach report, is to change the selection criteria to reduce the relevance of advocacy skills and emphasize instead other intellectual and practical abilities such as communication skills. This proposal has been implemented and the Department for Constitutional Affairs stressed that advocacy skills were not, of themselves, part of the selection criteria. Nevertheless, senior barristers almost exclusively remain the recruiting pool for the senior judiciary.

17.33 It is also necessary to consider structural and cultural factors which might deter applicants from non-traditional backgrounds from applying for judicial office. For example, the requirement that High Court judges go on circuit for periods of several weeks or longer is a potential barrier to anyone with family responsibilities. Similarly, the requirement that applicants for full-time posts should have first been appointed as a part-time judge is also particularly difficult for solicitors who, unlike barristers, are not usually self-employed and must obtain the agreement of their partners to taking unpaid time off to sit as a judge.

17.34 The fact that the current system contains discriminatory practices is not evidence of a conspiracy to exclude certain groups, but is the inevitable result of a system which evolved around the working practices and social circumstances of a small predominantly London-based and all-male Bar which was the recruiting pool for the judiciary, as the following comment by a judge in 1970 illustrates:

> The Lord Chancellor and members of his department and the judges would nearly all know a good deal about every member of the bar whose practice is big enough to justify his being considered for appointment to the bench. (Judge Henry, 1970)

17.35 The enormous growth and diversification of the Bar and the legal profession generally combined with the eligibility of solicitors for appointment require considerable changes to the appointments process to accommodate different career patterns and experiences. Under the current system, many lawyers cannot compete for judicial office equally because the nature of their work means that they are not known by the judges and so cannot be recommended by them in the consultations process.

The current system can be described as a 'merit-plus' system. Merit is a necessary but not always sufficient criterion for appointment. Other factors, such as being known by senior judges, are required in addition to ability in order to be appointed.

17.36 The Constitutional Reform Act recognized the need for the new Judicial Appointments Commission to take seriously the issue of diversity and includes the provision that: 'The Commission, in performing its functions under this Part, must have regard to the need to encourage diversity in the range of persons available for selection for appointments' (s 64(1)). However, in the first two years of the Commission's work, the proportion of women and BME lawyers appointed to the bench did not rise significantly, leading to criticism that the statutory duty was proving ineffectual. In an attempt to focus attention on the problem and promote further change, in March 2009, the Ministry of Justice announced the creation of an Advisory Panel on Judicial Diversity to work with the Judicial Appointments Commission with the aim of 'identifying the barriers to a more diverse judiciary and making recommendations to achieve speedier and sustained progress to a judiciary more representative of the people it serves'.

Implications of the new judicial appointments process

17.37 England and Wales is not alone in adopting a judicial appointments commission. Elsewhere in the UK, Scotland, and Northern Ireland have recently established commissions (called the Judicial Appointments Board in Scotland). Around the world there has been a tendency to replace elections (in the US state level) or executive appointment with some form of commission. Even in the continental civil law countries, where judges are chosen through examination and trained at judicial colleges, commissions contribute to the selection process.

17.38 These commissions cover a wide range of different models, so that generalizations about their effectiveness are difficult to make. Nevertheless, it is possible to conclude that the evidence we have as to their functioning is generally positive. Overall, it seems that judges appointed by commissions are as competent as those selected by the executive alone, while the record of commissions in improving the diversity of the judiciaries they select is generally better than other selection methods. In Canada, for example, the introduction of an appointments commission at federal level in 1989 led to a rise in the number of female applications for federal appointments from 12 per cent to 26 per cent over the following five years. The establishment of the judicial appointments committee in Ontario resulted in an even more dramatic rise in the number of women appointed; between 1989 and 1992, 41 per cent of new appointees were women compared to under 20 per cent before the establishment of the commission. Recent research from the Brennan Centre in New York comparing the record of different commissions in the US in improving diversity on the bench concluded that those which saw themselves as 'background checkers' were less effective than those which were 'headhunters', who actively set out to recruit candidates from under-represented groups. But perhaps the greatest strength of commissions is that they tend to generate increased public confidence in the appointments process and, in turn, the judiciary. If the primary goal of reform to the system is to bolster its levels of legitimacy, this benefit is very significant.

17.39 Commissions are not, however, without their critics. In Ireland and some US states it has been claimed that they are unacceptably politicized. Two factors seem to be present in those jurisdictions where this claim is made. First, an excessive degree of control of the membership of the commission by elected politicians, such as the Governor in some US states and, second, a strong culture of partisan politics within the judicial system generally.

17.40 Those commissions that work best in other countries appear to be the ones which have a wide-ranging membership, so that no one faction or interest group dominates the process. A key issue, therefore, is the composition of the commission. There is no doubt that the model adopted in the CRA has a strong judicial presence. This may ensure that judicial independence is preserved, but also runs the danger that diversity may be downgraded and the risk of 'self-replication' is increased. Supporters argue, on the other hand, that it is well balanced and that the strong judicial membership is countered by the fact that the Commission is chaired by a non-lawyer. Ultimately, the way in which the Commission works in practice will depend on the particular attitudes of the members and the dynamics of the different interest groups. A key question is whether the lay members will be sufficiently confident and authoritative to influence the judicial members of the Commission so as to develop a reflexive and modern appointments process.

Summary

17.41 The quality of the bench in terms of independence, integrity, and intellectual standards is generally high and compares well with other jurisdictions. In addition, the appointments system has undergone significant changes in recent years designed to make it a more professionalized, fair, and open process. Nevertheless, the recent reforms are the product of a growing consensus that more root and branch change is needed to counter the risks of politicization on the one hand and lack of account-ability on the other.

17.42 The challenge facing the new system will be to retain the high quality of the appoint-ments made while opening up the system so that all well-qualified lawyers can com-pete for judicial office on a level playing field rather than in a system designed for the needs of a small group of elite members of the Bar. The extent to which the process promotes diversity in the composition of the judiciary and opens up the recruitment pool to a wider range of candidates has become the litmus test by which the new judicial appointments system will be measured.

FURTHER READING

Judicial Diversity Strategy (May 2006, DCA) (http://www.dca.gov.uk/publications/reports_reviews/judicial_diversity_strat.pdf).

Constitutional Affairs Committee *Third Report Constitutional Reform Bill [Lord]: The Governments' Proposals* (28 January 2005) (http://www.publications.parliament.uk/pa/cm/cmconst.htm).

Roger Hood, Stephen Shute, and Florence Seemungal *Ethnic Minorities in the Criminal Courts: Perceptions of Fairness and Equality of Treatment* (2003). Summary avail-able on Department for Constitutional Affairs website at: http://www.dca.gov.uk/research/2003/2-03es.htm.

Lord Woolf *The Needs of a 21st Century Judge*, Address to the Judicial Studies Board, London (22 March 2001) (http://www.jsboard.co.uk/downloads/annual_lecture_2001.pdf).

Judicial Diversity: Finding of a Consultation with Judges, Solicitors and Barristers (2006, DCA) (http://www.dca.gov.uk/publications/reports_reviews/jd_cbsj06.pdf).

C. Torres-Spelliscy, M. Chase, and E. Greenman, (2008) *Improving Judicial Diversity*, Brennan Center for Justice, New York (http://brennan.3cdn.net/96d16b62f331bb13ac_kfm6bplue.pdf)

Kate Malleson 'Creating a Judicial Appointments Commission: Which Model Works Best?' (Spring 2004) Public Law.

Lord Taylor 'The Judiciary in the Nineties' (1993) 19(1) Commonwealth Law Bulletin 323.

USEFUL WEBSITES

Judicial Appointments Commission
http://www.judicialappointments.gov.uk/

1   Outline the process by which High Court judges are appointed.

2   'The judicial appointments process will continue to lack transparency and fairness until the consultations process is abolished.' Discuss.

3   What are the advantages and disadvantages of the consultations process?

4   What lessons can the appointments process in England and Wales learn from the judicial selection processes in other jurisdictions?

18

Lay adjudication

SUMMARY

This chapter reviews the ways in which jurors and magistrates are selected and the tensions which exist between the competing goals of random selection, impartiality, and the need for representativeness. It scrutinizes the justifications for the strong attachment to the jury and assesses the relative quality of the justice dispensed by juries, lay magistrates, and District Judges. Lastly, it describes the gradual reduction in the use of jury trial and examines the reasons for this trend.

18.1 In contrast with most other legal systems, England and Wales still relies heavily on the use of lay personnel in the courts, most particularly in criminal cases. With the exception of about 100 District Judges (Magistrates' Court) the magistrates' courts are staffed by around 28,000 lay magistrates. In the Crown Court, all fact-finding is carried out by a jury. In the civil system the decision-making in the courts is largely undertaken by professional judges, but many tribunals have at least some lay participation.

Rationale for lay participation

18.2 Observers from countries which use only professional judges are often mystified by the strong attachment which is retained in England and Wales to the participation of lay decision-makers and argue that their use is likely to result in inconsistency, low standards, and subjective decision-making.

18.3 These claims can be countered with the argument that lay justice is democratic, local, and legitimate. Its advantages are that it ensures the participation of citizens in the justice system, providing a potential check on abuse of power by those in authority, thus allowing for the values of society as a whole to inform the decisions of the courts and to reflect local conditions and circumstances. If judging is an expression of values and standards, and fact-finding requires the ability to weigh up the credibility of one version of events against another, then it is arguable that the characteristics required of an adjudicator are common sense and experience of the world rather than technical legal skills.

History of the role of the jury

18.4 Whatever the arguments for and against lay adjudication, the continuing popularity of the jury is largely a result of the particular role which it played in the development of English political history. For many centuries it has fulfilled both a symbolic and practical role as a tool for resisting the oppressive rule of the monarch or executive. The Magna Carta of 1215 recognized the right of trial by one's peers as a means of preventing arbitrary justice from the throne. Trial by jury was later the standard against which the oppressive procedures of the Star Chamber were judged and the Bill of Rights of 1689 reasserted the right to jury trial as an 'ancient liberty'. However, the notion of jury sovereignty was only gradually established. At one time, jurors could be fined and incarcerated if they did not return a guilty verdict. In 1670 a jury refused to convict William Penn, a Quaker (and later founder of Pennsylvania), who was accused of sedition for preaching outside the Church of England. The jury were imprisoned for nine weeks in Newgate prison before being set free by the Lord Chief Justice.

18.5 In the context of this political history, the jury has come to be seen as a key feature of the democratic system. Lord Devlin, one of the most influential judges of the twentieth century and a strong advocate of the jury, wrote of this aspect of its role:

> Each jury is a little parliament. The jury sense is the parliamentary sense. I cannot see the one dying and the other surviving. The first object of any tyrant in Whitehall would be to make Parliament utterly subservient to his will; and the next to overthrow or diminish trial by jury, for no tyrant could afford to leave a subject's freedom in the hands of twelve of his countrymen. So that trial by jury is more than an instrument of justice and more than one wheel of the constitution; it is the lamp that shows that freedom lives. (Devlin, 1956)

18.6 The practical expression of the jury's function in protecting individual liberty against state oppression or unjust laws is found in cases in which so-called 'perverse verdicts' have been reached (without the threat of punishment for an acquittal as in William Penn's day). In 1985, for example, a civil servant, Clive Ponting, was acquitted of breaching the Official Secrets Act for informing the press of the sinking of an

Argentine ship in safe waters during the Falklands War. The 'not guilty' verdict was returned despite the fact that the judge had directed the jury that there was no defence in law to the charge. Similarly, two defendants, Pottle and Randall, were acquitted in 1991 of helping the escape of the spy, Peter Blake, 26 years earlier. They defended themselves in court and argued that: '... we do not deny the things we are accused of. Not only do we not deny it. We say it was the right thing to do.' The jury either agreed or, alternatively, considered that to prosecute the men nearly three decades later was an injustice. Most recently, defendants charged with criminal damage to genetically modified crops and those suffering from multiple sclerosis charged with possession of a class B drug who claimed to have used cannabis to relieve their symptoms have similarly been acquitted.

18.7   Controversially, the Auld report on the criminal courts in 2002 recommended that the law should be changed so that juries have no right to acquit in defiance of the law or in disregard of the evidence and that there should be a right of appeal against a 'perverse verdict'. The Lord Chief Justice, Lord Woolf, gave his support to this proposal, provided the jury's decision was against the rational weight of the evidence, but not if the perverse verdict was one of principle. He did not give any guidance on how the Court of Appeal was to distinguish these two types of decisions. These proposals from the Auld report were not, however, implemented.

Selection and composition of the jury

18.8   Originally juries were made up of witnesses, those who had some personal knowledge of the events and people involved in the case, and they worked closely with the judge in reaching a verdict. Over the years, the precise opposite came to be the case. Jurors must now be wholly unconnected with the case and are expected to reach an independent verdict uninfluenced by the views of the judge on the facts. Members of a jury are selected from a jury panel which is made up of citizens between 18 and 70 years of age chosen at random from the electoral register. Service is compulsory and is unpaid except for a modest daily allowance to cover expenses. Jury service normally lasts around 10 days and under the provisions of the Employment Relations Act 2004, it is now illegal to sack someone because they have been summoned for, or completed, jury service.

18.9   There is a constant tension in the jury system between the requirement of random selection and the need to ensure that its members are impartial. Two mechanisms are used to influence who can sit on a jury. The first is the prosecution's 'right of standby' whereby a juror can be put back onto the panel of jurors from which the 12 are chosen. This right is usually only exercised by the prosecution in cases involving terrorism or national security where, with the approval of the Attorney-General, the prosecution can 'vet' the jury by checking the records of the police and security services to see whether any jurors have a particular political affiliation which would make them unsuitable to sit on the case. Jury vetting is carried out in a relatively small number of cases each year, but the fact that it is used in politically sensitive cases in which the actions of officials may be under scrutiny, coupled with the fact that the prosecution does not have to give reasons for asking a juror to 'stand by', has meant that the practice is extremely controversial.

18.10 The second method of influencing the membership of the jury is the right to challenge jury members 'for cause' as each juror is sworn in. Both the prosecution and the defence have the right to show some reason (such as that the juror knows someone in the case) why he or she should not serve. At one time the defence had a pre-emptory right to challenge three jurors who would then be asked to step down. Unlike the prosecution's right of 'stand by', it was regularly exercised. This right was abolished in 1988 because of concern that it was used to manipulate unfairly the make-up of the jury in the defendant's favour. The abolition of the right was strongly contested by defence lawyers who argued that it helped to protect the defendant from trial by prejudiced or partial jurors. A review of over 2,000 cases carried out by the Crown Prosecution Service in 1986 found that there was no difference in the acquittal rates of those who exercised the right of pre-emptory challenge and those who did not.

18.11 The debate over the selection process for juries is based on the assumption (surprisingly difficult to prove) that the composition of the jury affects its decision-making. Although service is technically obligatory, there were, until recently, a wide range of circumstances in which people either were not allowed to serve, or could choose not to. Before 2004, around 480,000 people were summoned annually for service, of whom more than half were ineligible, disqualified or excused from service. For this reason, there was concern that the make-up of juries was not representative. This contention was not, however, supported by research into jury composition carried out by the Royal Commission on Criminal Justice in 1993 which concluded that in terms of gender, ethnicity, and class juries were broadly representative of the population as a whole. The Commission did, however, recommend that the rules governing who could sit on a jury should be changed to improve the diversity of the composition of juries. Under these rules, some groups, such as those with certain criminal records or mental illnesses, were disqualified from sitting on a jury. Others were deemed ineligible to sit, including members of the clergy and people who worked in the criminal justice system such as judges, lawyers, and police officers. Lastly, others who might be called up for jury service could be excused as of right, such as doctors and MPs. In addition, many of those who were called up would be allowed to defer their service if it would cause personal or financial hardship. Those caring for small children or self-employed people often fell into this category.

18.12 The Auld report in 2001 supported the argument of the Royal Commission that these rules should be reformed in order to increase the representativeness of juries. This recommendation was included in the Criminal Justice Act 2003 which removed the concept of exclusion as of right and abolished the categories of ineligibility (with the exception of mentally disordered persons and certain groups of convicted persons). Only those who can prove that they have 'compelling reasons' to be excused will be released from the obligation to undertake jury service. In 2004, Lord Justice Dyson became the first Court of Appeal judge to be called to do jury service. Similarly, in January 2005, a Government minister, Alun Michael, was also called up. Both expressed their willingness to undertake their service, but whether, in practice, judges and ministers will seek to be excused on the grounds that they have compelling reasons to be allowed to step down remains to be seen. In terms of public confidence, there is clearly something to be gained by the participation of high-profile and important figures in the jury system. But whether this gain is worth the cost in terms of time and resources of judges and ministers leaving their jobs for days or weeks to sit on a jury is open to question.

18.13 These reforms to the composition of juries were challenged as being contrary to Article 6 ECHR in *R v (1) Abdroikov (2) Green (3) Williamson* (2005). The juries in the first two cases contained serving police officers and the jury in the third case contained an employed CPS prosecuting solicitor. The House of Lords, by a majority of 3 to 2, held that the appeals of Green and Williamson should be allowed. As Baroness Hale explained, just because a person *can* be called for jury service it does not mean that they should sit on the case they have been summoned for. The majority therefore held that whether members of the criminal justice system could sit in particular cases depended upon whether there was an appearance of bias which rendered the trial unsafe. In Abdroikov's case there was no appearance of bias because there was no real dispute over the evidence between the police and the defendant and no link between the police witnesses and the policeman juror. However, there was an appearance of bias in the case of the CPS employee because the prosecution was being brought by the crown prosecutor's employer. The Court of Appeal gave further guidance on these issues in *Khan* (2008). The mere fact that a police officer works in the same locality as a witness does not provide evidence of bias, not does the fact that he works on similar cases. Furthermore, crown prosecutors are only ineligible for jury service where the CPS is the prosecuting authority.

18.14 Another topical question which has attracted considerable debate in recent years is whether juries should ever be required to have a certain ethnic composition in cases involving a racial element. A random jury is not necessarily a representative one, so that it may quite often occur that the defendant or victim comes from a different background from all those on the jury. The Royal Commission recommended allowing the defence or prosecution the right to request at least one juror of the same ethnic origin as the defendant or victim. The Auld report supported this change but it has not, to date, been implemented. Recent research carried out by Thomas and Balmer does, somewhat surprisingly, suggest that there is no significant under-representation of ethnic minority groups among those summoned for jury service at virtually all Crown Courts.

Reliability of jury verdicts

18.15 Critics of juries argue that jurors are often discriminatory, do not understand the evidence and reach a verdict based on inappropriate criteria or methods (Darbyshire, 1991). Occasionally, evidence emerges which supports this contention. In one infamous case, a conviction was quashed by the Court of Appeal when it was found that the verdict was reached using a ouija spirit board (*Young* (1995)).

18.16 However, obtaining reliable evidence about the overall quality of jury verdicts is hampered by the fact that under the Contempt of Court Act 1981 it is a contempt to publish or solicit for publication details of what happens in a jury room. In the 1990s the Royal Commission on Criminal Justice argued for the repeal of this provision to allow for academic research into juries and the Government indicated its support for this change. However, no progress was made on this issue until 2005 when the Lord Chancellor, Lord Falconer, issued a consultation paper on the jury which sought opinions on a proposal to change the law to allow research into how jurors in England and Wales reach their decisions. To date, the restrictions imposed by the Contempt of Court Act have meant it is has been necessary to develop indirect ways of assessing the jury system. One such method is the use of a 'shadow' jury whereby 12 people are asked to sit in the public gallery and shadow the real jury, hearing the evidence and retiring to deliberate when they do. Researchers scrutinize their deliberations and interview them about their experiences. Another indirect method of assessing the effectiveness of the jury system is to interview the other participants in the court process such as lawyers, judges, the police, and defendants in order to find out their views on the work of the jury.

18.17 The research which has been carried out using these methods is somewhat contradictory. Baldwin and McConville's review in 1979 involved questioning the participants in just under 400 jury trials (Baldwin and McConville, 1979). They found that a significant number of acquittals and some convictions were considered doubtful by those in court, leading the authors to question the effectiveness of the jury. Their findings were contradicted, however, by a Home Office study in 1986 which found that there were generally acceptable reasons for acquittals in a sample of 320 cases reviewed (Vennard, 1986).

18.18 Research findings from the Royal Commission's Crown Court survey in 1993 also indicates continued support for the jury system from those who participate in the trial process. 79 per cent of jurors who were asked their opinion on the jury system thought that it was either good or very good, as did 79 per cent of judges, 82 per cent of prosecution barristers and 91 per cent of defence barristers (Zander and Henderson, 1993). These findings were supported in 2004 by the findings of a large survey conducted for the Home Office of people who had undertaken jury service. The research found that, overall, respondents had a very positive attitude towards the experience. The respondents generally expressed the view that juries were an essential component of providing a fair and just trial process and that diversity amongst jurors was important in avoiding bias and ensuring a sound verdict. The researchers concluded that for the vast majority of respondents: 'jury service was a unique experience which increased their sense of social solidarity and citizenship, while enhancing their confidence in the jury system' (Matthews, Hancock, and Briggs, 2004).

18.19 One way in which the quality of jury decision-making could be improved would be by providing the jury with a summary of the facts which are agreed and those which are in issue. This proposal was put forward in the Auld report and has support from recent research findings from the New Zealand Law Commission (where direct jury research is allowed) which argued for the need for improvements in the way the information is provided to juries (*Juries on Criminal Trials* (New Zealand Law Commission (1999)).

Reduction of the jury system

18.20 The amount of space which the jury occupies in public debate on criminal justice would suggest that it is a major feature of the system. In fact, only around 2 per cent of criminal cases are decided by a jury. About 95 per cent of cases are heard in the magistrates' courts and of the remaining 5 per cent most plead guilty and so do not come before a jury. But although the jury may only hear a small fraction of cases, the fact that around 200,000 people sit on juries each year is evidence of its continuing role as a means of ensuring participation by ordinary people.

18.21 Because research findings are so limited and the subject of the jury is such an emotive one, views about the appropriate role of the jury tend to be based less on empirical evidence and more on political instinct. While many academic commentators and lawyers strongly defend the right to jury trial, some have questioned the uncritical approach to this form of decision-making: 'The jury is an antidemocratic, irrational and haphazard legislator whose erratic and secret decisions run counter to the rule of law' (Darbyshire, 1991).

18.22 Successive governments, both Conservative and Labour, would appear to agree with this view and have introduced a range of measures which have reduced the role of the jury. These changes are, however, probably driven as much by reasons of economy as any empirically grounded assessment of the reliability of jury verdicts. Legislation in the 1970s restricted the range of offences for which the defendant could elect trial by jury. More recently, the Criminal Justice Act 1988 recategorized certain offences such as driving while disqualified and common assault and battery as summary only. In 1986, the Roskill Committee on Fraud Trials recommended that the jury trial should be replaced by an expert panel in a small number of complex fraud cases. The recommendation was supported in a modified form by the Auld report and included in the Criminal Justice Act 2003. In Northern Ireland the right to a trial by jury has been removed in terrorist cases, which are now tried in the 'Diplock courts' by a judge alone. The evidence suggests that these trials are generally well regarded as fair and efficient and there has been very little suggestion that juries should be brought back as the instances of terrorism activity in the region has receded.

18.23 In 1999, the Government introduced a Bill in Parliament which would have removed the right of a defendant to elect trial in the Crown Court in either way offences and transferred the decision to the magistrates. The Bill was twice defeated in the House of Lords. Its provisions were broadly supported by the Auld proposals which also proposed that defendants charged with indictable or either way offences be given the right to elect trial by judge alone in the Crown Court.

18.24 The Criminal Justice Act 2003 did not seek to reinstate the proposals of the Mode of Trial Bill for complete transfer of the decision on venue to the magistrates, but it did include a provision that defendants be given the right to choose trial by judge alone. What is not in doubt is that the increase of magistrates' sentencing powers from six to twelve months in custody will substantially increase the number of cases being dealt with at summary level. The Government's goal of reducing the number of more costly jury trials below the current 2 per cent is therefore likely to be achieved despite the defeat of the Mode of Trial Bill.

Magistrates

18.25 The reduction in the number of jury trials will not, of course, reduce the role of lay participation in the system. With the exception of those cases tried by District Judges (Magistrates' Court), all cases which would have been heard by a judge and jury will now be heard by lay magistrates. The Department for Constitutional Affairs National Recruitment Strategy has been seeking an additional 5,000 magistrates in anticipation of the increasing workload of the magistrates' courts. Each magistrate is required to sit for a minimum of 26 half days per year. They have no legal qualifications, but they do receive training from the Judicial Studies Board. This covers both practical skills concerning procedure and sentencing and issues around discrimination. Magistrates sit with a legally qualified clerk who advises them on the law and their powers.

Selection and composition of magistrates

18.26 Lay magistrates are appointed by the Department for Constitutional Affairs after consultation with local advisory committees made up of magistrates and other local people. Because they are meant to be representative of the community, no formal qualifications are required for the job and all citizens can put themselves forward. In practice, because the work is voluntary and unpaid only those with the time and resources can apply. Moreover, the strong role of the advisory committees has meant that, in the past, only those who are part of the work or social network of its members have tended to be appointed.

18.27 The result is that the magistracy is overwhelmingly drawn from professional and managerial groups and is generally made up of older people (Morgan and Russell, 2000). And although it is balanced in terms of gender and race overall, in urban areas the ethnic mix of the bench is also often unrepresentative of the local communities. To address these limitations in the background of magistrates, the Department for Constitutional Affairs has undertaken a number of initiatives to recruit more widely. Advertisements have been placed in a wider range of publications to try to attract more working people and younger people and a Magistrates' Shadowing Scheme has been established to encourage those who do not come from the traditional recruitment pool to see at first hand what the job involves.

18.28 One aspect of the selection process for magistrates which has differed significantly from that of professional judges is the role of party politics. For judges, their personal political views are not expected to play any part in the selection process. In relation to the magistracy, the local advisory committee is required to try to ensure a balanced bench in terms of social and political background. In practice this is not generally achieved, and there are a disproportionate number of Conservative voters among those appointed. In 1998, the LCD put forward proposals in a consultation paper that this arrangement should be replaced by a more sophisticated geodemographic system in which the pool of candidates would be drawn from a range of geographical areas according to the known background of its residents. This new approach has not been implemented although the Ministry of Justice is still considering a better mechanism for ensuring the selection of magistrates with a diverse range of experiences, backgrounds, and views. In 2003, the Lord Chancellor, Lord Falconer, announced that questions about magistrates' political affiliations would be removed from the application form as these were: 'no longer an effective guide to social background'.

18.29 Research carried out for the Home Office in 2000 on the relative merits of lay and professional magistrates found that, although the magistrates were not representative of the community, the use of lay magistrates generally commanded public confidence and should be retained (Morgan and Russell). This conclusion was supported by the Auld report, which also recommended that efforts should be made to ensure a more representative composition.

Comparison between professional and lay magistrates

18.30 The Home Office research also concluded that the magistrates' courts generally work well and provide a satisfactory quality of justice. It found that District Judges were more efficient in the sense that they were faster and needed to confer less with their clerk than lay magistrates, the result being that they can deal with a case load which is 30 per cent higher. In terms of cost per hearing, District Judges were found to be more expensive than lay magistrates, but when all the indirect costs were taken into account, such as court and administrative time and the extra costs in lost time for court users, there was found to be relatively little difference in the costs (£52.10 per hearing for lay magistrates and £61.78 for District Judges). However, District Judges were also more likely to remand in custody and to pass longer custodial sentences with the knock-on increase in costs to the prison service.

Comparison between magistrates and juries

18.31 The gradual reduction in the use of the jury and the increasing role of magistrates raises the question of whether this change improves or reduces the quality of justice in the courts. An important factual difference between the two is that more defendants plead guilty in the magistrates' courts – approximately 88 per cent compared to 58 per cent in the Crown Court (see chapter 13).

18.32 Among the minority of defendants who plead not guilty, the conviction rate is higher in the magistrates' courts (approximately 80 per cent compared with 50 per cent in the Crown Court). However, it is important to realize that just over half the acquittals in the Crown Court are directed by the judge because the prosecution has decided not to proceed or because the evidence is, in her or his view, too weak to safely convict.

18.33 One commonly heard explanation for these differences in conviction rates is that juries are not 'case-hardened' as magistrates become and are more likely to believe the defendant's explanation of events. Another is that the more representative make-up of juries makes them more able to relate to the circumstances and lifestyle of many defendants and to give credibility to their stories.

18.34 Since it is difficult to conduct research into jury verdicts, there is no reliable empirical evidence to support or refute these theories. But even if more rigorous research into jury decision-making was carried out, it could not tell us whether these verdicts were correct. It will never be possible to know which decision-makers are more accurate – whether juries are acquitting significant numbers of guilty people, or whether magistrates are convicting significant numbers of innocent people. Moreover, the answer to that question also depends on what definition of 'significant' is adopted and whether or not the maxim that 'it is better that 100 guilty people go free than one innocent person is convicted' is applied (or perhaps modified to a different ratio, whether higher or lower).

18.35 Apart from the vexed question of verdict accuracy, there are other factors which are relevant in comparing the two systems. The fact that juries do not give reasons for their decisions is often criticized as fundamentally unjust since the obligation on decision-makers to give reasons is increasingly recognized as a basic requirement of a fair trial under Article 6 of the European Convention on Human Rights.

18.36 On the other hand, the jury system is praised because it allows the judge to decide whether or not evidence should be admitted, such as the previous convictions of the defendant, in the absence of the jury. If the decision is to exclude, the jury will not hear the evidence, whereas in the magistrates' court the magistrates must try to put out of their mind what they have heard if they rule it inadmissible.

18.37 In terms of public confidence in the quality of justice between the two courts, one recent research study suggests that the magistrates' courts may be perceived by defendants, at least, as fairer. About one-third of defendants in the Crown Court and about one-quarter in the magistrates' courts said their treatment had been unfair in court.

18.38 Lastly, jury trials are generally longer and more expensive, the average cost of a jury trial being £8,500 and a trial in the magistrates' court being £550. It is this factor, rather than any other, which probably plays the most significant role in Government policy in this area.

The use of mixed panels

18.39 In response to the concerns which have been raised about both systems, there is increasing support for the use of mixed panels of lay and profession judges for middle-ranking offences. The Auld report, for example, proposed that an intermediate court between the magistrates' courts and the Crown Court consisting of a District Judge and two lay magistrates should be created.

18.40 However, critics of this proposal urge caution, arguing that rather than ensuring the best features of the two systems, the use of mixed panels can result in the worst of both worlds. Evidence from other countries suggests that the role of the lay personnel is usually very limited and the professional judges dominate the proceedings. In addition, the presence of District Judges is likely to drive up the severity of sentencing.

Summary

18.41 The principle that a person accused of a crime should be tried by her or his peers is entrenched in the legal and political culture of England and Wales. Interestingly, it is generally the jury, rather than the magistracy, which attracts passionate support. The image of the jury as a bastion of freedom and protection from authoritarian control lives on despite the fact that very few cases are actually tried by a jury and most which are so tried are relatively routine criminal matters without a political content.

18.42 Even this limited role seems likely to be eroded still further as magistrates' sentencing powers increase thereby enabling more cases to be dealt with summarily. While the role of the jury seems set to continue to diminish, the future of the magistracy appears more secure for the time being and the criminal courts will still be in the hands of lay adjudicators. The quality of the decision-making of the magistrates, therefore, should be the subject of greater debate and more rigorous research in the years ahead as the proportion of the caseload which they hear grows to encompass more serious cases.

FURTHER READING

Department for Constitutional Affairs *Jury Research and Impropriety*, Consultation paper on jury research (January 2005) (http://www.dca.gov.uk/consult/juryresearch/juryresearch_cp0405.htm).

Roger Matthews, Lynn Hancock and Daniel Briggs *Jurors Perceptions, Understanding, Confidence and Satisfaction in the Jury System: A Study in Six Courts* (2004, Home Office No 05/04) (http://www.homeoffice.gov.uk/rds/pdfs2/r227.pdf).

Darbyshire et al *What can the English Legal System Learn from Jury Research Published up to 2001* (2001).

Rod Morgan and Neil Russell *The Judiciary in the Magistrates' Courts* (2000, Home Office Occasional Paper No 66) (http://www.homeoffice.gov.uk/rds/pdfs/occ-judiciary.pdf).

Lord Justice Auld *Review of the Criminal Courts* (2001), ch 5 (http://www.criminal-courts-review.org.uk/auldconts.htm).

Penny Darbyshire 'The Lamp that Shows that Freedom Lives: Is It Worth the Candle?' (1991) Criminal Law Review 740.

Lord Devlin *Trial by Jury* (1956, London: Stevens and Sons).

John Baldwin and Mike McConville *The Jury* (1979, Oxford: Clarendon).

Julie Vennard *Evidence and Outcome: a Comparison of Contested Trials in Magistrates' Courts and the Crown Court* (1986, Home Office Research and Planning Unit, Research Bulletin No 20).

Michael Zander and Paul Henderson, Royal Commission on Criminal Justice Research Study No 19, *The Crown Court Study* (1993).

Michael Zander *The State of Justice* (2000, London: Sweet and Maxwell), pp 53–62.

Cheryl Thomas and Nigel Balmer *Diversity and Fairness in the Jury System* (2007)

http://www.justice.gov.uk/publications/docs/PagesfromJuries-report2-07C1.pdf

USEFUL WEBSITES

Directgov website magistrates' section

http://www.direct.gov.uk/en/CrimeJusticeAndTheLaw/Becomingamagistrate/index.htm

SELF-TEST QUESTIONS

1   What rationale is there for retaining lay participation in the criminal justice process in the form of magistrates and juries?

2   Give three possible explanations for the higher conviction rate of magistrates compared to juries.

3   What explains the continuing popularity of the jury system in criminal cases? Why is the jury used so rarely in civil cases?

4   What is meant by 'jury vetting'?

19

Funding of legal services

SUMMARY

This chapter outlines the history of the legal aid system and the extensive reforms introduced under the Access to Justice Act 1999. It analyses the role of the Legal Services Commission, the Community Legal Service, the Criminal Defence Service, contracting, and Conditional Fee Agreements. It argues that these changes have led to reductions in public spending but have not, overall, increased access to justice. It finishes by reviewing the continuing pressure to reduce the legal aid budget and the proposals for reform of the criminal legal aid system set out in the 2006 Carter report.

19.1 The question of how legal services are funded raises many of the themes identified at the beginning of this book. In particular, it highlights the debate over the public or private nature of the system. In order to determine the best way to fund the legal system it is necessary to consider whether the justice system is a public service in the same way as, for example, the National Health Service, to which every person has an entitlement should they need it and which should be free at the point of delivery, or whether it is a consumer service which should be self-funding and purchased privately, or some mixture of the two. Assuming that it is at least to some extent a public service, on what basis should legal services be rationed? Should, for example, the funding basis of civil and criminal justice be different?

19.2 Whether funding is public or private, the problem remains of ensuring that services are efficient and that users receive value for money while at the same time maintaining high standards of justice. These are the issues which the government, lawyers, and judges have been grappling with in recent years. Over the last decade or so, the system of funding has undergone more change than at any time since the Second World War.

Funding civil justice

19.3 Access to the civil courts is widely accepted as being a key component of a democratic system. If citizens do not have the ability to seek redress for breaches of contract and civil wrongs or to challenge illegal government action, the rule of law is meaningless. In practice, however, the cost of bringing or defending civil actions is beyond the reach of most people and criticisms of the 'affordability gap' in civil justice are as strong today as they ever were. In 2003, a leading High Court judge, Mr Justice Lightman, argued at a reception organized by a mediation group that methods of alternative dispute resolution should be given a higher priority in the light of the costs of the civil court system:

> The already outrageous and ever-increasing costs of litigation are beyond the means of the more advantaged members of the public including the middle class and small to medium size business entities. They are ruinous, and the threat and risk of the burden of costs must daunt all but the most gung-ho litigant.

19.4 If litigation is beyond the means of the relatively wealthy, then the majority of the population have no hope at all of accessing the courts without government assistance in funding their litigation. It was for this reason that the legal aid system was developed.

Legal aid

19.5 In 1949, the legal aid system was set up with the aim of establishing a comprehensive system of public funding for both criminal and civil cases for those who needed it. The system was envisaged as a key part of the welfare state but, unlike the National Health Service, legal services were not restructured into a national system and most legal work continued to be carried out by solicitors and barristers in private practice. The legal aid system allowed these lawyers to undertake publicly-funded criminal and civil work paid for by the state on a case-by-case basis.

19.6 The test for deciding whether someone could receive legal aid in bringing or defending a case was, broadly, whether the person lacked the means to pay for it privately and whether the case merited funding (whether it had a reasonable chance of success and whether it was reasonable for public money to be spent). The Legal Aid Board administered the fund through which lawyers were paid for advice and representation in those cases which satisfied these criteria.

19.7 The system therefore remained a mixed private and public one. Any lawyer could offer to undertake legally aided work for a client who passed the means and merit test. There has never been an obligation on solicitors to undertake publicly funded work and many, particularly those doing commercial work, do not. In contrast, other providers such as the Citizens Advice Bureau, advice centres, and law centres, undertake almost exclusively publicly funded work, either legally aided or funded indirectly through local authority or charitable grants. These different means of supplying publicly funded legal services together make up one of the most extensive legal aid systems in the world, and levels of public spending on legal aid in the UK are significantly higher than any other country in Europe. The total budget for 2005 was over £2 billion.

The Access to Justice Act 1999

19.8 These relatively high levels of spending, which for some are a measure of the success of the system, have also been a source of growing political attention. During the 1980s and 1990s, the increasing cost of civil legal aid in particular led to pressure for reform of the system to reduce costs and increase efficiency. In 1991, the budget for civil cases was £685 m and by 1996 had increased to £1.4 billion. This increase in expenditure cannot easily be attributed to one single cause, but the general increase in the amount of litigation, particularly in the area of divorce and employment disputes, accounted for some of this growth. However, there was also evidence that the legal aid budget was covering the costs of a smaller number of cases. In response to the rising budget, eligibility for legal aid was reduced in an attempt to cut expenditure. By 1995, 10 million people were removed from eligibility by the tighter thresholds of the means tests.

19.9 These figures were the impetus for Lord Mackay, then Lord Chancellor, to identify ways of reducing costs and improving efficiency by seeking out alternative means of funding and by reorganizing the legal aid system. His proposals, which were developed first in a Green Paper and in a modified form in a White Paper, aroused much debate and controversy, but were nonetheless broadly implemented by the Labour Party after it came to power in 1997.

19.10 Under the Access to Justice Act 1999 (AJA 1999), two new funding schemes were established: the Community Legal Service (which replaced civil legal aid) and the Community Defence Service (which replaced criminal legal aid). These two new services were to be managed by a new body, the Legal Services Commission, which was set up in place of the Legal Aid Board.

Legal aid budget

19.11 The most dramatic change brought about by the AJA 1999 was the ending of a demand-led system and the establishment of a fixed civil budget set annually and capped, rather than, as in the past, being supplemented by extra granting of funds by Parliament, if required. Moreover, the sum allocated to civil cases was, for the first time, limited to the amount left over after the criminal legal aid fund budget had been spent.

19.12 This prioritization of criminal over civil funding was explained by the Government as a requirement of the Human Rights Act 1998. The argument is that the right to a fair trial under Article 6 of the European Convention on Human Rights requires that funds are available for a defence to a criminal charge so that this part of the budget must remain demand-led. The HRA 1998 also requires, however, that people have access to the courts in the resolution of their civil duties and claims. The limitation of the civil legal aid budget to that which is left over once the criminal requirements are paid for could, theoretically, leave no money for assistance with civil claims, however serious. If this situation arose, there is little doubt that it would be the subject of challenge under the HRA 1998.

Scope and availability of legal aid

19.13 Although legal aid remains available for cases in areas such as family law, welfare law, housing, medical negligence, and human rights cases, a key feature of the new system was the removal of legal aid from personal injuries and business disputes cases and the introduction of a new funding code for all other areas. The old 'means test' and 'merit test' was replaced by a quantitative formula based on likely success rates. The main criticisms of the new system are firstly, that calculating the likelihood of success in percentages is problematic and, secondly, that the likely success rates which must be achieved before funding is granted have been set too high.

19.14 There is evidence that the introduction of the new funding code has led to a significant reduction in legal aid orders. In 2001/2 there was a 12 per cent fall in family certificates being granted and a 30 per cent reduction in other cases, even after allowing for the removal of personal injuries which are now funded through the new Conditional Fee Agreements (outlined below). As with the rise in legal aid spending, there is probably no one explanation for this drop in the number of legal aid certificates. But the more demanding threshold for qualification is undoubtedly one factor, combined with the reduction in the number of firms undertaking legal aid work as a result of the new contracting arrangements (described below) and the relatively low rates of remuneration which legal aid solicitors receive. Rates of remuneration are likely to fall even further as a result of the Ministry of Justice's current consultation on the issue of reform to the fees paid to litigators and advocates in publicly-funded criminal cases and measures to reduce spending on experts' fees in all legal aid cases.

Matching need and supply

19.15 In the light of concerns about the falling numbers of legal aid orders, there has been growing interest in trying to identify the amount of unmet legal need which exists in England and Wales. By definition, this is not an easy task since it requires detailed research on disputes which could result in legal action but which are not pursued. In 1999, a survey conducted by Professor Hazel Genn into people's experiences of dealing with legal problems found that most people seek to resolve a justiciable legal problem without legal advice and assistance. However, half the people in the survey who had sought to deal with a problem in this way failed to resolve it and abandoned the matter. Genn concluded that:

> This is a relatively high figure that demonstrates the difficulty of achieving a resolution for many types of problem and the need for advice and assistance in enforcing rights and defending claims ... what emerges clearly from the approach of the public to the resolution of justifiable disputes is the very limited use made of formal legal proceedings. (Genn, 1999)

19.16 The research concluded that there was a 'profound need' for knowledge and advice about legal rights and obligations and the procedures available for resolving disputes.

19.17 This conclusion has been supported by research carried out in 2002 by the Legal Services Commission Research Unit which found that over 1.5 million people do not take any action to resolve their legal problems because of lack of knowledge about how to do so. The study also found that people from disadvantaged groups such as those with a long-term illness or disability were more likely to experience legal problems. Interestingly, the research also identified the important role played by advisers without legal qualifications. 40 per cent of respondents did not seek help with legal problems from traditional sources of legal help such as solicitors or advice centres, but turned to social workers, health professionals, social security offices, and religious organizations. This finding challenges our assumptions about the most effective way to try and improve access to legal advice and assistance.

19.18   One way in which the Government sought to address the problem of unmet legal need when setting up the Community Legal Service was through the development of a 'joined-up' approach to legal services which tried to ensure that the right number of providers were available offering sufficiently high standards of service in the right places. Working together with solicitors, the not-for-profit sector, and local authorities, the Legal Services Commission was required to develop a network of good quality value-for-money legal providers through Community Legal Service 'partnerships'.

19.19   One particular aim of the new system was to ensure a better match between the supply and demand for legal services in rural and urban areas. There was particular concern about the rural poor who had few accessible services since most were clustered in urban areas and there was general agreement that a geographical redistribution of supply to meet demand was necessary. However, since no additional resources were made available for this change there is understandable scepticism about whether the Legal Services Commission can make any significant headway in this reform. The early evidence suggests that, to date at least, the goal of ensuring a more appropriate geographical spread of legal provision has achieved no more than some minor rearrangement of existing resources at the margins.

Contracts

19.20   In addition to restructuring the system through which legal aid is managed, the way in which legal services providers operate has been fundamentally reorganized through the introduction of a contract system. Under the old arrangements, lawyers were paid on a case-by-case basis for the work they did. Under the current system, lawyers either in the not-for-profit sector or private practice bid for a contract to undertake work in a certain area or work for a certain period of time. If their bid is successful, they enter into a contract with the LSC for the provision of these legal services. In relation to civil work, this usually takes the form of a block contract covering a certain fixed amount of work in a certain period. For example, an advice centre might have a contract to undertake 1,000 hours of welfare benefit work over a 12-month period for a fixed sum.

19.21   The advantage of these arrangements for the provider is that, if they are successful in their bid, they are guaranteed the contract and paid regularly without having to wait for the individual bills to be checked. Delay in paying legal aid bills by the Legal Aid Board was, in the past, a source of grievance for solicitors and sometimes of serious financial hardship. The advantages for the funder of contracting are value for money, the ability to predict costs and to scrutinize quality control by requiring certain standards to be met before a contract is granted.

19.22 These advantages are offset, however, by certain dangers: first, an increase in bureaucracy because of the enormous amount of paperwork generated by applications and quality control systems; second, the risk that the introduction of competition will result in the prioritization of cost-cutting over quality of work. This danger is less acute if the system is based on the number of hours of work undertaken rather than the number of cases.

19.23 If, as in the above example, an advice centre is contracted to undertake 1,000 hours of welfare work, it can allocate as much or as little time to each case as is needed. If anything, the danger might be of spending too long on each case in order to ensure that the hours are completed. However, if the contract is for, say, 2,000 cases in a 12-month period, any complex case which requires extra time is unlikely to receive it. Another concern about the quality control aspect of the contracting arrangements is that it depends on the ability of the Legal Services Commission to identify and set standards. Critics of the system argue that it more effectively measures the ability of providers to comply with the necessary quality control paperwork rather than the real quality of legal services they are providing to clients.

19.24 Contracted providers have complained that they are deluged with unnecessary monitoring requirements, often having to provide the same information in different forms to different funders such as the Legal Services Commission and the local authority. In particular, there is concern that solicitors' firms run by members of minority ethnic groups which are often only made up of one or two partners do not have the extra resources to support this bureaucracy and, as a result, have been notably under-represented among contract-holders.

19.25 Perhaps the most serious long-term problem facing the system is the reduction of the number of firms undertaking legal aid work. Around 6,000 firms have been granted contracts compared with approximately 11,000 legal aid practices under the old system. While some of this reduction may be desirable in that it may have weeded out poorer quality firms, it has also significantly reduced the choice available to those looking for legal advice and increased the distance which many people have to travel to reach a firm or law centre. In rural areas this lack of competition may ultimately have a serious effect on the service since one provider may now have a monopoly in an area. If the standards of that firm fall through lack of competition, the removal of its contract by the Legal Services Commission may leave a large geographical area without any provision at all.

19.26 The reduction in the number of firms undertaking legal aid work as a result of the contracting system is compounded by evidence that the low rates of pay which legal aid lawyers receive is causing firms to drop legal aid work altogether. In its 2002 annual report the Legal Services Commission warned that fewer young lawyers were willing to undertake criminal legal aid. It concluded that: 'Our studies show that at current legal aid rates many firms are at best marginally profitable.' It argued that without significantly increased funding the problem was likely to get much worse.

Conditional fees

19.27 A key feature of the new system was that the gaps left by the reduction in eligibility for legal aid should be filled by a new form of funding called conditional fee agreements (CFAs). These are no-win-no-fee arrangements whereby solicitors and barristers undertake work on the basis that if they win the case, they receive their fees plus a 'success fee'. If they lose, they receive no costs, so that the success fees on cases which are won must cover the cost of those which they lose. The success fee is calculated as a percentage of the costs and can range from anything from 5 per cent to 100 per cent depending on the risks which the lawyers estimate of losing the case.

19.28 The first and main area to be opened up to CFAs was personal injury cases. In 1998, it was extended to all civil work except family cases and in 2000 legal aid was removed completely from personal injury cases with the exception of medical negligence cases. The Government accepted that this category of case was often time-consuming, difficult, and costly to pursue and might not be attractive to solicitors on a CFA basis and so should remain available to public funding. Since CFAs were established, tens of thousands of cases have been funded on this basis.

19.29 The popularity of the new arrangements shows that CFAs have provided an important new source of funding and allowed many cases to be pursued which would previously have been abandoned because of lack of funding. Nevertheless, there are serious problems with the way the system works.

19.30 There has been considerable criticism about the levels of success fee with claims that solicitors are setting unreasonably high fees for straightforward personal injury cases with a very high success rate in which the risk taken in bringing the case is very low. Clients, particularly those with little experience of litigation, are unlikely to be able to assess the plausibility of the risk which the solicitor claims to be taking in proceeding with the case. The temptation for solicitors to exaggerate the risks is therefore an obvious one.

19.31 Research carried out in 2000 found that 93 per cent of completed CFAs were successful and that solicitors tended to over-estimate the risks with the result that the average fee of 43 per cent was too high for most cases (Yarrow, 2000). Evidence in support of this argument is found in the fact that lawyers working for trade unions have for many years taken on personal injury cases without charging if they lose and without any success fee at all, simply receiving their costs from the other side if they win. Because the success rate for personal injury cases is generally very high, this meant that in almost all cases their fees would be paid by the losing side and from these they would cover the cost of the occasional lost case.

19.32 The Government's response to concern about the level of success fee was not to impose limits on the percentage of costs which could be charged, but to relieve the claimant of the burden of paying it completely by allowing the success fee to be paid by the losing side, as has always been the case in relation to the actual costs incurred. This change has made litigation easier for claimants and their solicitors but has led to an increasing amount of litigation (often called satellite litigation), on the part of defendants (usually insurance companies who fund the litigation) challenging the reasonableness of the level of success fee. A number of judges have expressed the view that the recoverability of the success fee and insurance premium is the main reason for the current problems in the area of costs.

19.33 In 2002, it was hoped that some resolution of this problem would be provided by a definitive ruling from the House of Lords on the levels of recoverable success fees in *Callery v Gray (Nos 1 and 2)* (2002) in which the Court of Appeal had, essentially, rejected a challenge by insurers to both the level and process for calculation of the success fee. Instead, the Law Lords determined that the Court of Appeal was the right court to decide such matters and declined to interfere with its decision, while at the same time, however, expressing serious reservations about the level of fee set in that case and the general danger of excessive success fees and insurance premiums being set in a system in which these are payable by the other side. As Lord Hoffmann noted, the situation amounted to a cost-free, risk-free environment for claimants which inevitably lead to cost inflation:

> I am bound to add that I feel considerable unease about the present state of the law. In this respect I do not think that I am alone. There seems to be widespread recognition among those involved in personal injury litigation that costs … are getting out of hand.

19.34 Within months of the decision in *Callery v Gray (Nos 1 and 2)* (2002) the uncertainties of the costs situation were compounded in *Halloran v Delaney* (2002) which imposed a limit of a 5 per cent success fee in relation to cases which settled before proceedings. The decision represented such a swing of the pendulum against claimants' solicitors that it raises the danger that such firms may decide not to take on CFAs because of the low success fees and the degree of uncertainty over costs which now blights the system.

19.35 One effect on the weaknesses in the current system has been to reopen the debate about whether contingency fee arrangements such as those that operate in the US, in which lawyers can claim a percentage of the damages if they win, rather than a percentage of the costs, would be a better system. This system is already used in some areas such as tribunal work and general legal advice and assistance, but it cannot be used for litigation in the courts. Some commentators have argued that this form of no-win-no-fee arrangement might be fairer after all since it links the fee to the amount of the damages and has the advantage of greater simplicity (Zander, 2003). A contingency fee system was originally rejected by the government on the grounds that it gave the lawyers a more direct vested interest in the outcome of the litigation and would therefore encourage them to fight for excessive damages.

19.36　On the other hand it can be argued that the current CFA arrangement suffers from the opposite problem in that it gives lawyers no incentive to do the best for their client. Provided damages are awarded, however small, they will receive their success fee. From the lawyers' point of view, a settlement of one pound is all that is needed. When CFAs were first introduced the Law Society recommended that solicitors should impose a voluntary cap on the success fee of 25 per cent of the damages to ensure that clients did not lose a significant part of their damages in costs. However, since the rules were changed to allow the success fee to be recoverable from the losing party, the pressure to uphold this cap has weakened.

19.37　In 2002, a step was taken towards resolving the uncertainty and excessive costs in the area of CFAs at a meeting involving representatives of all the parties and groups involved. It was decided that fixed costs plus a fixed contingency fee element would be agreed in road traffic cases of less that £10,000 in value. If this formula is successful, the intention is to develop it for other areas of CFA litigation.

Legal insurance

19.38　Ultimately the success of CFAs is dependent on the availability of insurance against losing and having to pay the other side's legal fees, disbursements, and success fee, as well as the cost of their own solicitor's disbursements which are still payable if they lose. Since the introduction of CFAs there has been a huge increase in the number and range of 'after-the-event' insurance packages. Initially, the insurance premiums for standard personal injury cases were low, usually less than £100, and could be paid by the client or the solicitor. However, as costs have risen with the inclusion of the winning side's success fee, the premiums have gone up to a point where they are becoming a barrier for claimants without funds.

19.39　Some solicitors will still fund the premium themselves, to be recovered if the case is won, or it can be paid by a loan arranged by the solicitor. In some cases the insurance schemes allow the premium to be deferred and paid at the end of the case. The degree of complexity in these arrangements is in itself becoming a disincentive for ordinary people to bring an action. Moreover, the rising costs of premiums may more than cancel out any saving to the tax payer in the removal of personal injury cases from the legal aid scheme: 'The predictable result of the rising costs is that a relatively modest benefit to the public purse will in the end be paid for in increased insurance premiums' (Zander, 2003).

19.40 In an important test case in 2002, the Senior Costs Judge reduced the insurance premium claimed by a claims management company from £1,250 to £451. This ruling was expected to reduce the premiums in 100,000 unsettled cases. The judge also reduced the costs claimed by the company for handling the case. The case highlighted concern over the high costs charged by claims management companies which have marketed their services aggressively through television and the press. A number of clients who have used their services have claimed that their costs left them with a small fraction of the damages won.

19.41 The 'after the event' insurance schemes are an integral part of the funding of CFAs, but they are not the only method by which insurance can fund litigation. Many ordinary household or motor insurance policies include cover for the cost of litigation. This has not yet developed into a primary means of funding litigation in England and Wales, but may well become more common in the future. In many other countries this is a commonly used funding system. Indeed, in Sweden, where there has recently been a dramatic reduction in the availability of legal aid for civil cases, almost all actions are now funded through this 'before the event' insurance.

Funding criminal justice

19.42 In relation to the funding of criminal justice, the Access to Justice Act 1999 allows the Legal Services Commission to secure the provision of legal services through private practice (principally contracted firms) or salaried defence services, which are currently being set up. Free non-means-tested legal advice is available under the duty solicitor scheme in police stations. In contrast to civil legal aid, criminal legal aid has traditionally been granted by the courts rather than the LSC, though the LSC has a greater role in the process than did the Legal Aid Board and it is intended that it will gradually take over the functions of the courts in granting legal aid as the number of contracted firms increases.

19.43 Unlike civil legal aid, the trend in criminal legal aid has been the expansion of the numbers receiving legal aid. Previously most defendants qualified for legal aid under the old 'means' and 'merit' test, but the system was criticized as inconsistently applied and expensive. Because almost all defendants qualified for legal aid under the means test the scheme cost more to administer than was received back in contributions. In response to these criticisms a new system was set up. From 1999, legal aid was granted to all defendants who satisfied the 'interests of justice' merit test without any application of the means test. At the end of the case, if the defendant was convicted their means were assessed to determine whether a contribution is required. In 2003, however, the Government announced that it planned to reintroduce means testing for criminal cases and this change was implemented in 2006. The immediate impetus for the move appears to have been concern about the costs to the legal aid fund of payments to relatively well-off defendants facing relatively minor charges in the magistrates' courts. However, the u-turn is also a reflection of a wider concern about the increasing expansion of the criminal legal aid budget. Between 1999 and 2005, criminal legal aid expenditure rose by 37 per cent while high cost cases such as fraud trials which make up only 1 per cent of the total case load consume 50 per cent of the total budget.

19.44   One way in which the Government has sought to bring greater cost efficiency to the criminal legal aid system and so reduce costs is through the use of salaried defence lawyers, which has been one of the most controversial aspects of the changes to criminal justice funding. Pilot schemes have been set up to see if a state-run defence service can offer value for money and a good service. The Government claims that defendants will never be obliged to use the services of the criminal defence service and that the system will never replace lawyers in private practice, but that it will give greater choice to defendants and drive up quality by ensuring the presence of competition.

19.45   It is also hoped that new practices can be piloted through the criminal defence service which will then be adopted, if successful, by private practice. Critics argue that the service will be heavily subsidized and so amount to unfair competition designed to drive down legal fees at the cost of quality and so create a cut-price service. It is also argued that it will undermine the independence of defence lawyers and so threaten the justice system. They also doubt whether it will retain the limited role currently envisaged if it proves a cheaper option. The preliminary results of the pilot seems to show, however, that the system is no cheaper than private practice. In practice, such changes are likely to have no more than a marginal effect on the costs of the legal aid system.

19.46   More radical changes to the criminal legal aid system have recently been proposed in a report produced by Lord Carter who was asked by the Government to carry out a full review of the system. In 2006, he put forward a scheme to be introduced by 2008 whereby all criminal legal aid except very high cost cases would be paid for by fixed or graduated fee schemes rather than hourly rates. The aim of the new system is to reduce costs by £150 m by 2011. Whether or not the changes can achieve this goal without impacting on the quality of legal advice and representation in the criminal courts remains to be seen.

Assessing the changes

19.47 Critics have argued that the Access to Justice Act 1999 was a misnomer in that its ultimate effect was to save money by restricting access to the civil courts. Since the numbers of cases started in the civil courts have dropped very significantly in recent years, this suggests that the reforms are having that effect, whether intended or not.

19.48 However, one of the difficulties which besets any attempt to assess the effects of the reforms to the funding of legal services is lack of information. We do not have full or accurate data about who uses legal aid and with what result. We know in general that there has been a reduction in the amount of litigation started, the number of providers offering legal aid and in legal aid certificates granted, and a rise in the use of conditional fee agreements. However, while the legal aid budget stabilized for a short while after the introduction of the changes, it rose again significantly in 2003. Unravelling the causes and effects of these changes is very difficult. Moreover, we have very few economic analyses of the changes to funding. One recent study of the sources of personal injury litigation funding concluded that:

> ... the source of plaintiff finance was a significant factor determining delay (and consequently cost and settlement amounts), as a result of incentive effects on behaviour. The behaviour of litigants and their representatives is clearly influenced by the way financial risks are shared, and this must be taken into account when formulating and evaluating policy in this area.

19.49 Without considerably more economic research data on the incentive effects on behaviour in litigation, the extent to which policy makers can make informed choices when formulating and evaluating policy in this area is limited.

19.50 Despite these difficulties we can make some general comments about the effects of the changes to funding arrangements. Some are undoubtedly positive. CFAs have provided a service to some people who previously fell between the gap of the public and private provision. The Government claims that the system opens up justice to those too poor to pay privately and too wealthy to qualify for legal aid and encourages proactive lawyering by giving lawyers an incentive to succeed. By saving on the costs of civil cases, it allows public funding to be redirected to areas of real need such as welfare law.

19.51 Critics of the CFA system argue that it is simply a cost-cutting exercise and one that will increase lawyers' income with no increase in efficiency. The fear is that the system encourages solicitors to cherry-pick those cases which have few costs such as expert reports and to refuse more difficult and time-consuming but equally meritorious cases.

19.52 Ultimately, the cost of the litigation must be paid for by increases in insurance premiums to cover the increased legal costs which insurance companies will have to pay in the event of litigated loss and injuries. The danger is that the arrangements promote a two-tiered system in which those with difficult or less lucrative cases get no help while those with easy claims are pursued by ambulance chasers who make inappropriately large amounts of money from straightforward cases.

19.53 More positively, the reduction in litigation generally and legally aided cases specifically may indicate that unnecessary and wasteful cases which could best be resolved without legal channels have been weeded out of the system. But another equally plausible explanation may be that real need is going unmet and that those who previously would have been able to seek a remedy in court are now denied it. Whether, on balance, access to justice has been increased as a result of the Access to Justice Act 1999 seems unlikely.

FURTHER READING

Lord Phillips, Keynote Speech to the Law Society Litigation Conference (June 2003) (http://www.dca.gov.uk/judicial/speeches/lp190603.htm).

Lord Carter *Review of Legal Aid Procurement – A Market-based Approach to Reform* (July 2006, DCA) (http://www.legalaidprocurementreview.gov.uk/publications.htm).

John Peysner 'A Revolution By Degrees: From Costs to Financing and the End of the Indemnity Principle' (2001) 1 Web Journal of Current Legal Issues (http://webjcli.ncl.ac.uk/2001/issue1/peysner1.html).

Michael Zander 'Will the Revolution in the Funding of Civil Litigation in England Eventually Lead to Contingency Fees?' (Spring 2003) DePaul Law Review.

Stella Yarrow *Just Rewards?* (2000, London: Nuffield Foundation).

Paul Fenn, Alastair Gray, and Neil Rickman *The Impact of Sources of Finance on Personal Injury Litigation: An Empirical Analysis* (2002) available on the Judiciary website at: http://www.judiciary.gov.uk/docs/costs-review/empirical-analysis-litigation-funding.pdf.

Ministry of Justice *Legal Aid – Funding Reforms Consultation* (2009) (http://www.justice.gov.uk/consultations/legal-aid-funding-reforms.htm).

USEFUL WEBSITES

Legal Services Commission website home page

http://www.legalservices.gov.uk/

Directgov website information on legal aid and conditional fees

http://www.direct.gov.uk/en/MoneyTaxAndBenefits/BenefitsTaxCreditsAndOther Support/On_a_low_income/DG_10018868.

SELF-TEST QUESTIONS

1 'The growing demands on the civil justice system have made it impossible for the state to provide the necessary funds for an acceptably accessible system. The costs must ultimately be borne by the litigants themselves.' Discuss.

2 Has the time come to reconsider the acceptability of contingency fees?

3 What effect are the decisions in *Callery v Gray* (2002) and *Halloran v Delaney* likely to have on the funding of Conditional Fee Agreements?

4 What are the advantages and disadvantages of the pubic defender service?

5 'The Woolf reforms have failed to make civil litigation more affordable.' Discuss.

6 'Giving lawyers a financial stake in the outcome of litigation is dangerous and conditional fee agreements should be abolished.' Discuss.

Index